The most important educational breakthrough in recent years involves the identification of individual learning styles—and the subsequent matching of complementary strategies, resources, and environments. This diagnostic–prescriptive approach is crucial for teaching children to read.

Designed to assist parents, classroom teachers, reading specialists, and special educators, this book describes effective reading programs that promote success and achievement for the child. Here are useful suggestions and detailed explanations for increasing the reading ability of students ranging from the primary youngster thought to be learning disabled, to the potential drop-out—the turned-off student experiencing difficulty and gradually decreasing motivation.

Teaching Students to Read Through Their Individual Learning Styles will aid teachers and supervisors in dramatically reducing and even preventing failure through the early diagnosis of individual characteristics and the matching of methods and materials to specific individual strengths. Systematic approaches are presented that respond to the unique learning requirements of poor readers.

On the other end of the reading ability spectrum, this text includes scores of strategies that permit the successful introduction of reading and related skills to gifted children often thwarted in the conventional classroom, required to progress at the group—rather than their own individual—rate.

This is a text that provides practical, classroom-tested models and examples that can be used on a daily basis to promote a love of reading and reading efficiency at any level. It details specific techniques and accompanies explanations with sequential, easy-to-follow recommendations for designing and using the techniques in any class or Resource Room. Useful guides demonstrate how to select and adapt existing commercial materials, as well as how to design and create highly motivating teacher-, parent-, or student-made resources. Helpful recordkeeping charts, diagnostic instruments, illustrations, photographs, and how-to descriptions are included for easy and rapid adaptation to daily classroom procedures.

Use these instructional strategies and experiment with teaching your student to read through his or her individual learning and reading style. Research verifies that use of individualized techniques increases students' achievement, improves attitude, and reduces discipline problems.

Teaching Students to Read Through Their Individual Learning Styles

Previous Books by Marie Carbo

- *Happy To Be Me!* Activity Book Series (1976)
- *Soy Feliz Siendo Yo!* Activity Book Series (1976)
- *My Family History Activity Book* (1977)
- *La Historia De Mi Familia* (1977)
- World Record Activity Book Series (1978)
  Word Families, Reading Comprehension I (with Elizabeth H. Burton), *Vocabulary, The Sentence I and II, The Paragraph, Punctuation, Parts of Speech I and II, Correct Usage, Creative Writing, Spelling I and II, Addition and Subtraction I and II, Multiplication and Division I and II.*
- World Record Duplicating Master Book Series (with Nick Carbo) (1980)
  Reading Comprehension, Reading For the Main Idea, Reading For Meaning, Basic Word Families, Building Vocabulary, Reading For Details, Phonics I and II, Writing Sentences, Writing Paragraphs, Basic Grammar, Capitalization and Punctuation
- *Reading Style Inventory Manual* (1981)
- *Reading Style Inventory Research Supplement* (1983)

Previous Books by Rita and Kenneth Dunn

- *Practical Approaches to Individualizing Instruction: Contracts and Other Effective Teaching Strategies* (1972)
- *Procedimentos Practicos Para Individualizar La Ensenanza* (1975)
- *Educator's Self-Teaching Guide to Individualizing Instructional Programs* (1975)
- *Programmazione Individualizzata: Nuove Strategie Practiche Per Tuitti* (1979)
- *Administrator's Guide to New Programs for Faculty Management and Evaluation* (1977)
- *How to Raise Independent and Professionally Successful Daughters* (1977)
- *Teaching Students Through Their Individual Learning Styles* (1978)
- *Situational Leadership for Principals: The School Administrator in Action* (1983)
- *Learning Style Inventory Manual* (with Price) (1974, 1979, 1981, 1985)
- *Productivity Environmental Preference Survey Manual* (with Price) (1979, 1981, 1986)

Teaching Students to Read Through Their Individual Learning Styles

Marie Carbo
Rita Dunn
Kenneth Dunn

90-1752

A RESTON BOOK
PRENTICE HALL, Englewood Cliffs, New Jersey 07632

To teachers everywhere
who give students
the greatest gift of learning—
the ability to read.

Library of Congress Cataloging-in-Publication Data

Carbo, Marie.
   Teaching students to read through their individual
learning styles.

   "A Reston book."
   Includes bibliographies.
   1. Individualized reading instruction.   2. Reading—
Audio-visual aids.   I. Dunn, Rita
II. Dunn, Kenneth J.   III. Title.
LB1050.38.C37   1986   372.4'147   85-19599
ISBN 0-8359-7517-7

Illustrations by Bruce H. Bolinger

A Reston Book
Published by Prentice-Hall
A Division of Simon & Schuster, Inc.
Englewood Cliffs, NJ 07632

10   9   8

Printed in the United States of America

Contents

Chapter 4   How to Match Reading Methods to Individual Reading Styles   64

Chapter 5   Selecting and Adapting Reading Materials to Match Individual Reading Styles   87

Chapter 6   The Carbo Recorded Book Method: Matching Global/Visual Reading Styles   117

Chapter 7   Teaching Children to Read Through Tactile and Kinesthetic Resources   145

A Word From the Authors

The most important instructional breakthrough in recent years involves the identification of individual learning styles and the subsequent matching of complementary strategies, resources, and environments. A considerable and growing body of research verifies how crucial this diagnostic–prescriptive approach is for teaching students to read. This book, therefore, is designed to assist classroom teachers, reading specialists, and special educators to develop effective reading programs that promote academic achievement.

The text includes useful suggestions and detailed explanations for increasing the reading ability of students ranging from primary youngsters thought to be learning disabled to turned-off students experiencing difficulty and gradually decreasing motivation. It will aid teachers and supervisors in preventing and dramatically reducing failure through the early diagnosis of individual characteristics and the matching of methods and materials to specific individual strengths. In addition, the text presents systematic approaches that respond to the unique learning requirements of poor readers.

At the other end of the reading ability spectrum, chapters include scores of strategies that permit a successful introduction of reading and related skills to bright children often thwarted in conventional classrooms because of the need to progress at group—rather than individual—rates and through strategies appropriate for average, rather than gifted, youngsters.

The initial chapters establish a framework for increasing reading achievement and for preventing reading failure through the application of learning style concepts to direct reading instruction. Matching selected reading approaches and individual reading styles to facilitate success and a love for reading comprise the focus of the middle chapters. The largest section of this compendium details specific techniques accompanied by sequential, easy-to-follow, recommendations for designing and using them in any class or Resource Room. These include Recorded Books, Tactile/

Kinesthetic Resources, Programmed Learning Sequences, Contract Activity Packages for the very bright, and Multisensory Instructional Packages.

The causes of reading failure are analyzed, and the *Learning Style Inventory* and the *Reading Style Inventory* are introduced to help the teacher identify every student's learning style and reading style strengths and to assign appropriate, complementary techniques. Most traditional reading methods are analyzed and related to specific reading style traits so that students can learn easily and well. Once our approach is understood, the reader gradually is moved into an appraisal of more sophisticated techniques for matching each youngster's reading style characteristics with methods and materials that capitalize on existing strengths.

The second half of the text provides practical, classroom-tested models and examples that can be used on a daily basis to avoid and eliminate reading problems and to promote a love of reading and reading efficiency at any level. These useful guides demonstrate how to:

- select and adapt existing commercial materials
- design teacher-, parent-, or student-made materials
- create highly motivating games, activity cards, learning circles, task cards, pic-a-holes, flip chutes, and other tactile/kinesthetic resources
- develop Contract Activity Packages, Multisensory Instructional Packages, and Programmed Learning Sequences, and
- ensure a love of learning and proficiency in reading through recorded books.

In addition, many useful record-keeping charts, diagnostic instruments, illustrations, photographs, and how-to descriptions are included for easy and rapid adaptation to daily classroom procedures.

Teachers can use this book as a how-to guide to promote reading fluency or to overcome their students' reading difficulties. Sample resources and procedures are provided for the primary and intermediate levels which are easily adaptable for older students. Supervisors can use the descriptions and models to demonstrate how teachers can respond to the varying instructional needs of all learners. A support system for those who are willing to experiment with the strategies is provided by the many examples that can be duplicated, colored, cut out, assembled, bound, and then used with students for whom they are appropriate.

Practitioners can use this text as a basis for teacher education courses, in-service workshops, and training institutes focused on a broad range of students that include the young beginning learner, the child labeled Learning Disabled, the highly-achieving, and the gifted.

Teachers will be better able to understand their students' natural, biological development and the typical approaches to learning necessary at various stages of growth; they thus will be able to provide vital, effective reading instruction. Finally, special educators and reading teachers will find this book an invaluable aid when writing Individual Education Plans (IEPs) in response to Public Law 94-142. In addition to the above, a bibliography lists recent publications concerned with learning and reading styles.

This book, then, presents tried and tested materials for immediate classroom use. All resources and strategies are based on the well-designed, often prize-winning research described in the text. It may be used for college courses, in-service workshops, and as a daily reference for teachers concerned with employing sound and practical reading techniques based on the most recent research in academic achievement.

Epilogue

When children learn to read well, and enjoy reading on their own, we have been successful. But not all children can read well, and many who do, certainly resist reading unless they are required to do so. With those we have not been successful.

Since the late 1960s we, and others at St. John's University and in New York, began examining the phenomena of learning style. Research conducted by many teachers in both schools and universities has verified that children tend to learn better and more easily when the methods and resources are matched with their unique characteristics. Our findings in this regard have been reported in this book. In addition, we have described instructional strategies used to help children throughout the United States increase their achievement, improve their attitudes, and reduce their discipline problems.

We ask that you experiment with teaching children to read through their individual learning and reading styles. Begin with the underachievers; work with the dropouts; work with those you believe to be unsalvageable— but use the strategies suggested herein. Match the teaching method with the student's style. We are certain that you will realize the same success we have observed across the nation. Then expand your efforts to all students and watch reading momentum and achievement grow!

Marie Carbo
Kenneth Dunn
Rita Dunn

Preventing Reading Failure and Increasing Reading Achievement Through Learning Styles

Analyzing the Causes of Failure

Educators are loath to admit it, but our nation's schools have been in the midst of crisis for a long time. We have begun reading instruction earlier, continued it longer and spent countless hours and sums of money on developmental, remedial, and special education programs (Copperman, 1979). Despite continuing efforts and monumental costs, it is the rare urban high school whose students are not well below the fiftieth percentile on nationally normed reading tests; approximately 25 percent of our students have reading difficulties (Kintsch, 1979). Indeed, as many as 20 percent of all American 17-year-olds were functionally illiterate in 1975 (Lerner, 1981), and those figures do not include people who can, but consistently choose not to, read (Maeroff, 1982).

That inability of our schools to teach reading well is not a new problem; *Why Johnny Can't Read . . .* (Flesch) was the focus of national attention in 1955. Teachers have been trying to increase reading ability for decades but despite professional expertise, many innovations, and massive federal funding, *both past and present reading programs have produced a highly unacceptable and unnecessary number of children who read poorly* (Hart, 1983). In effect, we have wasted a great deal of time, money, and human energy in pursuit of a mythical best approach to teaching children to read. *There is no best way;* there are many different approaches—some of which are effective with some children and ineffective with others. Each youngster learns differently from every other one, and *it is the match between how the learner learns and how the method teaches* that determines who learns what—and how much.

Years ago we did not know how to teach every child to read. Many people preferred one method, others were successful with another, and in different sections of the country individuals developed their own approaches to help children who were unsuccessful with the two or three better-known techniques. Because selected strategies "worked" with many youngsters, we assumed that they *should* be effective for all—if the children paid attention, tried harder, and did their homework. When children did their very best to learn but remained unsuccessful, we assumed they were not intelligent enough and might not "be ready." Today we know better. Research has evidenced that normal youngsters with a minimum IQ of 90 can learn to read better, more easily and retain longer by being taught through approaches that complement their learning styles.

Learning Style: A Detailed Explanation

Everyone has a learning style. You have one, and so does your spouse if you are married. Your children have one too—both your biological offspring and the ones you teach. People's styles determine how they begin to concentrate every time they have new or difficult knowledge or skills to master.

Everyone has a learning style, but each person's is different—like fingerprints. Fingerprints are similar in many ways, but specialists trained to tell the differences can identify which belong to whom. Learning style specialists can do even more than diagnose and match styles; they can describe how to learn more with less effort and remember better than ever before, merely by capitalizing on each individual's unique characteristics.

Learning style is the way that students of every age are affected by their (a) *immediate environment,* (b) *own emotionality,* (c) *sociological needs,* (d) *physical characteristics,* and (e) *psychological inclinations* when concentrating and trying to master and remember new or difficult information or skills (see Figure 1-1). Children learn best *only* when they use their learning style characteristics advantageously; otherwise they study, but often forget what they tried to learn.

The Environmental Elements: Sound, Light, Temperature, and Design

Students are either stimulated or inhibited by the location in which they are trying to learn. Their reactions are determined by their biological makeup (Thies, 1979; Restak, 1979); they can't change their hearing, sight, temperature or body sensitivities any more easily than they can alter the color of their eyes.

SOUND IN THE ENVIRONMENT

In testing more than 950,000 students, we never have found one who has not been affected, in some way, by the environment in which he/she is

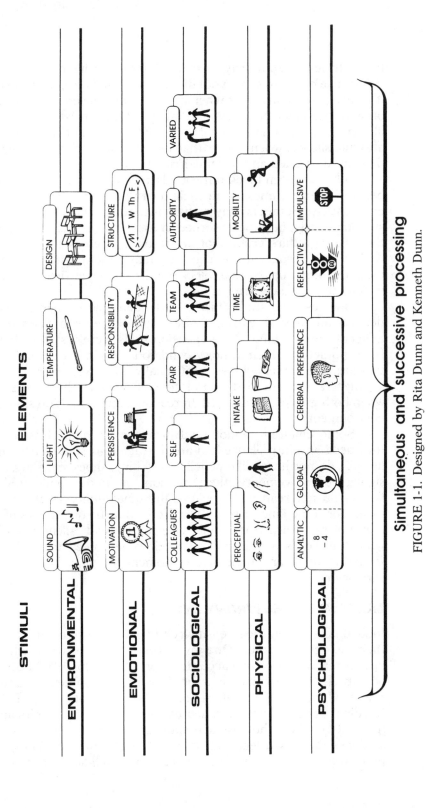

DIAGNOSING LEARNING STYLES

STIMULI   **ELEMENTS**

Simultaneous and successive processing

FIGURE 1-1. Designed by Rita Dunn and Kenneth Dunn.

3

trying to learn. Some say, "I can't *think* when it's noisy; I need quiet!" Others use music to screen out distracting sounds. Some can't study when it's warm, and many can't when it's cool. Some lie on floors, some curl up on a lounge chair or a bed, and others sit on a hard, wooden chair in a library or classroom for hours! Some children cannot concentrate without absolute silence; when noises (that sometimes others do not "hear") occur, they are distracted and become irritable.

Other children block out sounds; they can sit among classmates but become deeply enmeshed in their own thoughts and literally block out everyone else. Some can stay partially in tune and hear pertinent sounds but, simultaneously, become absorbed in their imagination or problems. And then there's a third group that *needs* sound, such as a radio or television, when trying to concentrate. The latter may be sound-sensitive and may be using the music or voices to block out distracting environmental noises of which others usually are not aware.

One research study (Pizzo, 1981) identified elementary school students who needed extreme quiet and those who needed sound to concentrate. Reading comprehension skills were tested in both groups, first in quiet and then in noisy conditions. When it was silent, the group that preferred quiet achieved statistically higher scores ($p. < .01$) than the youngsters who needed sound to concentrate; the reverse occurred when both groups were tested on reading comprehension skills in a noisy environment.

Some children cannot read in a conventional classroom because they need absolute silence and are distracted by sounds that many of us literally do not hear—like pencils scratching, shoes shuffling, youngsters sighing, or movement either outdoors or in our building's corridors. Others do not read well because the quiet unnerves them; they need music (or some kind of sound) to drown out the distractors of which we may not be aware. Some children need to read "silently" and *visualize* what the words are describing, while others need to read "out loud," *hear* the words and then take a moment to "play them back" in their ears or mind.

LIGHT IN THE ENVIRONMENT

Individuals vary in their sensitivity to light because of the differences in their biological makeup. One investigation of the ways in which lighting affects reading speed and accuracy scores (Krimsky, 1982) tested students who preferred learning in a brightly lit environment and those who preferred the exact opposite set of conditions in both types of classrooms. Reading speed and accuracy scores consistently were significantly higher ($p. < .01$) when the instructional lighting environment *matched* the student's diagnosed learning style preference for light. Thus, those who preferred bright light performed better in a well lit environment and less well in a dimly lit classroom, while the reverse occurred for the youngsters who preferred a dimly illuminated area.

One longitudinal study of students in grades 3 to 12 ("Which Learning Style Elements . . .", 1980) revealed that, generally speaking, the need for light *increases* over time. Thus, the older one grows, the more light is needed. However, we are not necessarily describing the differences between elementary school students and adults; the need for more and more light is evidenced among individuals almost every five to seven years.

One of the more interesting things we have learned about light and reading ability is that many *poor* readers prefer to read in dimly lit areas (Carbo, 1983(a); 1983(b); Dunn and Dunn, 1978; Dunn, Price and Sanders, 1981). It wasn't until breakthroughs were made into hemisphericity that we recognized the relationships that exist between right preferenced youngsters and their need for low light (Zenhausern, Dunn, Cavanaugh and Eberle, 1981; Dunn, Cavanaugh, Eberle and Zenhausern, 1982).

People's reactions to *all* the environmental elements of learning style are biological in nature; they exist because of the physical differences among us and no more can be controlled by school or parental commands than can the brain—which to a large extent tells *us* what to do rather than the reverse.

TEMPERATURE IN THE ENVIRONMENT

Most people say that they can't do their best thinking when they are either "too warm" or "too cool." Temperature, however, is relative; we do not react identically to the same amount of heat. Thus, in any given environment, some are comfortable while others are warm and still others are cool. If it is true that physical discomfort interferes with one's ability to concentrate—and it *is* true!—then it is understandable that children will not pay close attention to reading when they are physically ill at ease. It is important to remember, however, that while *we* may be comfortable, some students may feel cold or warm at the same time in the same physical location (Murrain, 1983).

FORMAL VERSUS INFORMAL DESIGN IN THE ENVIRONMENT

Youngsters who are *able* to remain still at a conventional desk and seat are *physically* capable of being seated for long periods in a formal design; those who prefer studying in a bed or on a lounge chair, a couch, the floor or carpeting, do better in an "informal" design. Parents often caution their children against doing homework on the floor or reading in unusual positions; as long as they *read*, ignore the position in which they place themselves.

Although many of us tell children to sit up and pay attention, there is no direct relationship between how one sits and the amount of concentration devoted to what is being studied. In fact, for many, because of biochemical considerations, even a chair that is anthropometrically correct may not be comfortable (Panero and Zelnick, 1980, p. 57). Most people do not realize that, while sitting on any chair, approximately 75 percent of the body weight is supported on only four square inches of bone. In addition, prolonged sitting without postural changes can cause decreased blood circulation which, in turn, causes aches, pains, cramps, and/or numbness (Shea, 1983). However, the more children squirm in their seats trying to find a comfortable position, the more likely it is that they will be accused of fidgeting and urged to sit still!

Students' reactions to sound, light, temperature and design—if those elements are *very important* to them—are beyond their control and will remain fairly stable over time. Environmental learning style characteristics can change, and they often do, but when they are strong, they change only gradually and over a period of time that is rarely fewer than two years and often is more than three or four. How quickly the characteristic changes depends on how *strong* it is and the person's age. The younger the student, the more likely it is that change will occur; the older the student, the more likely it is that the characteristic will change slowly—if at all.

The Emotional Elements: Motivation, Persistence, Responsibility and the Need for either Structure or Choice

The emotional elements are different from the environmental ones in some ways, and yet similar in others. They also are different from *each other*, which means that they must be viewed individually.

Whereas the environmental elements of learning style basically are *biological* in nature, the emotional elements appear to be essentially *developmental*—they emerge over time as an outgrowth of the experiences youngsters have at home, in school, on the playground, on trips and so on.

MOTIVATION

Motivation correlates with achievement. When youngsters *cannot* learn—either because of their inability or ours—they often turn off, tune out, or withdraw. Sometimes they become aggressive and rambunctious; other times they drop out of school or become either negative or apathetic. Those behaviors merely reflect their defeat.

Some students are extremely motivated to learn—but not what we are trying to teach them. Madison Prep, an alternative New York City junior high school for difficult-to-teach, delinquent students, was designed to translate the school curriculum into high-interest materials and, through studies of aerospace, taught its teenagers reading, spelling, grammar, writing, mathematics, science, psychology and human relations skills (K. Dunn, 1981; Hodges, 1982, 1983). When students become interested in learning, they can be taught basic skills *through* their interests and their learning style strengths. Sometimes students do not try to achieve because it is easier to say, "I don't care" than "I can't." When they are shown that they *can* achieve, their motivation to master requirements increases.

Sometimes the work is done, but not well. Often inadequate work is an outgrowth of an inability to perform, or a lack of confidence or skill, or a need for mobility, intake or an informal design, or the need to work in another style. Students permitted to work in their preferred learning styles perform better and "try harder" than when prevented from working in ways that are natural to them (Carruthers and Young, 1980; Wheeler, 1980).

Finally, students who appear to learn when in class or with a tutor, but who forget what they supposedly absorbed, probably have not been taught correctly—for them! That's precisely why some children forget; they cannot remember things taught in someone else's style.

Motivation can be reversed. We have seen "unmotivated" students become willing to learn when they are:

1. Taught through their unique learning styles;
2. Given material on their level and in small sequences;
3. Encouraged and given many opportunities to succeed;
4. Provided immediate feedback; and
5. Supervised during the learning process.

Once such students begin to achieve, their motivation *and* their academic success increase.

PERSISTENCE

Persistence is different from other elements. First, every time we test students with high IQ's who perform well academically, they are highly persistent (Dunn and Price, 1980; Price, Dunn, Dunn and Griggs, 1981). Thus, persistence is the only element that consistently correlates with IQ. Second, although students do appear to become increasingly persistent as they are better able to achieve, that is a quality that tends to change slowly; impersistent children may become increasingly motivated and able to learn more, but they continue to need frequent "breaks" and appear to have a short attention span when involved in academic pursuits. They have a *long* attention span when doing things that are interesting to them.

The general guidelines that tend to increase motivation (teaching through learning style and providing on-level material in short sequences with immediate feedback, encouragement, and supervision), also tend to increase persistence gradually.

RESPONSIBILITY

Every teacher recognizes and appreciates responsible students. Invariably, such youngsters follow through on assignments, complete them to the best of their ability, and often do so without continuing supervision. Such learners require only (a) a clearly stated objective or task that can be understood and mastered, (b) resources that teach the required information on a level with which they can cope, (c) a suggested time interval during which the task should be completed, (d) an indication of where assistance may be obtained if the task becomes difficult, (e) suggestions for testing themselves to note their progress and those aspects that require further study, and (f) alternative ways in which their achievement of those objectives may be demonstrated.

Many youngsters appear to be less responsible than they really are. When a task becomes difficult, rather than seek assistance, they often are diverted from learning to playing or daydreaming. Sometimes they annoy their classmates for want of interaction. At other times they become troublesome and cause a disturbance. For such youngsters it is necessary to use methods that are different from those suggested for responsible students.

Many youngsters who experience academic difficulties evidence learning styles that are extremely different from those of the gifted or highly achieving populations. Initially, underachievers often require an informal design; they find it difficult to sit on wooden or steel chairs for more than a few minutes. Such children also appear to prefer learning either with classmates through small-group techniques or directly with their teacher; they lack the independence skills and ability to learn alone, and they do not derive much satisfaction from large group instruction where they must patiently wait their turn and consistently compete with classmates. Underachievers usually find it difficult to learn by listening; the ability to remember what they have heard seems to be their most difficult task. Neither are they strong visual learners; but they do achieve well when involved kinesthetically and tactually. Such children learn most easily through a multisensory approach that introduces new material through their strongest perceptual modality and reinforces through their secondary and then tertiary strength (Carbo, 1980; Urbschat, 1977; Wheeler, 1983).

Underachievers often like to eat while they are learning; if food is not available, they will resort to snacks, gum, smoking or chewing on whatever is near—even pencils or fingernails. Unlike the gifted, they are *not* early morning, high energy people; they often are not fully awake until late morning, and many experience their highest vitality in the afternoon. Such youngsters need a great deal of mobility and find it difficult to sit still—even in an informal design.

When the learning style characteristics of underachievers are analyzed, they cluster into items that could be considered distractors; such youngsters seek movement, activities, interaction and "things to do"—traits very different from those manifested by higher achievers who like to sit quietly by themselves, for long periods of time, reading their books whenever the teacher requires, without food or supervision; the latter group often is easily distracted whereas underachievers *cause* the distractions.

Underachievers are not intrinsically "bad" children; they have not been able to learn easily in conventional schools and have become discouraged or angry. We can help such youngsters avoid experiencing self-defeating emotions by teaching them through the resources with which they are most likely to be successful. When students are taught through their learning styles, they achieve better and more easily; that revives their hopes and increases their motivation.

Although matching a child's style with complementary materials and approaches will *facilitate* achievement, academically unsuccessful children need to be taught specific study skills, i.e., how to initially attack new information (see Table 1-1), how to use their perceptual strengths and their other learning style characteristics, how to schedule time and allow for mobility needs, with whom to study, and so forth. Slow learners who do not read well should be given short assignments, written materials that are read to them on a supplementary cassette, frequent encouragement and supervision and much praise as each objective is completed. For youngsters who do not understand what they are reading, either an accompanying tape should explain the written content, or tactual and kinesthetic games that further teach the concept or skill should be made available. When students cannot learn alone, use small-group techniques such as Circle of Knowledge, Team Learning, Brainstorming or Group Analysis (see Chapter 9). For youngsters who need structure but cannot work well with their peers, use programmed learning sequences (see Chapter 8). If you want to help slow learners, or those experiencing difficulty with a specific concept or skill, try multisensory instructional packages (see Chapter 10).

As previously irresponsible boys or girls begin to achieve and to develop confidence, gradually lengthen and increase the difficulty of their assignments. Expect that individuals will behave responsibly when they are able to do what is required without fear of either embarrassment or failure. Continue to provide encouragement, frequent supervision and

TABLE 1-1. *How to . . . Learn/Remember . . . New/Difficult . . .
Information/Skills . . . Effectively

YOUR PERCEPTUAL** STRENGTHS OVER 60	INTRODUCE THROUGH: [1]	REINFORCE THROUGH: [2]	REINFORCE THROUGH:	USE NEW KNOWLEDGE CREATIVELY BY MAKING: [3]
AUDITORY	Lectures, cassettes, records, tapes, radio, discussions	Reading, films, filmstrips, television, transparencies	Taking notes from the introduction and reinforcement	A tape after the lecture, reading and notetaking; describe the important things that you have been learning and play the tape back until you remember well and can describe the major points without notes.
VISUAL	Reading, films, filmstrips, television transparencies	Taking notes as you read or watch resources	Reading your notes onto a cassette and playing the tape back until you recall the important points.	A written, graphic overview of all the major points. Illustrate each point as well as you can. Color the illustrations.
TACTUAL/ KINESTHETIC	Task cards, learning circles, electroboards, floor games[4]	Reading, films, filmstrips, television, transparencies	Making task cards, learning circles, electroboards, body games	Explain the Task Cards or other materials you made onto a cassette tape. Have a friend use the materials and simultaneously play the tape and answer your questions on the major points.

[1] This technique is based on extensive research that demonstrates that when students are taught through their strongest perceptual preferences, increased academic achievement is evidenced at statistically significant levels (see Table 2).

[2] Through more than a decade of field-based research, we repeatedly have found that when new and difficult knowledge or skills are introduced through the strongest perceptual preferences and then reinforced through secondary and tertiary preferences, students learn more, more easily and retain better that they did previously (see Roberta Wheeler, "Teaching Reading According to Students' Perceptual Strengths," *Kappa Delta Pi Record*, Indiana: Kappa Delta Pi 17, 2 (December. 1980): 59-63.

[3] Between 1967-1974 we found that if students had to *use* new material they were learning in a creative way, we could increase their ability to retain by approximately 20 percent (see Dunn and Dunn. *Teaching Students Through Their Individual Learning Styles: A Practical Approach* Englewood Cliffs. NJ. Prentice Hall. Inc. (1978): 89)

[4] These are tactual/kinesthetic resources that can be made easily. For explicit directions. see Dunn and Dunn. *Teaching Students Through Their Individual Learning Styles: A Practical Approach*, Englewood Cliffs, Prentice Hall, Inc. (1978): 317-358; also see, Angela Bruno. "Hands-On Wins Hands Down," *Early Years*, Darien, CT. Allen Raymond, Inc. 13, 2 (October. 1982): 60-67.

* Rita Dunn, "Now That You Know Your Learning Style—How Can You Make the Most of It?" *Early Years*, Darien, Connecticut, February, 1983, *13*, 6, 52.
** See Appendix A.

deserved praise. Do not demand more than the student can achieve, for many *become* irresponsible when they realize that their serious efforts cannot produce success.

Responsible students usually try to do the things their teachers ask, but the reverse is not necessarily true; students who do *not* do as they are directed are not always irresponsible. One prize-winning study (White, 1981) revealed a strong correlation between responsibility, as measured by the LSI, and achievement via conformity on the California Psychological Inventory (CPI). Some students *like* to be told exactly what to do, how to do it, when it is due, and so on; they then proceed to follow those directives and feel good about doing so. Some children, however, are nonconformists; often they will do exactly the *opposite* of what their teachers or parents suggest. Such youngsters may be responsible, but they find it difficult to follow directions consistently. If you want to help a nonconforming child to behave responsibly, you might be willing to experiment as we did. We began giving nonconformists *choices*. Instead of insisting that they do their homework in a specific way, we posed alternatives and asked that they select one way with which they would agree to follow through. We found that *once the nonconformists made a choice*, eighty percent of them would do what they had agreed to do. Thus, in a sense, when given appropriate choices, nonconformists *became* more conforming.

If nonconformists respond to explanations and choices by doing what they ought to do, they are being *reasonable* in the best sense of the word. If they become responsible as an outgrowth, we have hastened their maturation. If they do not become more responsible, we have lost only a little time and effort. *Any* child is worth that much.

STRUCTURE

Some people like to know *exactly* what is expected of them before they *begin* a project or assignment; others want only the end-objective or goal and prefer doing it *their* way; the latter group needs "breathing room"— opportunities for creativity and exploration.

Both Hunt (1979) and Price ("Which Learning Style Elements . . .", 1980) found that the older students become, the *less* structure (direction, a sense of external organization) they need. In many schools, the *younger* children are, the more choices they are given, and the *older* they are, the fewer choices they have. Kindergartners often are permitted to sit where they would like in the room; high schoolers rarely are afforded that luxury. Kindergartners often are encouraged to choose their activities; high schoolers usually are given directions and mandated assignments. According to both Hunt and Price, our educational system is upside-down in terms of the kind of structure it provides. However, generalizations are not the answer to improving instruction. *Some* students of any age require a great deal of structure; they feel secure and work well with it. *Some* students of any age are very self-structured; were we to impose more structure externally, they'd find it suffocating. Such youngsters need *some* direction, but many options and choices relieve the inner tension they usually live with on an ongoing basis.

The Sociological Elements: Learning Alone, with Others, or in a Variety of Ways—Perhaps including Media

Assigning children to learn with others can be extremely inappropriate in some cases and the best possible strategy for others. Knowing with whom a student can work is extremely important when trying to teach children through their individual learning styles. Other students resist learning with adults. It isn't that they don't like them; often their strong desire to please causes them to "freeze" when they are questioned. As a result, although they may know answers, sometimes students just can't think of them.

In addition, some youngsters prefer authoritarian personalities, structure, directives, detailed assignments and mandated expectations. Other students respond only to collegial, flexible instructors who offer choices, self-initiated and paced curriculum projects, and partnership in the learning process. A mismatch of student preference and teacher style in this regard usually causes learning problems, decreased motivation, and a dislike for school (Cafferty, 1980; Martin, 1977).

Adults and children are similar in their sociological preferences. Some like to learn alone; some can't study with others. Some prefer to study with others; when alone they can't concentrate or focus on the important items. With whom a student learns is not important; what *is* important is that he/she does learn!

The Physical Elements: Perceptual Strengths, Intake, Time of Day or Night Energy Levels, and Mobility

Like the environmental elements, those in the physical stimulus are *biological* in nature (Thies, 1979; Restak, 1979); they exist because of the way people's eyes, ears, nose, skin and bodies, in general, *are*. If these elements strongly affect how a person learns, they will remain fairly constant over a period of time. They can change, but they change gradually. How slowly or quickly change occurs depends upon the physical maturation of each person. Just as it is not possible to predict in advance when a certain young man will reach six feet, three inches, it is not possible to predict exactly when a person's need for mobility will dissipate, if indeed it ever will! Observing the kind of child the youngster is, whether he generally is extremely active, fairly active, or passive might give some clues, but even those could be misleading. Each person grows in his own fashion and rate, and how long it takes for specific physical characteristics to develop is *controlled by the genes*—not the child.

PERCEPTUAL STRENGTHS

People learn through their different senses. Approximately 20 to 30 percent of the school-aged population remembers what is heard; 40 percent recalls well visually the things that are seen or read; many must write or use their fingers in some manipulative way to help them remember basic facts; other people cannot internalize information or skills unless they use them in real-life activities such as actually writing a letter to learn the correct format. For such people, "making-believe" will not suffice; the letter should be written, mailed, and used to evoke a response.

Auditory Learners: Children Who Learn Easily by Listening

Most of us verbalize the things we want our children to learn or remember, but do most people *learn* by listening? We define an "auditory learner" as one who recalls at least 75 percent of what is discussed or heard in a normal 40 to 45 minute period. The younger children are, the less likely they are to be auditory (Carbo, 1983(a); Dunn and Carbo, 1981; Keefe, 1979; "Which Learning Style Elements . . .", 1980). Based on that knowledge, we teachers are not using effective communication skills when we lecture, ask questions or discuss as our *major* mode of teaching.

Auditory learners remember what they hear and can recreate what they heard by concentrating on previous discussions or lectures. They store spoken words in their brains almost like a recording and can play them back at will—when concentrating and motivated. The ability to do that is a physical gift; it may evolve with training and effort, *but only if the sense of hearing is sufficiently well-developed physiologically.*

Students who learn easily and well by listening should be *introduced* to new information or skills by *hearing* about them. Since their auditory sense is strong, that is the logical one to use at the *beginning* of a lesson.

After *hearing* about the new material, auditory children should reinforce what they learn through their *second* strongest sense. Thus, if the second strongest sense is *visual,* the youngster should *hear* the new material first and then *read* it. If the second strongest sense is tactual, the youngster first should hear the new material and take notes from that lecture or discussion. *Then* the child should read, which would be a visual tertiary reinforcement. (See Table 1-1.)

Because so few of our students find it easy to remember a great deal of what they *hear,* teachers who are lecturing or discussing important information with their classes should always *write* the key words that are being discussed on the chalkboard or on acetate on an overhead projector. In that way, the auditory children are receiving instant visual reinforcement while the visual children are being exposed to the new information visually and simultaneously are receiving verbal reinforcement. If possible, pictures, slides, drawings and photos should appear near the words for youngsters who learn best with pictures and images.

Auditory children should be encouraged to read printed material aloud onto a tape recorder and then to play it back and listen again. Such youngsters find things "clear" when they *hear* them, and, therefore, difficult class lectures should be recorded for playback in case of confusion or a lack of understanding.

Visual Learners: Children Who Learn Easily by Viewing, Watching, and Observing

Visual learners remember what they see and can retrieve details and events by concentrating on the things they have seen. It is only recently that studies indicate that left hemisphere preferenced people tend to remember words; rights recall pictures (Zenhausern, 1980).

Children who learn easily and well by seeing should be *introduced* to new material, information or skills by reading about or seeing them in use. Since their visual sense is strong, that is the logical one to use at the *beginning* of a lesson.

After *seeing* or *reading about* the new material, visual children should reinforce through their *second* strongest sense. Thus,

- If the second strength is auditory, after reading they should hear about and discuss the content
- If the second strength is tactual, they should take notes *as* they read and *then* hear about and discuss what was learned.

It is always a good practice for teachers to assign visual students the readings about a new concept the night *before* the lesson is "taught" (discussed) in class and to assign the same reading material to the auditory students for the night *after* the lesson. Thus, the visual student may read the material on Tuesday evening, attend the class lecture on Wednesday, and will have been *introduced* to the material visually and reinforced auditorially. By contrast, the auditory student will hear about the new concept in class Wednesday (constituting an introduction to it) and be reinforced visually by reading it Wednesday evening. (See Table 1-1.)

Tactual Learners: Children Who Learn Easily by Touching, Manipulating, and Handling

Students who use their fingers and hands while concentrating usually are tactual learners. They remember more easily when they write, doodle, draw, or move their fingers. Often they are talented people who do creative things well with their hands such as sewing, baking, repairing, designing, painting or molding.

Our schools rarely *introduce* new information tactually. Rather, that is a sense that historically has either been ignored or used only for reinforcement for underachieving youngsters (Barbe and Swassing, 1979). Because teachers do not introduce concepts or skills tactually, tactual learners find it difficult to learn as easily as auditory youngsters (who only have to listen to the teacher) or visual youngsters (who can go home and read what the teacher said). Tactual children are *not* less able than their classmates; they simply are not taught correctly (for them) in conventional classes (Dunn, 1971).

Today there are many tactual resources that can be adopted/duplicated easily and in little time (see Chapter 7). Such devices are unnecessary and inappropriate for auditory youngsters (except, perhaps, for a "fun" review); they should be used to *reinforce* visual youngsters, and they and Floor Games should be used to *introduce* new information to tactual students. (See Table 1-1.)

Kinesthetic Learners: Children Who Learn Easily by Doing and Experiencing

Young children, and those who seem to have problems in conventional classrooms, often are *kinesthetic learners*. These are youngsters whose perceptual strengths appear to mature more slowly than among average children; thus, they do not remember a great deal of what they are told and need frequent reminders; they often can't remember too much of what they are shown, and appear unable to recall specifics; and they learn most easily by a combination of tactual and kinesthetic experiences—a great deal of experiencing, doing, and involvement.

For such youngsters, introducing new and difficult information through trips, baking, cooking, building, making, interviewing, and acting experiences—to name but a few, produces the mental imprinting that helps them to focus on what needs to be learned. Reinforcement through secondary and then tertiary senses causes gradual internalization.

INTAKE

Many learners relate to the need for intake when studying or concentrating. Physicians suggest reasons why some people need to eat, chew, drink, bite, lick, smoke, or in some way ingest while they are engaged in new or difficult cognitive efforts. Some may deplete their physical energy and seek to replenish the supply that is being diminished as they concentrate. Others become nervous or tense while trying to learn and reach for a cigarette or gum; they may be seeking relief from their anxiety. Those who are bored with what they are doing seek to revitalize themselves with a reward "break" to provide incentive. Whatever the reason, some people of all ages involve themselves in food or drink *as* they learn.

Price's comparative study of the learning styles of students in grades three through twelve throughout the United States (1981) revealed that the need for intake parallels the growth curve. During each period of rapid growth, youngsters' needs for intake increased. Having raw carrots, celery, green pepper, cauliflower, and other vegetables available for children who really needed to eat while reading resulted in increased reading achievement at the elementary school level (MacMurren, 1985).

The only words of caution we suggest include the establishment of ground rules, e.g.: (1) no remnants; (2) all discarded food must be placed in a designated receptacle; (3) no "sweets" or junk food may be brought; (4) no chewing or digesting noises may intrude on others' concentration; (5) no "wetting" or otherwise soiling books; (6) eating is permitted *only* in room(s) of acquiescing teachers.

TIME OF DAY

Learning at the right time can improve reading achievement. Many administrators require that reading and math be taught early in the morning when, they believe, children are most alert. However, studies of students throughout the grades and over a seven-year period reveal that *at any time of day, at least one-fourth of the student population is experiencing an energy low* (Carruthers and Young, 1980; Freeley, 1984; Lynch, 1981; Price, 1981; Progress Report . . . , 1981; Virostko, 1983). Thus, morning, late morning, and afternoon—the hours of usual classroom instruction—are inappropriate concentration/learning periods for a large percentage of youngsters who are required to be there.

Virostko (1983) identified the time preferences of 286 third, fourth, fifth, and sixth graders with the *Learning Style Inventory* ® (1978). Students were assigned administratively to one hour of mathematics and one hour of reading each day for a two-year period. During the first year, each child was matched for one subject and mismatched for the other; during the second year, the matching was reversed.

During the first year, students whose time preferences were congruent with their reading or mathematics class schedules achieved statistically higher scores than those who were not matched with their time preference. During the second year, *when the reading and mathematics class schedules were reversed,* students who were matched with their time preferences again scored statistically higher than those who were mismatched— verifying the impact of time on achievement!

Kindergarten classes should be available both morning and afternoon, and children should be selected for participation on the basis of their individual energy levels so that their first school experiences are positive. Children should be taught to read at their best time of day; they should also be read to when they are most likely to concentrate on the story and the vocabulary.

PROVIDING FOR STUDENTS' MOBILITY NEEDS

When children are *not* interested in what they are reading, they tend to lose concentration. Sometimes they do not focus on the content because they do not read well or easily. Often they lose interest because the material, vocabulary or concept is difficult; when that happens, they become nervous or fidgety and, in turn, require a great deal of mobility.

The more children squirm in their seats and the more negative attention they receive, the more difficult it is for them to *refrain* from moving. Examining their learning styles may provide a vital clue to why some youngsters cannot sit still. Look for the youngster's mobility needs, perceptual strengths or weaknesses, sound, light, temperature, design, intake or time of day needs. Observe the child sociologically. Does he learn best alone? with peers? with the teacher? with another adult? or with media? Does he like alternatives, or does he prefer stability and appear to become disoriented by changes in routine or resources? The wrong response by a teacher to a student's strong learning style element easily can cause nervous reactions and mobility needs. Many adults react similarly under stressful conditions.

Some students learn best in a formal design (a straight, upright, wooden chair) and others in an informal environment (on carpeting, floor, lounge, bed, pillows and so on). Whichever is better for the individual will reduce the amount of mobility needed. Encourage children to read wherever they feel comfortable, for the preferred learning area will increase their reading and pleasure and, simultaneously, will help them to understand the differences among us!

Permit "breaks" when children appear to require them. There is no specific amount of time that is appropriate for all children to study, practice, or do homework. Because of their differing persistence levels, some are able to work for long periods of time consecutively, others need frequent opportunities to relax and then return to their studies, and others vary in their periods of concentration based on how important persistence, design and mobility are to them.

Examine individual needs for intake. Permit children to read while nibbling if they need to. Encourage reading at the best time of day; some cannot go to sleep when their parents think it is the appropriate bedtime; others find it difficult to remain awake when they have company, tasks or obligations they don't enjoy. Children's mobility needs often are related directly to their willingness, abilities, interests and energy levels—and adults have similar patterns.

Once you begin responding to individual learning style differences, you will be amazed at how much more each student learns, how much better he or she enjoys learning and how much better he or she behaves.

The Psychological Elements: Global/Analytic, Hemispheric Preference, and Impulsive/Reflective

GLOBAL/ANALYTIC

Surely you've taught a lesson that evokes affirmative nods from many students and simultaneously leaves certain ones in a quandary; the latter group is not able to make sense of what has been presented while it is all extremely clear to the others. It may be that you are teaching analytically and that some of your students are global or vice versa.

Analytic people piece details together to form an understanding that is "backwards" from the way globals learn. Globals require an overall comprehension first, and then they can attend to the details. Each group is as intelligent and as capable as the other, and, indeed, each learns equally as well *when taught through resources and approaches that complement its style* (Trautman, 1979). Trautman worked with junior high school students in social studies while Douglass (1979) was experimenting with high school biology classes; both matched and mismatched the populations with complementary and uncomplementary materials, and in each case, globals taught globally and analytics taught analytically achieved significantly better (p. < .01) when the strategies responded to their characteristics.

How To Teach Globally and Analytically

First it is necessary to identify your own predisposition, for students achieve better when their styles match those of their teachers' (Cafferty, 1980); they also like learning better when such matches occur (Farr, 1981; Copenhaver, 1979, 1979–1980; Pizzo, 1981). Then, regardless of your style, at least part of the time use the opposite style for each lesson. For example, if you are used to introducing a topic with a story and then zeroing in on its substantive facts midway through a lesson or unit, reverse the strategy and begin with the important facts and then overview the topic. Building the topic or lesson both globally and analytically will reach both types of students.

You might consider intentionally varying your technique so that each group has its turn at having its learning style matched first. Or you could team-teach important subjects with a colleague whose style is different from yours. Still another approach might involve a list of the details or rules for students; then show them the written or illustrated outline at the same time you are introducing the overview; in that way, they can hear the overview and see the detailed outline. If students take notes and then develop a set of task cards for the lesson, they also will have reinforced tactually—making the lesson multisensory. Thus, any resource to teach or improve reading skills can and should be developed in both ways if it is to be effective with both types of students.

Most young children (up to approximately eight years of age) are global; after that period, some become analytic. More *adults* appear to be global than analytic. However, *of the teachers we've tested,* more tend to be analytic than global. It may be that education attracts analytic people who become teachers and teach analytically to youngsters who find it difficult to learn mathematics, grammar or foreign language in other than global ways.

Since most young children we have tested are global, they should be taught to read through global methods. Thus, reading stories to young children is one effective technique for acquainting them with the concept of what reading is. One of the best ways we know to teach global students to read is to tape-record many different short high-interest stories and have them available for selection (Carbo, 1978). Each should have the text on a cassette and a tactile or tactile/kinesthetic reinforcement activity to supplement it. Thus, whenever a youngster wishes to hear a story—or wants something to do—he can choose a booklet, put its cassette into a tape recorder and follow the directions that tell him to "Open the book to page 1—the page with the silver rocket floating on the white cloud. The first word is 'Lost!'. Put your finger under that word and read along with me."

After hearing the story, the child then can follow the directions (in the back pocket) that describe how to use the "game" (tactile reinforcement). By hearing the same story several times, most children begin to remember the words and read along. After a while, they recognize the words out of context, and before long, they are "reading!"

That is one global approach to reading—hearing a story in its entirety rather than reading individual words or sounds. Analytic methods focus on the practice of words out of context and isolated letters and sounds. Often the latter procedures denigrate the value of reading—which is for understanding and pleasure! Reading *skills* are not reading; they are the intellectual components of the process that develops after a child understands how to read—and does. But more about that in Chapters 3 and 5.

HEMISPHERIC PREFERENCE

The past few decades have witnessed remarkable scientific advances in understanding the human brain. Investigations of both split brain patients and normal people have verified that the two sides of the brain perform different functions; characteristically, one has a higher arousal level than the other. It is believed that the differences caused by either the right or left side's higher arousal responses may be related to cognitive and personality functions (Levy, 1982a).

Those differences in brain functioning partially are what *cause* individual learning style differences among people; they suggest that learning is better accomplished for different people through different approaches.

> ... the child with a biased arousal of the left hemisphere may gain reading skills more easily through a phonetic, analytic method, while the child with a biased arousal of the right hemisphere may learn to read better by the sight method ... the *gateway* into whole-brain learning may differ for different children ... (Levy, 1982b, p. 181).

Our investigations of the differences between students who are extremely left or right hemisphere preferred revealed that the two learn under very different conditions from each other (Dunn, Cavanaugh, Eberle and Zenhausern, 1982). For example, right preferenced students: (a) are less bothered by sound when studying; in fact, they may *like* things that appear to be distractors to lefts—such as noise, people, movement or food while learning; (b) often prefer dim illumination; (c) usually require an informal design; (d) are less motivated toward conventional schooling than lefts; (e) are less persistent; (f) prefer learning with peers, and (g) prefer tactual more than either auditory or visual stimulation—even at the high school level.

Apparently right and left dominant students have different environmental and organizational needs when concentrating as well as different motivational and personality characteristics. Both groups learn equally as well—but differently. Conventional schooling accommodates the left preferenced students and imposes a handicap on their extreme counterparts—particularly in reading.

For example, in a comparative study of good and poor readers, Zenhausern (1982) reported that those who read well were divided evenly between left and right preferenced individuals; however, 17 of the 19 *poor* readers were right preferenced. When we re-examine the conditions preferred by right preferenced students (sound, low light, an informal design, shorter tasks and more rest periods for the less persistent, learning with peers rather than alone or with adults, and tactual and/or kinesthetic instruction rather than auditory or visual learning) it is not surprising to understand why they find it difficult to achieve academically in schools that impose identical environments on everyone.

IMPULSIVENESS VERSUS REFLECTIVITY

Conventional teachers find it difficult to tolerate impulsive youngsters—the ones who become exuberant and call out, behave spontaneously, and act before they think! Conversely, reflective students are considered more intelligent—perhaps because they generally behave contemplatively and appear more responsive to controls. Nevertheless, often the one quality is thought to be positive and the other negative—which is inaccurate. Both characteristics are valuable when used at appropriate times. Risk-takers may be far more impulsive than analytic; reflectives may be far more cautious—or fearful—than impulsives. When the student has both qualities and knows when and how to use them effectively, he is likely to be successful in learning and living.

How Is Learning Style Identified?

Several fine instruments exist for identifying individuals' styles, but some were designed solely for adults or post high school populations, and others are limited to effective usage with high schoolers. Because our concern is with teaching children to read, the best instruments that we can recommend are the *Learning Style Inventory* (LSI) (Dunn, Dunn and Price, 1974, 1979, 1981, 1985) and the *Reading Style Inventory* (RSI) (Carbo, 1979, 1981).

The LSI assesses each youngster's strong positive and strong negative preferences for each of 18 important elements and reveals relative strengths and weaknesses. Based on those identified characteristics, specific approaches and resources are suggested, as well as complementary ways to make the classroom environment more responsive.

The RSI has a slightly different focus. Whereas the LSI reveals learning style as it is important for overall student achievement, the RSI specifically examines how each youngster is most likely to learn to read (see Chapter 2).

Appendix A explains how to administer and how to interpret the LSI findings. If you are concerned with students in grades 3 to 12 who have not been achieving generally, use the LSI and follow its prescriptions. If your concerns are associated more directly with children's inability to read, use the RSI as explained in Chapters 2 and 4.

Examining Students' Learning Styles

Before continuing with this book, we suggest that you try to analyze one or more youngsters whom you know fairly well, using the Learning Style Profile (see Table 1-2) to record your judgments. Review the first 18 elements described earlier in this chapter and determine which you believe strongly affect the individuals you have in mind. Then reconsider the elements, and should you change your opinion concerning the students' styles, make the appropriate changes on their Profiles. If you want to know how accurate your assessment is, administer the Learning Style Inventory (LSI), send the Answer Sheets to Price Systems for scoring, and then compare your observations with the computer printouts that will be sent to you. (For information concerning the LSI, see Appendix A.)

Suggested Guidelines for Matching Selected Learning Style Characteristics with Complementary Instructional Methods

During the past 18 years, many classes and school districts have experimented with varied instructional resources and methods in efforts to determine which might be most appropriate for which students. Many publications have reported the comparative successes experienced by youngsters who were assigned to complementary strategies and/or materials (Cavanaugh, 1981; Fiske, 1981; Jenkins, 1982; Lemmon, 1983;

TABLE 1-2. Learning Style Profile

Student's Name _____ Teacher _____ School_____

Class _____ Counselor _____ Date_____

LSI Consistency Score

Comments based on highest ratios noted on LSI or teacher observations:

I. Environment

    Sound _____

    Light _____

    Temperature _____

    Design _____

II. Emotional

    Motivation _____

    Persistence_____

    Responsibility_____

    Structure _____

III. Sociological—Appears to work best (alone, with one friend, small team, peers, adult, in a variety of ways rather than consistent patterns)

    1. _____

    2. _____

    3. _____

IV. Physical

    Perceptual Preferences_____

    Intake _____

    Time _____

    Mobility _____

Pizzo, 1982). The following guidelines for providing specific materials for identified student characteristics are suggested on the basis of their previous successes with children with certain unique traits. If a youngster does not experience success with a resource within several days of usage, by all means discontinue use and experiment with alternative materials. For an overview of these guidelines, see Table 1-3.

Contract Activity Packages (CAPs)

These are self-contained units of study that include clearly stated objectives, multimedia resources, specific ways of creatively *using* new knowledge or skills and then sharing those original activities with classmates, at least three small-group techniques for use with peer-oriented students, a pre- and post-test, and varied other materials dependent on the topic (Dunn and Dunn, 1978). Youngsters who are motivated, persistent, have at least three perceptual strengths, and who like to learn alone, usually perform extremely well with the CAP system. For step-by-step descriptions concerning how to develop CAPs at each level and examples, see Chapter 9.

Programmed Learning Sequences (PLS)

Any information can be programmed, but such a system tends to appeal essentially to strongly visual students who require a great deal of structure. Again, for directions for developing PLS and samples, see Chapter 8.

Multisensory Instructional Packages (MIPs)

These are units of study that teach a single concept or skill through four different sensory activities—each of which reinforces the other. MIPs have been extremely effective for essentially tactual/kinesthetic students (who do not learn easily by listening and who rarely read well) or for those who have no strong perceptual modalities. They also may be used to teach highly achieving students exceptionally difficult new information or skills. Directions for designing MIPs and samples are available in Chapter 10.

Tactual/Kinesthetic Materials

Many young children learn most easily by touching, doing and being actively involved rather than through listening or reading. For those, tactual/kinesthetic materials facilitate achievement in ways that lectures/discussions and questioning cannot begin to rival. For directions and examples, see Chapter 7.

Children whose learning styles are not usually responded to by conventional schools, such as those who are peer- rather than authority-oriented and who learn best in an informal design with intake and mobility, generally learn more easily with either tactual/kinesthetic materials or MIPs. Underachievers thrive on them; the gifted enjoy learning through them occasionally.

Small-Group Techniques

For youngsters who are peer-oriented, small-group techniques like Circle of Knowledge, Team Learning, Brainstorming, and Case Studies provide effective strategies for learning and retaining new and difficult information and skills. Those, too, are available with complete directions and examples in Chapter 9.

Redesigning the Learning Environment

Whatever students' reactions to sound, light, temperature, and design, be certain that they are surrounded by an area that permits those environmental elements that they require to concentrate, or they won't do their best work. Neither a great deal of space nor money is necessary to redesign a conventional classroom so that it responds to each youngster's preferred characteristics. It is important that we recognize that everyone learns and produces differently and under varied conditions; what is "normal" to one is "ridiculous"—or impossible for another.

Teaching Students through Their Individual Learning Styles (Dunn and Dunn, 1978) clearly describes how to redesign a classroom with no money, no assistance, and little time. That it is effective cannot be doubted (Alloway, 1982; Fiske, 1981; Lemmon, 1982; Pizzo, 1982b).

Is It Important to Teach through Individual Learning Styles?

Extensive research corroborates the need for identifying each student's strong preferences and for teaching in ways that complement them. Table 1-4 verifies the increased academic achievement that was evidenced when students were taught through their individual styles. Copenhaver (1979), Domino (1970) and Pizzo (1981) documented the improved attitudes toward learning that resulted from working through a student's strengths, and Carruthers and Young (1980), K. Dunn (1981) and Lynch (1981) revealed the decreased number of discipline problems that were evidenced when learning styles' based instruction was used.

Because of the extensive research (see Table 1-4) and our own experiences, we believe that children who are taught through their natural learning styles *become* the achievers in school; those who experience difficulty do so because they are not being taught in ways that respond to how they learn. Thus, we believe in identifying each student's unique characteristics and providing complementary methods and resources to insure academic success; there is nothing as important as determining each youngster's unique learning style.

TABLE 1-3

Method or Resource	Learning Style Characteristics to Which It Responds	Learning Style Characteristics to Which It Does Not Respond	Learning Style Characteristics to Which It Can Be Accommodated
1. Programmed Learning	Motivation, persistence, responsibility, and a need for structure; a need to work alone, a visually oriented student.	A lack of motivation, persistence, or responsibility; a need for flexibility or creativity; a need to work with peers or adults; auditory, tactual, or kinesthetic perceptual strengths.	Sound, light, temperature, and design; a need for intake, appropriate time of day, and a need for mobility.
	Note: Where programmed learning sequences are accompanied by tapes, they will appeal to auditory learners; when they include films or filmstrips, they will reinforce the visually oriented student; when teachers design small-group techniques such as team learning, circle of knowledge, or brainstorming, peer-oriented students may develop an ability to use programs more effectively than if they use them exclusively as individual learners.		
2. Contract Activity Packages	A need for sound and an informal design; motivation, persistence, and responsibility; a need to work either alone, with a friend or two, or with an adult, all perceptual strengths and weaknesses and the need for mobility.	None	Sound, light, temperature, and design; motivation, persistence, responsibility; sociological needs; perceptual strengths, intake, time of day, and the need for mobility.
	Note: Contract Activity Packages respond to all learning style characteristics provided that (1) they are used correctly and (2) multisensory resources are developed as part of them.		
3. Instructional Packages	A need for sound or structure; a need to work alone; all perceptual strengths.	A lack of responsibility; a need for peer or adult interactions.	Light, temperature, and design; motivation, persistence; intake, time of day, and mobility.
	Note: Because of their multisensory activities, instructional packages are very effective with slow learners. Unless the curriculum is extremely challenging, they may be boring to high achievers.		
4. Task Cards and Learning Circles	Motivation, persistence, responsibility, and the need for structure; visual or tactual strengths.	A lack of motivation, persistence, responsibility, or a need for structure; auditory or kinesthetic strengths; a need for mobility.	Sound, light, temperature, and design; the need to work alone, with peers, or an adult; intake and time of day.
5. Tapes, Audio Cassettes	A need for sound; motivation, persistence, responsibility, and a need for structure; a need to work alone; auditory strengths.	A need for silence; a need to work with peers or an adult; visual, tactual or kinesthetic strengths, and a need for mobility.	Light, temperature, and design; intake and time of day.

Rita Dunn and Kenneth Dunn, *Teaching Students Through Their Individual Learning Styles: A Practical Approach.* Englewood Cliffs, NJ: Prentice-Hall (1978), p. 39.

TABLE 1-4. Learning Styles Research

Researcher, University Date	Population	Findings
Elsie Cafferty, "An Analysis of Student Performance Based Upon the Degree of Match Between the Educational Cognitive Style of the Teachers and the Educational Cognitive Style of the Students," Ed.D. Dissertation, University of Nebraska (1980).	High School Teacher/ Student Pairs	1. The greater the match between the student's and the teacher's style, the higher the grade point average. 2. The greater the mismatch between the student's and the teacher's style, the lower the grade point average.
Marie Carbo, "An Analysis of the Relationships Between the Modality Preferences of Kindergartners and Selected Reading Treatments as They Affect the Learning of a Basic Sight-Word Vocabulary," Ed.D. Dissertation. St. John's University (1980).[1]	Kindergarten Children	1. Children taught through their strongest perceptual modalities learned more easily and retained better than when taught through either their secondary or tertiary strengths. Results were significant at the .01 and .05 levels, respectively, for immediate and delayed word recall.
Joan Della Valle, "An Experimental Investigation of the Relationship(s) Between Preference for Mobility and the Word Recognition Scores of Seventh Graders to Provide Supervisory and Administrative Guidelines for the Organization of Effective Instructional Environments," Ed.D. Dissertation, St. John's University (1984).[2]	Seventh Graders	1. When students were matched with their learning style mobility preferences, they scored significantly higher word-pair recognition scores at the .001 level. 2. When mismatched, students achieved statistically less well.
George Domino, "Interactive Effects of Achievement Orientation and Teaching Style on Academic Achievement," ACT Research Report 39 (1970): 1–9.	College Students	1. Students taught in ways they believed they learned scored higher on tests, fact knowledge, attitude, and efficiency than those taught in a manner dissonant from their orientation.
Claudia B. Douglass, "Making Biology Easier to Understand," *The American Biology Teacher*, 41, 5(May, 1979): 277–299.	High School Students	1. Deductive students taught through deductive biology materials and inductive students taught through inductive materials each achieved better than when mismatched.
Helene Hodges,"An Analysis of the Relationships Among Preferences for a Formal/Informal Design, One Element of Learning Style, Academic Achievement, and Attitudes of Seventh and Eighth Grade Students in Remedial Mathematics Classes in a New York City Alternative Junior High School," Ed.D. Dissertation, St. John's University (1985).	Seventh and Eighth Graders	1. Students who preferred an informal design performed statistically better when taught and tested in that type of environment; those who preferred a formal design performed better in the formal condition. 2. Both groups' attitudes were significantly higher when they were in responsive environments.

TABLE 1-4. (*continued*)

Researcher, University Date	Population	Findings
Harold MacMurren, "A Comparative Study of the Effects of Matching and Mismatching Sixth-Grade Students With Their Learning Style Preferences for the Physical Element of Intake and Their Subsequent Reading Speed and Accuracy Scores and Attitudes," Ed.D. Dissertation, St. John's University (1985).	Sixth Graders	1. When students were matched with their preferences for intake, they achieved significantly higher scores (.01) than when mismatched. 2. When they were mismatched, they achieved significantly less well. 3. Their attitudes were also significantly higher when students' styles and environmental conditions were congruent.
Jeffrey S. Krimsky, "A Comparative Study of the Effects of Matching and Mismatching Fourth Grade Students with Their Learning Style Preferences for the Environmental Element of Light and Their Subsequent Reading Speed and Accuracy Scores," Ed.D. Dissertation, St. John's University (1982).[3]	Fourth Graders	1. Students who preferred bright light performed statistically better when tested in brightly lit areas; those who preferred reading in dim light did equally as well in a low-light setting. Both groups performed statistically less well when tested in mismatched situations.
Jeanne Pizzo, "An Investigation of the Relationships Between Selected Acoustic Environments and Sound, an Element of Learning Style, as They Affect Sixth Grade Students' Reading Achievement and Attitudes," Ed.D. Dissertation, St. John's University (1981).[4]	Sixth Graders	1. When students were matched with learning style preferences, statistically higher reading and attitude scores resulted at the .01 level. 2. Students who were mismatched, achieved significantly below the matched students.
Thomas C. Shea, "An Investigation of the Relationship Among Preferences for the Learning Style Element of Design, Selected Instructional Environments, and Reading Achievement of Ninth Grade Students to Improve Administrative Determinations Concerning Effective Educational Facilities," Ed.D. Dissertation, St. John's University (1983).[5]	Ninth Graders	1. When students were matched with their learning style preferences for a formal versus informal design, they achieved statistically higher scores at the .01 level. 2. When mismatched, students who preferred an informal design, achieved significantly below their matched counterparts (.01). 3. Mismatched students who preferred a formal design were better able to adjust the environment to their needs than were the mismatched youngsters who preferred an informal design.

TABLE 1-4. (*continued*)

Researcher, University Date	Population	Findings
Paul Trautman, "An Investigation of the Relationship Between Selected Instructional Techniques and Identified Cognitive Style," Ed.D. Dissertation, St. John's University (1979).	Junior High School Students	1. Whenever the instructional materials were matched correctly to the student's identified style, significant academic gains were made; whenever the materials and styles were mismatched, achievement fell below that of both matched groups. 2. There is no difference between the relative achievement of analytic and global students when they each are taught through materials that match their styles.
Rhoada Tannenbaum, "An Investigation of the Relationship(s) Between Selected Instructional Techniques and Identified Field Dependent and Field Independent Cognitive Styles as Evidenced Among High School Students Enrolled in Studies of Nutrition," Ed.D. Dissertation, St. John's University (1982).	Tenth, Eleventh and Twelfth Graders	1. Field independent students provided low structure and field dependent students provided high structure performed significantly better when taught through complementary (matched) methods.
Karen S. Urbschat, "A Study of Preferred Learning Modes and Their Relationship to the Amount of Recall of CVC Trigrams," Ph.D. Dissertation, Wayne State University (1977).	First Graders	1. Modality strengths can be identified among first graders. 2. Superior and significant results occurred when a treatment was matched to the appropriate modality. 3. Most of the first graders in the study found it easier to learn through either a visual or a combined auditory/visual treatment than solely through an auditory approach.
Joan Virostko, "An Analysis of the Relationships Among Academic Achievement in Mathematics and Reading, Assigned Instructional Schedules, and Learning Style Time Preferences of Third, Fourth, Fifth and Sixth Grade Students," St. John's University (1983).[6]	Third, Fourth, Fifth, and Sixth Graders	1. When students were matched with their learning style time preferences, they achieved significantly higher mathematics and reading test scores at the .001 level. 2. When mismatched, students who preferred another time of day achieved statistically less well.

TABLE 1-4. (*continued*)

Researcher, University Date	Population	Findings
Frederick H. Weinberg, "An Experimental Investigation of the Interaction Between Modality Preference and Mode of Presentation in the Instruction of Arithmetic Concepts to Third Grade Underachievers," Ph.D. Dissertation, St. John's University (1983).	Third Graders	1. Visual and tactual/kinesthetic children taught through their strongest perceptual modalities achieved significantly better (.05) than when mismatched. 2. Auditory children achieved significantly better when taught through their tactual/kinesthetic senses.
Roberta Wheeler, "An Investigation of the Degree of Academic Achievement Evidenced When Second Grade, Learning Disabled Students' Perceptual Preferences Are Matched and Mismatched With Complementary Sensory Approaches to Beginning Reading Instruction," Ed.D. Dissertation, St. John's University (1983).	Second Graders	1. Learning disabled children taught through their strongest perceptual modalities learned significantly better than when taught through either their secondary or tertiary strengths or weaknesses.
Regina T. White, "An Investigation of the Relationship Between Selected Instructional Methods and Selected Elements of Emotional Learning Style Upon Student Achievement in Seventh and Eighth Grade Social Studies," Ed.D. Dissertation, St. John's University (1980).[7]	Seventh and Eighth Graders	1. Persistent and responsible students achieved significantly higher than students with low persistence and responsibility scores. 2. Students identified as being persistent and responsible also were identified as manifesting conforming behavior. 3. Less persistent and less responsible students do not learn through conformity.

[1] Recipient, Association for Supervision and Curriculum Development National Award for the Best Doctoral Dissertation (1980).

[2] Finalist, National Association of Secondary School Principals Distinguished Middle Level Award (1984); Finalist, Association for Supervision and Curriculum Development Supervision Award (1985); Recipient, Phi Delta Kappa Research Award (1985).

[3] Finalist, Association for Supervision and Curriculum Development National Award for the Best Doctoral Dissertation (1982).

[4] Finalist, Association for Supervision and Curriculum Development National Award for the Best Doctoral Dissertation (1981).

[5] Finalist, National Association of Secondary School Principals Distinguished Middle Level Dissertation Award (1984).

[6] Recipient, Kappa Delta Pi International Award for Best Doctoral Dissertation (1984).

[7] Recipient, Delta Kappa Gamma International Award for the quality of the dissertation proposal (1980).

2

Reading Styles: Applying Learning Styles Concepts to the Teaching of Reading

Developing Effective Reading Programs for Poor Readers

After years of working with poor readers and conducting research on reading and learning style, Marie Carbo developed the concept of "reading styles," coined the term, and designed observation guides and checklists that evolved into the Reading Style Inventory (RSI) (Carbo, 1979, 1981). The RSI, an adaptation of the Dunn and Dunn learning styles model, is described in the second half of this chapter.

Initial Experiments in Reading and Learning Style: Setting the Stage

In 1974, the "back to basics" movement was beginning, "decoding" sections had been added to some standardized achievement tests, the popular whole-word method was being supplemented with or replaced by phonics, basal reader publishers were including extensive phonic exercises in their reading workbooks (Chall, 1979), and some school districts were instituting perceptual remediation programs to improve reading achievement. In most classrooms, all children were taught to read with the same reading methods and materials. Students who performed poorly in reading attended remedial reading classes and sometimes perceptual training classes.

In the early 1970s a number of educators believed that poor readers had perceptual disorders which had to be remedied before any real reading progress could occur. Often, tactile/kinesthetic youngsters who were not strongly visual and/or auditory had to attend perceptual training classes and were taught in unstimulating, austere surroundings with few, if any, tactile/kinesthetic materials. In such programs, the students' learning style strengths and preferences were largely ignored while their learning style weaknesses were highlighted. As a result, many poorly achieving students felt even more unsuccessful because their learning style weaknesses were the focus of so much attention and concern. Not surprisingly, most attempts to remediate perceptual deficits were largely ineffective, and did not result in academic gains (Hammill and Larsen, 1974).

Identifying the Learning Style Characteristics of Poor Readers

Following three investigations in which Marie Carbo experimented with providing: (a) remediation for students who had severe deficits in visual and auditory perception, (b) high-interest materials to encourage reading for students with similar sensory problems, and (c) instructional resources that complemented each student's perceptual strengths, she recognized that those underachieving students were highly tactile/kinesthetic, only moderately visual, and were low auditory.

Apparently, they had not learned to read because their previous reading instruction had mismatched their learning styles in many ways. In fact, they had been taught to read with strategies diametrically opposed to those that should have been used. For example, their conventional classrooms required them to sit still in hard chairs, by themselves, for fairly long periods—even though most of them needed mobility, peers, and an informal environment while learning. Most important, those poor readers had been told to listen carefully, although they were not auditory; at best, they had great difficulty following directions. When the instruction, however, was responsive to their learning styles, they made rapid reading gains and became attentive, enthusiastic students. (See Figures 2-1 and 2-2.)

As Carbo further experimented, gradually introducing alternative reading methods, she recognized that phonics—requiring strong auditory discrimination skills which those students lacked—appeared to be the least effective approach for those underachievers. The Fernald reading method which capitalized on students' tactile senses produced noticeable gains within a short period of time. When Fernald was supplemented by games, students evidenced both increased achievement and a joy of learning. And when special recordings were made of their favorite stories, the youngsters became more attentive, comprehended most of what they read and retained words better than they ever had before (Carbo, 1978, 1979, 1981, 1982).

RESULTS OF IMPLEMENTING LEARNING STYLES PROGRAM

After four months of experimenting, the following results were noted:

1. Perceptual training had little or no effect on perception abilities or reading scores.

(a)

(b) Photograph by Marie Carbo, courtesy of the Robert Carbonaro School, District 24, Valley Stream, New York.

(d)

Photograph by Mike Kasnic, courtesy of Butcher Children's School, Emporia University, Kansas.

FIGURE 2-1. Most students prefer to read in an informally designed environment (Carbo, 1983a). Informal reading areas can contain a variety of soft, comfortable seating, such as couches (a), rugs (b), bean bag chairs (c), washtubs and cardboard boxes (d), bathtubs filled with pillows (e), and even pillows tucked inside a reading castle, (f).

(c) Photograph by Lois LaShell, courtesy of the Hillcrest Elementary School, Lake Stevens School District, Everett, Washington.

(e) Photograph by Jan Sutherlin Lane, courtesy Glynn County Schools, Brunswick, Georgia.

(f) Photograph by Patricia Lemmon of the Roosevelt Elementary School, Hutchinson, Kansas.

32

(a)

Photograph by Bill Benish, courtesy of the Hamblen School, District 81, Spokane, Washington.

(b)

Photograph by Marilyn Gardner, courtesy of the Lycoming Valley Middle School, Williamsport, Pennsylvania.

(c)

Photograph by Mike Kasnic, courtesy of the Butcher Children's School, Emporia, Kansas.

FIGURE 2-2. Some youngsters like to read alone in separate, private areas (a and b), while others prefer to read alone near their peers (c).

2. Teaching students to read through their perceptual strengths produced excellent reading gains.

3. Attitudes, behavior, and attention worsened when students were taught through their perceptual weaknesses, and improved significantly when students were taught through their perceptual strengths.

4. Tactile/kinesthetic materials and experiences (see Chapter 7) and high-interest tape recorded books (see Chapter 6) were especially effective techniques, particularly for youngsters with visual memory problems and auditory weaknesses.

Matching Reading Programs to Individual Learning Styles

During a three-year period, the learning styles of hundreds of students were identified with the Learning Style Questionnaire (Dunn and Dunn,

1975), and complementary reading methods, materials and strategies were designed and implemented. It was obvious that no single reading approach was best for all students. Specific profiles, however, did match particular reading methods closely (Carbo, 1980; 1982) (see Chapter 4). For example, students who were successful with phonics invariably:

- had strong auditory preferences,
- were teacher motivated,
- enjoyed reading with a teacher and peers,
- were able to sit and listen to a lecture for moderately long periods of time, and
- often preferred a formal, quiet environment.

On the other hand, the characteristics of those who learned easily with the language-experience method were quite different. Those students:

- had strong tactile/kinesthetic and visual preferences,
- were primarily self- and/or peer-motivated,
- needed mobility, and
- liked to learn in an informal environment.

Rarely did a reading method match a youngster's learning style exactly; most had to be adapted in some way to the individual.

Identifying Individual Reading Styles

After years of research, checklists and instruments were developed that identified a student's learning style for reading, or "reading style." The Reading Style Observation Guide (Table 2-1) can be used to identify and diagnose students' reading styles quickly and on-site. An in-depth analysis is provided by the Reading Style Inventory (RSI) (Carbo, 1979, 1981).

Observing and Recording Individual Reading Styles

The Reading Style Observation Guide (RSOG) identifies student behavior, diagnoses it, and then recommends compatible teaching strategies (Carbo, 1981) (see Table 2-1). There are 20 items listed that characterize possible student behaviors. For example, item 1 portrays a student who is distracted by noise, looks up from reading at the slightest sound, places hands over ears, and tries to quiet others. That youngster probably needs quiet when reading and would benefit from quiet reading areas such as study carrels and quiet carpeted sections.

TABLE 2-1. Reading Style Observation Guide (RSOG)*

Observation	Reading Style Diagnosis	Suggested Strategies for Teaching Reading
The student:	*The student:*	
1. Is distracted by noise, looks up from reading at the slightest sound, places hands over ears, tries to quiet others.	Prefers to read in a quiet environment.	Provide quiet reading areas such as study carrels and magic carpet sections; use rugs, stuffed furniture, drapes to absorb sound; make available tape recorded reading materials with headsets to block out noise.
2. Can read easily when people are talking or music is playing.	Prefers to read in an environment with talking and/or music.	Permit student to listen to music through headsets while reading; establish small-group reading areas where youngsters may read and talk.
3. Squirms, fidgets, squints when reading near a window on a sunny day.	Prefers to read in soft or dim light.	Use plants, curtains, hanging beads, dividers to block and diffuse light; add shaded lamps to reading sections; suggest student read in darker area of room.
4. Seeks brightly lit areas for reading.	Prefers to read in bright light.	Allow student to read under bright lights and near windows.
5. Wears many sweaters indoors.	Prefers a warm environment.	Encourage youngster to read in a warmer section of the room and suggest sweaters.
6. Perspires easily; wears light clothing.	Prefers a cool environment.	Encourage pupil to read in a cooler section of the room and suggest light clothing.
7. Is restless and moves in his/her seat when reading.	Prefers an informal design.	Allow the student to read while sitting on a pillow, carpeting, soft chair or the floor.
8. Continually asks for teacher approval of reading work; enjoys sharing reading interests with teacher.	Is teacher-motivated.	Encourage child to discuss reading interests with you and to do reading work and then share it with you; praise him/her; try small, teacher-directed reading group.
9. Enjoys reading with the teacher.	Prefers reading with adults.	Schedule youngster to read with you often; try older tutors and adult volunteers.
10. Cannot complete lengthy assignments.	Is neither persistent nor responsible.	Give short reading assignments and check them frequently; try programmed reading materials or multisensory instructional packages.
11. Becomes confused by many choices of reading materials.	Requires structure.	Limit choices; give clear, simple directions; try a structured reading approach such as a basal reader or programmed materials; provide a limited selection of reading resources based on child's interests.
12. Enjoys choices, demonstrates creativity when reading.	Does not require structure.	Provide many choices of reading materials; try an individualized reading program with many options for project work.

TABLE 2-1. Reading Style Observation Guide (RSOG)

Observation	Reading Style Diagnosis	Suggested Strategies for Teaching Reading
The student:	*The student:*	
13. Participates actively in group discussions; chooses to read with friends.	Prefers to read with peers.	Establish isolated areas where small groups can meet and read together; provide reading games, activity cards, small-group techniques; encourage writing and acting in plays or panels; try a language-experience approach.
14. Shies away from others; reads best alone.	Prefers to read alone.	Provide independent activities such as programmed materials if the child also needs structure, tape recorded books, computers, multisensory instructional packages if the child is only tactual/kinesthetic or is unmotivated; try an individualized approach.
15. Notices and remembers details in pictures; is a good speller; does not confuse visually similar words ("stop" and "spot" or "was" and "saw") or letters ("m" and "n" or "b" and "d"); has a good sight vocabulary.	Is a visual learner.	Try a whole-word reading approach; if the child also needs structure, try programmed learning sequences.
16. Remembers directions and stories after hearing them; decodes words with ease; does not confuse similar sounding words ("pot," "hot," "dot"); enjoys listening activities.	Is an auditory learner.	Try a phonic or linguistic reading approach; if the child also needs structure, for variety, occasionally try a programmed learning sequence.
17. Enjoys learning by touching; remembers words after tracing over and "feeling" them, likes to type, play reading games; is very active.	Is a tactual/kinesthetic learner.	Try a language-experience approach; use clay, sandpaper, and so on to form words; try many reading games, model building, project work and multisensory instructional packages.
18. Continually asks if it is lunchtime or time for a snack when reading.	Prefers intake while reading.	Permit nutritious snacks (carrots, celery, nuts, fruit) during reading periods.
19. Has difficulty reading in early morning; becomes animated and attentive in the afternoon.	Is better able to read in the late afternoon; may be even better at night!	Schedule student to read in the late afternoon or send home "talking books" (see Chapter 6) for evening work.
20. Cannot sit still for long reading periods; becomes restless and sometimes misbehaves.	Either requires mobility or different types of studies or methods.	Allow the youngster to get a drink or snack and then return to reading work; provide many manipulatives and reading games; try reading on soft couch and/or carpeting where child can move or stretch while reading; schedule movement to different areas and centers in the room.

*From the *Reading Style Inventory Manual* by Marie Carbo, 1981, pp. 6–7.

Items 15 and 16 deal with the important element of perception. The student depicted in item 15 is a good speller—a strong indication of visual ability, since English is not essentially a phonetic language, and good spelling, therefore, requires good visual memory. In addition, the youngster does not confuse words or letters that are visually similar. Such a student probably would do well with whole-word and individualized methods emphasizing the visual characteristics of words—provided, of course, that the child is interested in the materials. A very different learner has been recorded under item 16. He is highly auditory, enjoys listening to and repeating stories, remembers what he hears, does not confuse words that sound alike, and finds decoding activities easy. For that student, phonic and linguistic approaches are recommended as beginning reading methods.

Recording student behaviors anecdotally, analyzing them, and testing compatible teaching strategies are first steps toward understanding how to teach children to read through their individual styles. The Reading Style Inventory® is described in the next section.

Obtaining and Using the Reading Style Inventory®

Which reading method would allow Tony to make the best progress? At what time of day should reading be scheduled? Why isn't our reading program working in first grade? What kinds of reading materials should be ordered for next year? Why don't Carrie, Pat, and David enjoy reading?

Those are some of the questions that can be answered by the computerized printouts of the Reading Style Inventory (RSI). While there are many tests that assess a child's reading level, the RSI is the first diagnostic instrument that reveals the many conditions under which a student is likely to learn to read and become a good reader (see Table 2-2 and Figure 2-3). The RSI is a multiple-choice, self-report questionnaire (see Appendix B for sample statements). It can be administered in about 20 to 30 minutes with a computer diskette, or a pencil-and-paper test, to selected first graders individually toward the end of the school year, to small groups of second graders, and to large groups of most students in grades three through twelve. Specific instructions for administering the RSI are in the *RSI Manual* (Carbo, 1981). As a student's RSI is processed, the computer compiles the answers into patterns; those reading methods and materials that most nearly match a youngster's reading style are recommended on the RSI computer printouts, along with any needed modifications.

Both individual and group RSI computerized profiles can be obtained after the RSI has been administered. The RSI Individual profile is recommended particularly for any student who is experiencing difficulty learning to read, does not read well, and/or does not enjoy reading (see Figures 2-4 and 2-5). The RSI group profile summarizes and condenses the infor-

TABLE 2-2. Elements of Reading Style Identified by the *Reading Style Inventory*

I. Environmental Stimulus	Does the student prefer to read:
Sound	with music, with talking, in silence?
Light	in bright or dim light?
Temperature	in a warm or cool temperature?
Design	in a formal design (hard chair at a desk) or an informal design (soft chair, rug, floor)?
II. Emotional Stimulus	When reading, is the student:
Motivation	self-motivated; not self-motivated, motivated by peers, motivated by adults?
	Does the student:
Persistence	complete reading tasks?
Responsibility	do the reading work agreed upon or assigned?
Structure	prefer: little or much direction when reading? many or few choices of reading materials? reading work checked immediately or seldom? reading work checked by peers, adults, self?
III. Sociological Stimulus	Does the student prefer to read:
Peers	with five or six students?
Self	alone?
Pair	with one student?
Teacher	with a teacher?
Varied	with a teacher and students?
IV. Physical Stimulus	Does the student read best:
Perceptual	when taught through his/her visual modality, auditory modality, tactual modality, kinesthetic modality, and/or with a multisensory approach?
	Does the student prefer to read:
Intake	when permitted to eat and drink?
Time	in the morning, early afternoon, late afternoon, evening?
Mobility	when permitted to move?

From: The *Reading Style Inventory Manual* by Marie Carbo, 1981, p. 2.

mation on the individual profiles, and provides both group totals and individual diagnoses and recommendations (see Figures 2-6 to 2-8). The group profile enables educators to: (a) order the kind and number of reading materials needed to match individual reading styles; (b) plan reading groups; (c) decide overall reading strategies; (d) schedule groups; and (e) redesign the reading environment. (For information on the RSI, see Appendix B.)

FIGURE 2-3. Thanks to the RSI recommendations, Thornton is now an avid reader. His RSI profile indicates that he prefers the individualized method, storybooks, reading alone in an informal design, warmth, music, snacks, and dim light.

OPTION 1: COMPUTERIZED RSI INDIVIDUAL PROFILE
(Recommended to: teachers, diagnosticians and parents.)

The information contained in the computerized individual profile provides answers to questions, such as those that follow, about the reading style of a particular youngster:

- Why can't John learn with the whole-word method?
- Which reading method most closely matches his reading style?
- Can John's reading style be accommodated sufficiently by the classroom reading program? If not, which reading program is most appropriate?
- On which pages of the *RSI Manual* can I find additional suggestions for teaching John to read?
- Would he respond well to a peer tutor?
- What special modifications will help him compensate for his visual and auditory perception difficulties?

The RSI individual profile is ideal for discussing the reading style of a child at a case conference, and during a teacher-parent conference (Carbo, 1984a). We especially recommend it to reading specialists, special education and classroom teachers, diagnosticians, and parents. The RSI individual profile is a three-page computer printout that identifies a youngster's reading style and recommends reading strategies, methods and materials (see Figures 2-4 and 2-5). Each page has the student's name, grade, date of birth, date of processing, reading level (optional), predominant reading method(s) already used (optional), identification number and special code number.

The first page of the individual profile (Figure 2-4) describes the youngster's reading style preferences, and strengths, lists appropriate strategies, and provides reference pages for additional teaching sug-

```
    DATE OF PROFILE:06/26/85        INDIVIDUAL READING STYLE PROFILE            SC:0020

    STDNT NAME: GAFFNEY JOHN       GRADE:06  RL:00.0  RM:       DOB:12/04/71  SEX:M  STDNT ID:

     DIAGNOSIS                  RECOMMENDED STRATEGIES FOR TEACHING READING         RSI MANUAL PAGE

PERCEPTUAL STRENGTHS/PREFERENCES
    POOR AUDITORY STRENGTHS     LIMIT LISTENING ACTIVITIES THAT FOCUS ON DECODING       P. 21#27C
    FAIR VISUAL STRENGTHS       LIMIT USE VISUAL AIDS:WORD FLASH CARDS,CHARTS,BOARD WORK P. 22#28C
    MODERATE TACTUAL PREFRNCES  USE TACTUAL ACTIVITIES:WRITING,TYPING,MANIPULATIVES      P. 22#29B
    STRONG KINESTH PREFRNCES    COMBINE READG W/MAKING/BUILDG/DOING; USE FLOOR GAMES     P. 23#30A

PREFERRED READING ENVIRONMENT
    QUIET (NO MUSIC)            PRVIDE QUIET AREAS,STUDY CARRELS,HEADSETS TO BLOCK NOISE P. 15#1A
    QUIET (NO TALKING)          PRVIDE QUIET AREAS,STUDY CARRELS,HEADSETS TO BLOCK NOISE P. 15#2A
    DIMLY LIT                   PRVIDE SHADED LAMPS,PLANTS/CURTAINS TO DIFFUSE LIGHT     P. 15#3B
    WARM TEMPERATURES           ALLOW STDNT WEAR WARM CLOTHING AND READ WARMEST AREA OF ROOM P. 15#4B
    INFORMAL DESIGN             PRVIDE SOFT CHAIRS/COUCHES,RUGS,PILLOWS                  P. 16#5B
    HIGHLY ORGANIZED            PRVIDE READG MATERIALS THAT ARE COLOR-CODED,NUMBRD,LABLD P. 16#6A

EMOTIONAL PROFILE
THIS STUDENT IS:
    PEER-MOTIVATED              ENCOURAGE TO SHARE READG INTERESTS W/PEERS              P. 16#7
    NOT ADULT-MOTIVATED         DO NOT REQUIRE STDNT SHARE READG INTERESTS W/ADULTS
    NOT SELF-MOTIVATED          PRVIDE MATERIALS BASED ON STDNT'S INTERESTS; PRAISE OFTEN P. 17#9
    NOT PERSISTENT              PRVIDE ONE OBJECTIVE,BRIEF ASSGNMNTS;PRAISE             P. 17#10C
    NOT RESPONSIBLE             GIV SHORT ASSGNMNTS;ONE OBJECTIVE;FEW/NO OPTIONS        P. 18#11C
THIS STUDENT PREFERS:
    FEW/NO CHOICES              PRVIDE NARROW SELECTION HIGH-INTEREST MATERIALS         P. 18#12C
    MUCH DIRECTION              SET CLEAR, SIMPL OBJECTIVES;TIME LIMITS,FEW OPTIONS     P. 18#13A
    WORK CHKD IMMEDIATELY       PRVIDE BRIEF TASKS;CHECK AS COMPLETED                   P. 19#14A
    WORK CHKD BY ADULTS         CHECK WORK AT REGULAR INTERVALS;OFFER PRAISE/GUIDANCE   P. 19#15B

SOCIOLOGICAL PREFERENCES
    TO READ TO A TCHR           SCHDULE STDNT TO READ TO TCHR                           P. 19#16
    NOT TO READ W/PEERS         DO NOT SCHDULE STDNT TO READ W/PEERS OFTEN
    NOT TO READ ALONE           DO NOT SCHDULE STDNT TO READ ALONE OFTEN
    TO READ W/PEERS/TCHR        SCHDULE STDNT TO READ W/PEERS/TCHR                      P. 20#19
    TO READ W/ONE PEER          SCHDULE STDNT TO READ W/ONE PEER                        P. 20#20

PHYSICAL PREFERENCES
    INTAKE WHILE READG          PRMIT STDNT TO EAT/DRINK WHILE READG                    P. 20#21A
    NOT TO READ IN THE MORNING  DO NOT SCHDULE READG WORK IN THE MORNING OFTEN
    TO READ EARLY NOON          SCHDULE READG WORK IN EARLY NOON                        P. 20#23
    TO READ LATE NOON           SCHDULE READG WORK IN LATE NOON                         P. 20#24
    TO READ IN EVENING          ASSIGN READG WORK TO BE DONE IN EVENING                 P. 21#25
    MUCH MOBILITY               PRMIT STDNT TO TAKE FREQUENT BREAKS WHILE READG         P. 21#26A
```

FIGURE 2-4. RSI Individual Profile. The first page of the RSI individual profile: (a) identifies the youngster's reading style preferences and strengths (column 1), (b) lists appropriate strategies for teaching the child to read (column 2), and (c) has reference pages for additional teaching strategies which are described in detail in the *Reading Style Inventory Manual* (column 3).

```
DATE OF PROFILE:06/26/85          READING MATERIALS RECOMMENDATIONS              SC:0020

STDNT NAME:GAFFNEY JOHN        GRADE:06  RL:00.0  RM:        DOB:12/04/71  SEX:M  STDNT ID:

HIGHLY RECOMMENDED
    GAMES,EG.,DLM,CURRIC ASSOC (P.50 RSI MANUAL;ALSO SEE PP.57-9,61 FOR TCHR-MADE GAMES AND
    MULTISENSORY INSTRUC PKGS).

RECOMMENDED
    COMPUTERS WITH A VARIETY OF READING SOFTWARE.

    TCHR-MADE RECORDED BOOKS(PP.54-5 RSI MANUAL)IF STDNT IS IN PRIMARY GRADES AND/OR IS READG BELOW
    GRADE LEVEL.USE MODFCATIONS UNDER CARBO METHD P.2 OF PRINTOUT.

ACCEPTABLE
    AUDIO-VISUALS,EG.,FILMSTRIPS,FILM LOOPS,ELECTRONIC TCHG MACHINES (P.53 RSI MANUAL).

    USE LANGUAGE-EXPERIENCE MATERIALS WITH EITHER LANG-EXPERIENCE METHD OR FERNALD WORD-TRACING METHD,
    EG., ENCYC BRITANNICA LEIR KIT(P.48 RSI MANUAL) AND/OR ACTIVITY CARDS
    P.50 RSI MANUAL). ALSO SEE P.56 FOR TCHR-MADE ACTIVITY CARDS. USE MODFCATIONS UNDER
    LANG-EXPERIENCE METHD OR FERNALD METHD P.2 OF PRINTOUT.

NOT RECOMMENDED
    READING KITS,EG.,SRA READG LAB,AUDIO READG PROGRESS LAB (P.51 RSI MANUAL;ALSO SEE P.60 FOR
    TCHR-MADE PROGRAMMED LNG SEQUENCE).

    SKILL BUILDER WKBKS & DUPL MASTERS,EG.,BARNELL LOFT,WRLD RECORD PUBL,MILLIKEN (P.52 RSI MANUAL).

    BASAL RDRS W/PHONIC OR LINGSTC EMPHASIS,EG.,OPEN COURT,LIPPINCOTT(PP.46-7 RSI MANUAL).

    GLASS-ANALYSIS MATERIALS (P.51 RSI MANUAL).

    BASAL RDRS USING WHOLE-WORD METHD,EG.,SCOTT FORESMN,MACMILLAN, HOLT
    (P.45 RSI MANUAL),UNLESS WORD-FOR-WORD RECORDINGS ACCOMPANY MATERIALS.

    INDIVIDUALIZED MATERIALS,EG.,SCHOLASTIC BOOKS,RANDOM HOUSE(P.49 RSI MANUAL),UNLESS
    WORD-FOR-WORD RECORDINGS ACCOMPANY MATERIALS.
```

```
DATE OF PROFILE:06/26/85          READING METHOD RECOMMENDATIONS              SC:0020

STDNT NAME:GAFFNEY JOHN        GRADE:06  RL:00.0  RM:        DOB:12/04/71  SEX:M  STDNT ID:

HIGHLY RECOMMENDED
    NONE LISTED

RECOMMENDED
    THE CARBO RECORDED-BOOK METHD (PP.54-5 RSI MANUAL),IS RECOMMENDED IF STDNT IS IN ELEMENTARY GRADES
    AND/OR RDG BELOW GRADE LEVEL.MAKE THE FOLLOWING MODFCATIONS:
        -RECORD SMALL AMOUNTS OF BOOK FOR STDNT          -HAV STDNT READ IMMDTLY AFTER LISTENG TAPE
        -PRVIDE EXACT DIRCTIONS FOR WORK                 -SCHDULE STDNT TO READ TO TCHR
        -SCHDULE STDNT TO READ W/ONE PEER

ACCEPTABLE
    THE LANGUAGE-EXPERIENCE METHD IS ACCEPTABLE W/THE FOLLOWING MODFCATIONS:
        -PRVIDE QUIET WRITG/READG AREA                   -PRVIDE HI-INTEREST ASSGNMNTS
        -PRVIDE SPECIFIC WRITG ASSGNMENTS                -PRVIDE FEW OPTIONS/CLEAR DIRCTIONS
        -CHECK WORK IMMEDIATELY                          -SCHDULE STDNT TO READ TO TCHR
        -DO NOT SCHDULE STDNT TO READ W/PEERS OFTEN      -DO NOT SCHDULE STDNT TO READ ALONE OFTEN
        -SCHDULE STDNT TO READ W/PEERS & TCHR            -PRVIDE SHORT-TERM ASSGNMNTS

SPECIAL MODIFICATIONS
    FOR ALL READG METHODS LISTED ABOVE,THE FOLLOWING SPECIAL MODFCATIONS ARE RECOMMENDED FOR THIS STDNT:
        -WRITE DIRECTNS FOR WORK,GIV TO STDNT            -HAV STDNT USE CURSIVE TO LESSN B&D REVERSALS
        -PRVIDE REPETITION OF WORDS THRU MANY SENSES     -HAV STDNT USE INDEX CARD UNDR WORDS WHILE READG
        -DO NOT HAV STDNT SOUND OUT WORDS WHILE READG    -LIMT BOARD COPYG;GIV WRITTN COPY OF ASSGNMNT
        -PRMIT STDNT PUT FNGR UNDER WORDS WHILE READG

NOT RECOMMENDED
    THE PHONIC METHD AND THE LINGUISTIC METHD ARE NOT RECOMMENDED FOR THIS STDNT.

    THE WHOLE-WORD METHD IS NOT RECOMMENDED FOR THIS STDNT.

    THE FERNALD WORD-TRACING METHD IS NOT RECOMMENDED FOR THIS STDNT.

    THE INDIVIDUALIZED METHD IS NOT RECOMMENDED FOR THIS STDNT.

    THE ORTON-GILLINGHAM METHD IS NOT RECOMMENDED FOR THIS STDNT.




    FOR A DETAILED DESCRIPTION OF ABOVE READING METHODS, SEE PP.39-43;54-5 RSI MANUAL.PAGES 24-9 EXPLAIN HOW
    READING METHODS ARE SELECTED BASED ON READING STYLE DIAGNOSIS.
```

FIGURE 2-5. RSI Individual Profile. The second page itemizes reading methods in order—from *Highly Recommended* to *Not Recommended*—and describes how each approach can be modified to match the student's reading style. Recommended reading materials are listed on page three.

gestions in the *Reading Style Inventory Manual.* Page two of the RSI individual profile lists reading methods in order from Highly Recommended to Not Recommended. Following each method are the modifications that can help the youngster learn more easily with a particular technique (see Figure 2-5). Note that the Special Modifications section of page two provides specific strategies that can help the student compensate for particular visual and/or auditory perception problems. The third page of the RSI individual profile, itemizes the reading materials that match the youngster's reading style, in descending order, from those resources that are Highly Recommended to those that are Not Recommended (Figure 2-5).

Interpreting an RSI Individual Profile

Let's look at John's RSI individual profile (Figures 2-4 and 2-5). The first page indicates that John is a tactile/kinesthetic learner with fair visual and poor auditory strengths (Figure 2-4). When reading, John prefers quiet, dim light, warmth, soft furniture, highly organized reading materials, intake, and mobility. Like many poor readers, he is peer-motivated, not responsible or persistent, and does not like to read in the morning.

John needs a great deal of structure. For example, line 17 (first column) states that he prefers "Much Direction." The recommended strategy in the second column is for the teacher to "Set Clear Simple Objectives, Few Options, Time Limits;" the third column indicates that a detailed description of the strategies for providing "Much Direction" is on "P. 18#13A" of the *RSI Manual.*

Page two of John's RSI lists the reading methods that do match his reading style. For example, since John's visual perception is "fair," and he does not have an independent reading style, the individualized method is not recommended (Figure 2-5). The Carbo Recorded Book Method is one of the methods recommended for John because this approach provides the auditory and visual reinforcement he needs, and requires no decoding skills. His tactile preferences, combined with his fair visual perception, make the language-experience method advisable. John's RSI indicated that he had certain visual and auditory perception difficulties. Several Special Modifications are listed to help him to overcome those problems.

Page three of John's RSI individual profile lists commercial and teacher-made materials needed to implement his reading program. Note that games are highly recommended because he has strong kinesthetic preferences.

To summarize, the RSI individual profile has important information for educators and parents. The first page identifies the student's reading style, and itemizes teaching strategies and reference pages in the *RSI Manual.* Page two lists reading methods that are and are not recommended for a youngster, and describes how reading instruction should be modified to give a student the best opportunity to learn to read. And, finally, the materials needed to implement a student's reading program are contained on page three (addresses of publishers of those reading materials are listed in Appendix D).

OPTION 2: COMPUTERIZED RSI GROUP PROFILE (Recommended to: administrators, teachers and supervisors.)

The nine-page RSI group profile summarizes the individual profiles, reveals group patterns and provides: (a) specific information about the reading style preferences and strengths of each member of the group (Figure 2-6); and (b) recommended teaching strategies, reading methods and materials for the overall group; and for each individual youngster (Figure 2-7). At the bottom of each page are reference pages for the teaching strategies contained in the *RSI Manual.* Group totals are located directly under each reading style category on every page, so that teachers and administrators can plan schedules easily, order materials, and so on.

DATE OF PROFILE: 05/31/85   SC: 0000   PAGE 02

READING STYLE GROUP PROFILE — PERCEPTUAL STRENGTHS/PREFERENCES

STUDENT NAMES	GRD	AUDITORY STRENGTHS				VISUAL STRENGTHS				TACTUAL PREFRNCES				KINESTH PREFRNCES			
		EXC	GOOD	FAIR	POOR	EXC	GOOD	FAIR	POOR	STRG	MODR	MILD	NONE	STRG	MODR	MILD	NONE
TOTALS		03	06	09	06	04	09	07	04	08	10	04	02	17	05	02	00
1. ANZALONE LOUIS	02			X		X					X			X			
2. BURNETT JACK	02	X				X					X			X			
3. CERRERA LENNY	02		X						X		X					X	
4. COHEN PAUL	02		X			X				X				X			
5. DONAHUE DAVID	02			X			X			X				X			
6. DOWNING JOHN	02	X				X					X			X			
7. GAFF HUGH	02	X				X						X		X			
8. HARRIS RITA	02			X			X				X						X
9. HODGES JOANN	02				X				X			X		X			
10. JACKSON LISA	02		X			X						X			X		
11. JOHNSON PAULA	02		X				X				X			X			
12. KAZANZAKIS LIT	02			X		X				X				X			
13. MENDOZA RAUL	02			X			X				X				X		
14. MEYER MANNY	02				X	X					X			X			
15. OCONNOR EUGENE	02				X				X		X			X			
16. OLSEN DONALD	02		X				X			X				X			
17. OXFORD TED	02		X			X					X			X			
18. REUTHER VIOLA	02	X					X					X			X		
19. ROBFRTS MICHEL	02			X				X		X					X		
20. SCHROEDER BARB	02			X					X				X			X	
21. SELBY SY	02			X			X			X				X			
22. SWIFT DENNIS	02			X			X			X				X			
23. TSAO LIN	02			X				X					X	X			
24. ZALEWSKI IDA	02				X			X		X				X			

SEE PP. 21-23 RSI MANUAL FOR TEACHING STRATEGIES.

FIGURE 2-6. RSI Group Profile. Pages one through six provide group totals and individual diagnoses for each reading style element.

READING STYLE GROUP PROFILE – READING MATERIALS RECOMMENDATIONS

STUDENT NAMES	GRD	READING GAMES 1	2	3	4	ACTIVTY CARDS 1	2	3	4	AUDIO-VISUALS 1	2	3	4	COMPUTERS 1	2	3	4	RECRDED BOOKS 1	2	3	4
TOTALS		17	05	02	00	05	08	07	04	07	13	04	00	03	20	01	00	13	07	04	00
1. ANZALONE LOUIS	02	X					X			X					X			X			
2. BURNETT JACK	02	X					X				X				X			X			
3. CERRERA LENNY	02		X				X					X			X					X	
4. COHEN PAUL	02	X					X			X					X			X			
5. DONAHUE DAVID	02	X						X		X					X			X			
6. DOWNING JOHN	02	X					X			X					X			X			
7. GAFF HUGH	02	X						X	X					X				X			

READING STYLE GROUP PROFILE – READING MATERIALS RECOMMENDATIONS

STUDENT NAMES	GRD	BASAL RDR/PH 1	2	3	4	BASAL RDR/WW 1	2	3	4	READING KITS 1	2	3	4	WORKBOOKS 1	2	3	4	STORYBOOKS 1	2	3	4
TOTALS		00	08	06	10	02	10	03	09	00	10	05	09	00	08	05	11	07	06	07	04
1. ANZALONE LOUIS	02		X			X					X				X				X		
2. BURNETT JACK	02	X						X			X				X		X				
3. CERRERA LENNY	02		X					X				X			X						X
4. COHEN PAUL	02	X					X					X				X			X		
5. DONAHUE DAVID	02			X		X				X				X				X			
6. DOWNING JOHN	02	X					X			X				X				X			

READING STYLE GROUP PROFILE – READING METHOD RECOMMENDATIONS

STUDENT NAMES	GRD	PHONIC/LING 1	2	3	4	WHOLE-WORD 1	2	3	4	INDVDLIZED 1	2	3	4	LANG-EXP 1	2	3	4	FERNALD 1	2	3	4	CARBO 1	2	3	4
TOTALS		00	08	06	10	02	10	03	09	07	06	07	04	05	06	06	07	00	02	01	21	13	07	04	00
1. ANZALONE LOUIS	02		X			X				X				X					X			X			
2. BURNETT JACK	02	X					X			X				X					X			X			
3. CERRERA LENNY	02		X					X				X				X		X							X
4. COHEN PAUL	02	X					X			X				X					X			X			
5. DONAHUE DAVID	02			X		X				X					X				X			X			
6. DOWNING JOHN	02	X					X			X					X				X			X			
7. GAFF HUGH	02	X					X			X						X			X			X			
8. HARRIS RITA	02		X						X		X				X				X				X		
9. HODGES JOANN	02		X						X			X			X			X							X
10. JACKSON LISA	02	X					X			X					X				X			X			
11. JOHNSON PAULA	02	X						X		X				X					X				X		
12. KAZANZAKIS LIT	02		X				X			X					X				X			X			
13. MENDOZA RAUL	02			X				X		X						X			X			X			
14. MEYER MANNY	02			X			X			X					X				X			X			
15. OCONNOR EUGENE	02			X				X			X				X		X								X
16. OLSEN DONALD	02		X					X			X				X				X			X			
17. OXFORD TED	02	X					X				X				X				X			X			
18. REUTHER VIOLA	02	X					X			X					X				X			X			
19. ROBERTS MICHEL	02			X				X			X				X				X			X			
20. SCHROEDER BARB	02			X				X				X			X				X						X
21. SELBY SY	02		X		X					X					X				X			X			
22. SWIFT DENNIS	02			X		X				X				X					X			X			
23. TSAO LIN	02			X			X			X					X				X			X		X	
24. ZALEWSKI IDA	02			X				X		X					X				X			X			

1=HIGHLY RECOMMENDED; 2=RECOMMENDED; 3=ACCEPTABLE; 4=NOT RECOMMENDED
SEE PP. 40-3; 54-5 RSI MANUAL FOR TEACHING STRATEGIES.

FIGURE 2-7. RSI Group Profile. Pages seven to nine list recommended reading methods and materials that match the individual reading styles of the students in the group.

Interpreting an RSI Group Profile

Figures 2-6 to 2-8 represent an actual RSI group profile of a second grade class. Perceptually, these second graders are kinesthetic, tactile, visual, auditory—in that order (Figure 2-6). Totals appear under each perception category.

Like many second graders who have taken the RSI, this is a tactile/ kinesthetic class that is not highly auditory. Only nine youngsters qualify for the excellent or good auditory category, while 15 have fair to poor auditory strengths. Therefore, most of these children should not learn to read primarily by listening to lessons, or with the phonic method. Instead, they need tactile/kinesthetic involvement, such as field trips, "real" experiences, games, writing stories, manipulatives, and so on (Carbo, 1981, 1982, 1983a).

Subsequent pages of the RSI group profile indicate that most of the youngsters prefer quiet while reading, almost half like to read in dim light,

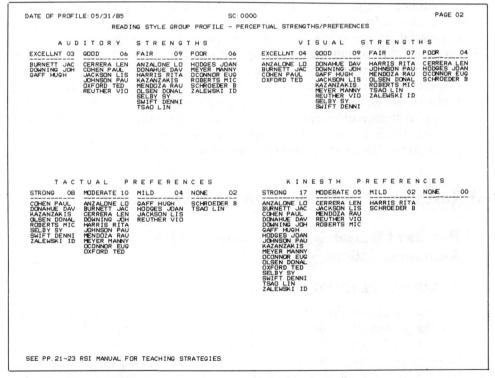

FIGURE 2-8. The RSI group profile is available in two formats. The first format (Figures 2-6 and 2-7), lists all the students in the group and indicates individual reading style preferences with an "X." The second format (above) lists each student's name under the categories that match the youngster's reading style.

temperature is not a factor for 17, none of the students wants to read in a formal design for an entire reading period, and 14 prefer to read in a highly organized environment. Clearly, these are children who need to read in a quiet, well organized room that has some informal and dimly lit areas. When reading, these second graders tend to be adult-motivated and they prefer clear directions, some choices of reading materials, and to read with one peer. The last three pages recommend reading methods and materials that match the reading styles of the youngsters in the group (Figure 2-7). Categories 1, 2, 3 and 4, listed under each reading method, refer to the degree to which that reading approach matches the reading style of the student (see bottom of printout page for explanation).

Information about the reading style of one youngster is provided on the RSI group profile, but not in the same detail as the RSI individual profile.

In summary, each page of the RSI group profile has a specific purpose: the first has detailed information about perceptual strengths and preferences; pages two and three can aid teachers in designing the room arrangement for reading; page four contains descriptions of each student's emotional profile; page five itemizes students' sociological preferences and is helpful to plan various group and individual activities, as well as for whom parent and peer tutors are advisable; page six, which lists physical preferences, is useful for scheduling groups and determining intake and mobility needs; and, the last three pages of the group RSI profile enable administrators and teachers to select the reading methods and materials that most closely match the groups' reading style, and to design alternate programs for those students requiring different methods and materials.

Initial Research with the Reading Style Inventory®

Results of Research Implementing the RSI Recommendations

IMPROVED READING ACHIEVEMENT

After being taught through their individual reading styles for three to ten months, youngsters in both remedial and developmental reading programs have made excellent progress in reading. Notably, 37 of 40 of LaShell's handicapped youngsters achieved mainstreaming reading scores during the 1982–83 school year when the RSI recommendations were implemented, compared with 2 of 40 the previous year (Carbo, 1984c,d). In a subsequent one-year study with 90 learning-disabled youngsters, LaShell reported that students whose reading styles were matched gained 1.4 years in reading, whereas mismatched subjects advanced less than 4 months (LaShell, 1986).

In the Roosevelt Elementary School in Hutchinson, Kansas, the 26 remedial reading students averaged a three-year increase in reading achievement in one school year (Lemmon, 1983). Sixth graders at Juanita Elementary in Kirkland, Washington, gained 11 percentile points, advancing to the 92nd percentile in reading comprehension (Adams, 1983); and junior-high poor readers at the Key School in District 4, New York City, gained 2.9 years on standardized reading tests in one school year (Hodges, 1984, 1985).

FEWER DISCIPLINE PROBLEMS AND IMPROVED STUDENT ATTITUDES TOWARD READING

Students' attitudes toward reading became far more positive when they learned through their individual reading styles: they were more relaxed and willing to try, they read more, discipline problems decreased markedly, and teachers reported that students became kinder and more helpful toward each other. Although Hodges' students were reading 4 to 7 years below grade level and had endured a long history of reading failure, they selected the RSI Reading Lab in place of their usual favorites, such as gym, music, art, dance and aerospace.

Both LaShell (1983) and Hamilton (1983) recorded similar, dramatically positive changes in their students' attitudes. LaShell's substitute observed, "The thing that amazed me over and over again was how the kids loved to read. They lined up to read to the parent volunteers or high school students and would argue over who got to read next."

At the beginning of the 1982 school year, Hamilton stated that some of her sixth-grade poor readers were discipline problems, and were absent often from her reading class. In May of 1983, Hamilton recorded the following transformation:

> I ended up with absolutely no discipline problems. . . . There was a much less stressful environment. They volunteered a lot more. My relationship with them was very good. They did their work, enjoyed it, and completed it in half the time.

INCREASED READING FOR PLEASURE

By implementing RSI profile recommendations, well-established, negative reading habits were altered in brief periods of time. For example, after a five-week RSI summer remedial reading program conducted by Adams (1983), 71% of the youngsters' parents said that their children enjoyed reading more, read more for pleasure, and did not want summer school to end (See Appendix B, Table 3).

POSITIVE CHANGES IN THE TEACHER'S ROLE AND ABILITY TO TEACH READING

An important outcome of reading programs that match students' reading styles has been, as Hamilton reported a "much less stressful" environment; the teacher's role has been perceived as changing from that of authoritarian to facilitator and helper. Hamilton (1983), a veteran teacher of twelve years, described that transformation:

> My relationship with the students became much friendlier. They no longer saw me as a threat to them, to their learning, or someone who was going to force them to learn. They saw me as a helper—helping them to learn more. . . . The students seemed to enjoy the class more, seemed to enjoy me more. I definitely enjoyed them more. (pp. 6–7).

Following four months of using the RSI recommendations, Adams found that his teachers were more willing to try a variety of approaches depending upon each child's reading style; they also developed and/or improved management techniques, and used more audio-visuals, computer software, and tactile kinesthetic materials than before working with the RSI profiles of their students.

Reliability and Validity of the Reading Style Inventory

Test–retest reliability coefficients for the 13 RSI subscales range from .67 to .77 (Carbo, 1981; 1982), and research with the RSI has demonstrated content, concurrent, predictive and construct validity (Carbo, 1981; 1982; 1983a,b,d; 1984c) (see Appendix B).

Reading Styles: Where Do We Go from Here?

The previous section was entitled "Initial Research with the Reading Style Inventory," because a great deal more cooperative investigation is needed to help educators and parents understand individual reading styles and how they can be accommodated. We are becoming increasingly aware of the large, complex variety of reading styles that exist, and the profound impact those style differences have upon learning to read. Even severely handicapped youngsters with a long history of reading failure have made excellent reading gains when their programs capitalized on their strengths and preferences. We are on the brink of an educational revolution—a breakthrough that may eliminate unnecessary and often fruitless remediation and enable all children to read naturally and easily.

3

Matching Reading Methods and Individual Reading Styles: A Crucial New Concept in Reading Instruction

The Best Reading Method for Every Student: Does One Exist?

In 1977, eight-year-old Jimmy was declared severely learning disabled and emotionally disturbed by his school's Committee on the Handicapped—but he was neither. Jim was a child of normal intelligence who could not learn to read with the methods his teachers used with him. Jim's severe reading failure made him physically ill, angry and argumentative. He hated school. By ninth grade he read on a second-grade level, and had spent a total of seven of his ten years of school in special classes, separated from the mainstream of school life.

How did Jimmy's reading failure start? He had trouble learning to read from the beginning. Just by chance, the reading approach used with Jimmy was phonics and, tragically, he did not have the auditory and analytic abilities needed to succeed with that method. To make matters worse, his reading difficulties led to repeated, intensive remedial drills in decoding: exactly what he could not do and did not need. The result? More anxiety, frustration and failure.

Although Jimmy's case is an extreme example of what can happen when a youngster's reading style is seriously mismatched, the potential for harm that can result from using the inappropriate reading approach is both real and pervasive in our schools. Selecting a reading method for a student is a crucial decision that can have a profound impact upon a youngster's desire to learn. We know that some students can learn to read with any method. They are fortunate because it is likely that they will learn whichever reading approach their teacher uses. But for others, the wrong reading method makes learning to read difficult or even impossible (Carbo, 1978, 1980a, b; Urbschat, 1977; Wheeler, 1983).

Importance of Matching Reading Styles and Learning Styles at All Levels

What happens when youngsters struggle to learn to read in the early grades? Like Jimmy, they generally dislike reading and avoid it. That sets a cycle of failure into motion. As a result of reading less, the gap between a student's grade and reading level widens. Eventually, in later years, that gap may seem insurmountable.

Once the failure cycle begins and continues for an extended period of time, it can be a Herculean task to reverse. Many school dropouts are poor readers who begin the failure cycle by suffering through the personal embarrassment of not being able to read well. New York City estimated that 45 percent of its high school population will drop out by 1985, regardless of the special alternative and remedial programs that have been instituted (Purnick, 1983). We believe that, in general, the failure to increase reading achievement on the junior and senior high levels is largely due to the continued mismatch of students' individual reading and learning styles.

Thus, it is absolutely imperative that programs match individual reading and learning styles at all levels—most especially in the primary grades where reading failure can be prevented from occurring in the first place (Carbo, 1978, 1980b, 1981; Dunn, Carbo and Burton, 1981). For example, both fictitious first graders described below are capable of learning to read well—provided that their first grade reading program matches their individual styles.

The Reading Gamble

Billy and Cindy are about to begin first grade. Both are bright, happy and eager to learn. By the end of the first week of school, Cindy still will be eager and happy, but Bill will be miserable. Their teacher will use phonics with every student. Phonics will be ideal for Cindy. She is analytic and learns most easily when information is presented in small, sequential steps. Cindy has excellent auditory perception skills, enjoys listening to adults and can sit for long periods. She likes the highly structured reading materials that her teacher uses.

Billy has a very different reading style. He will fail with phonics because he is a global learner. To get his attention, stories must have a strong emotional impact. Bill has excellent visual and tactile perception skills which help him to remember whole words that can be seen and even touched in manipulative tasks. He learns best in an informal reading environment where he can move about easily, and, is highly motivated to read interesting storybooks, as well as the stories he composes.

If Billy and Cindy lived just two blocks away in another school district, the odds would be reversed in Billy's favor. The first grade teacher there uses a visual-tactile, language-experience, reading approach with many word games. The classroom setting is informal with lots of rugs and interest centers. Cindy would be distracted by the noise in that classroom. She often would become argumentative during games, frustrated by the story-writing assignments, and confused by the choices of storybooks. She would complain that school was too much play and too little real work!

Ah, but Billy would blossom. He would write prolifically, become the center of attention for his writing ability, enjoy the games and storybooks, develop many friendships and beg his parents to take him to the library for more and more of those wonderful books (p. 34, Dunn and Carbo, 1979).

THE READING GAMBLE: INCREASING THE PROBABILITY OF SUCCESS

How can the odds for all the Billys and Cindys be improved so that no student has to suffer unnecessary reading failure? Like Billy and Cindy, most youngsters do come to school with ability, interest, and enthusiasm. They want to learn to read. That initial motivation is a powerful springboard for learning and should not be wasted.

To prevent reading failure and provide the most rapid remediation for those who already have failed, we urge that every child's style be identified before a reading approach is selected and that teachers then experiment with the recommendations suggested in Chapters 4 to 10 in this book (see Figure 3-1).

How Have Reading Methods Been Selected for Students in the Past?

For more than a century, most educators used whichever reading method was in vogue during that period. Before 1870, the alphabet method was used widely; by 1890 the whole-word method became popular; and, at the turn of the century, the sentence method gained wide acceptance. Then the cycle began to repeat itself. From the early twentieth century through the 1960s, first phonics, and then the whole-word method predominated. Throughout the 1970s and up to this writing, either phonics or whole-word plus phonic approaches have been used extensively.

Many reading innovations of the past have been reactions to contemporary reading techniques. For instance, during the 1930s when the whole-word method was used extensively, youngsters with visual perception problems probably had difficulty learning to read. Two researchers of that period devised different approaches for teaching such students to read: Fernald (1943) used a word-tracing, language-experience method, while Orton (1937) employed a multisensory phonic technique.

Merely shifting to a different method, without preliminary reading

FIGURE 3-1. Matching reading programs to individual reading styles helps to make learning to read a joy. (Photograph by Jan Sutherlin Lane, courtesy of Glynn County Schools, Brunswick, Georgia.)

style diagnosis, continues to be essentially a hit-or-miss approach which cannot assure success for all. Change without prior diagnosis will help only those youngsters whose styles happen to match the new method; it would cause difficulties for those who are mismatched. Such approaches are not the best way to help students avoid or overcome reading problems. No one reading method is best for every child.

Today's Preoccupation with Reading Subskills

School districts currently seem to be caught in a vicious cycle in which they consistently increase the amount of time and money spent on reading instruction but obtain only disappointing results; many students continue to find it difficult to read. Unfortunately, the following anecdotes are true (Carbo, 1983c).

Florida: A reading teacher was compelled to use meditation exercises to calm her poor readers because they had become so anxious and nervous about reading.

Washington State: Junior high school English teachers were required to avoid the term "reading" and substitute the word "literature" when teaching because their seventh graders had been so inundated with reading skill work that they reacted fearfully and negatively to the word "reading."

Pennsylvania: First grade teachers said they could not allow their students to read books for enjoyment because so much of the class period had to be devoted to the skill work which the children would be tested on at the end of the school year.

Georgia: A second grader able to read adult-level books fluently and with understanding, received a "C" in reading on his report card because he had difficulty doing his decoding work.

WHY THE PENDULUM SWUNG TO PHONICS IN THE '60s

Why is there concern about the hundreds, sometimes thousands, of so-called reading subskills that do not necessarily produce good, adult readers while, at the same time, so little attention is paid to what children are reading, and how they feel about learning to read? It is important to be aware of research that led to what is defined by current standards as a "good reading program" (one that emphasizes decoding skills).

During the 1960s, many books and editorials were written which advocated phonics. In 1967, Jeanne Chall gave credibility to the pro-phonics position with her book, *Learning to Read: The Great Debate*. Unfortunately, what few people realize is that nearly all the reading studies she had summarized were poorly conceived, conducted, and evaluated (Carbo, 1983c). Chall (1967) admitted:

> Most of the reading studies did not indicate how the experimental and control groups were selected, how much time was allotted to various aspects of reading, how the teachers were selected, whether the quality of teaching was comparable in both groups, or even whether the teachers followed the methods under study. Even more important, most studies did not specify clearly what a "method" involved, but instead merely assigned labels (e.g., "phonics"), expecting the reader to understand what was meant. . . . Many of the early studies did not use standard measures of outcomes or statistical tests of significance to determine whether the various results obtained could have been attributable to chance differences (p. 100–101).

Therefore, most of the research comparing reading methods included in *The Great Debate* could have been invalid; minimally they were less than adequate. Chall herself acknowledged: "Had I considered only studies that fulfilled all necessary experimental conditions, I would have been left with just a handful—if that many" (p. 102). Unfortunately, despite the lack of validity of the bulk of the research in *The Great Debate*, that book was largely responsible for the inclusion of decoding skills for the first time on achievement tests in 1972 (Chall, 1979).

Once children were to be tested on phonic skills, those skills had to be taught. Publishers began to include more and more decoding exercises in their reading materials to prepare youngsters for achievement tests.

PHONICS MATCHES ONLY CERTAIN READING STYLES

Some parents and educators appear to have forgotten that the original purpose of reading skill exercises was to make it easier for children to learn to read well. Phonics was never meant to be an end in itself. There are some students who must learn with phonics, some who cannot learn with phonics, some who need only a small amount of it, and still others who are capable of becoming excellent readers without learning any phonics at all.

It is highly probable that you are one of the many people who learned to read well with little or no phonic instruction because that method was only somewhat popular in the '30s, lost favor among educators in the '40s and '50s and was not widely advocated until the mid to late '70s. If you are knowledgeable about phonics, it is likely that you learned phonics in a Teacher Education course, or from a basal reader manual. It is not correct to assume that phonic instruction necessarily produces good readers; good readers may have had no phonic instruction.

Teaching Reading Through Modality Strengths

The story of Helen Keller demonstrates rather poignantly the enormous human potential that can be unlocked when individuals—even the most seriously handicapped—are taught through their modality strengths. Helen Keller became aware of the world around her because she was taught through the senses she did have—touch, body movement, smell and taste. Not only did she learn to read, she learned to speak and write, and became an inspiration to the nation's handicapped!

Just as deaf and blind children can and do learn through their best modalities, all students need to be taught to read through their strongest sense(s), and then reinforced through their next strongest. Children who are able to see and hear are fortunate because they can use both senses to learn to read. But sometimes youngsters who have their sight and hearing do not learn well or easily through those modalities; they may have other senses that are comparatively stronger which make it easier for them to learn and remember. That is why it is essential to determine youngsters' specific modality strengths and weaknesses and how those affect their ability to read.

Teaching Through Modality Strengths: State of the Art

Schools actually penalize tactile/kinesthetic learners and reward students with auditory and visual strengths because most instruction is either auditory (listening to the teacher), or visual (looking at what the teacher wrote on the chalkboard). As reported in Chapter 1, research verifies that beginning readers (Carbo, 1980, 1983a) and poor readers (Adams, 1978; Bakker, 1966; Carbo, 1983b; Price, Dunn and Saunders, 1980; Walters and Kosowski, 1963; Wheeler, 1983) tend to be strongly tactile/kinesthetic and have much lower preferences for learning visually and auditorially. At the age of six or seven, most children appear to be, in descending order of development: kinesthetic, tactile, visual, auditory; they learn most easily through their sense of touch and whole-body movement (see Figures 3-2 and 3-3).

Despite that data, researchers have not begun to examine modality development to the extent that its importance demands. Restak documented the auditory superiority of females over males, and that boys tend to be more kinesthetic longer than girls. In that regard, most studies test primary children for visual or auditory abilities and rarely include tactile/kinesthetic treatments; when they do, "kinesthetic" usually is restricted to tracing over words (which is tactile), rather than the use of tactile/kinesthetic resources such as task cards, electroboards, learning circles, body games, activity cards, trips, and "real life" experiences (Dunn and Carbo, 1981; Dunn and Dunn, 1978).

FIGURE 3-2. When games and electronic devices were introduced at Juanita Elementary, the tactile youngsters found that learning to read was "fun," and they learned their reading skills quickly. (Photograph by David Adams, courtesy of Juanita Elementary School, Lake Washington School District, Kirkland, Washington.)

Figure 3-3. These strongly kinesthetic second graders are learning first-hand about the carpenter's tools described in their basal reader story. (Photograph by David Adams, courtesy of Juanita Elementary School, Lake Washington School District, Kirkland, Washington.)

Research Matching Reading Methods and Modality Strengths: Flaws, Falacies, and Facts

Since teaching through modality strengths is so critical, why isn't it a standard practice in schools? The major problem has been the essentially negative results of nearly two decades of research investigating the importance of teaching students to read through their perceptual strengths. That research, however, reviewed in Carbo's doctoral dissertation, was found to be misleading because many of the studies had faulty designs, inadequate controls, and used incorrect, invalid, or unreliable instruments. Thus the investigators reached incorrect conclusions (Carbo, 1980 and 1983b). Carbo's doctoral study received the First National Dissertation Award from the Association for Supervision and Curriculum Development (ASCD) for contributing the "most to advance knowledge and understanding . . . in the field of curriculum in 1980."

Identifying Modality Strengths

When working with youngsters who had not achieved well in school, the Dunns (1971) found that such children were neither auditory nor visual. Although they did not read or compute well either, they often had excellent manual dexterity and were skillful when performing physical activities. Before that exploration of the learning styles of underachievers, most perceptual testing was limited to an evaluation of auditory and/or visual modalities—which often were weaknesses for youngsters with learning difficulties. Having identified the learning style that characterized underachievers, the Dunns experimented with tactile/kinesthetic resources and found significant gains resulted (Dunn, 1971). Thus, "tactile/kinesthetic" was added to their first instrument which identified students' styles, the Learning Style Questionnaire (1972; 1975; 1977). They also were identified in Dunns' and Price's *Learning Style Inventory* (1974, 1979, 1981, 1985).

In 1976, Carbo expanded the Dunns' work, and developed the *Reading Styles Checklist for Identifying Perceptual Strengths*—the first assessment to concentrate solely on the identification of each child's auditory, visual, tactile and kinesthetic strengths and weaknesses, as those either supported or hindered reading achievement. Figure 3-4 has selected samples from that original checklist.

INSTRUMENTS THAT IDENTIFY MODALITY STRENGTHS

Continued experimentation and revision of the Reading Styles Checklist for Identifying Perceptual Strengths resulted in inclusion of the most statistically reliable items on the *Reading Style Inventory* (RSI). Modality strengths and weaknesses comprise only one eighteenth of the categories investigated by the RSI, but perceptual abilities and global/analytic inclinations appear to be two of the more important elements of reading style.

The modality preferences of children at or above the second grade can be diagnosed either by administering the RSI or the Learning Style Inventory (LSI). If students are in a reading program—or should be—then use the RSI to identify modality strengths specifically for reading; to identify modality strengths for designing an overall instructional program, use the LSI; when students are below the second grade, try the *Learning Style Inventory: Primary (LSI-P)* (Perrin, 1981). If a first grader is capable of understanding the RSI statements, administer the RSI. These instruments are discussed in Chapters 1 and 2 and Appendixes A and B.

Teaching Students to Read Globally and Analytically

It is extremely important to match global and analytic styles when teaching reading because many studies verify that when analytic learners are taught analytically, and when global learners are taught globally, both achieve significantly better than when their learning and teaching styles are mismatched (Douglas, 1979; Trautman, 1979). Some youngsters (those

FIGURE 3-4. Reading Styles Checklist for Identifying
Perceptual Strengths (Carbo, 1976)

IDENTIFYING AUDITORY STRENGTHS

12–14 = Excellent

9–11 = Good

5–8 = Moderate

0–4 = Poor to Fair

The student can:

_____ 1. follow a short verbal direction
_____ 2. repeat simple sentences of eight to twelve words
_____ 3. remember a phone number after hearing it a few
times
_____ 4. recall simple math facts or a few lines of poetry after
hearing them several times
_____ 5. understand long sentences
_____ 6. remember and sequence events discussed
_____ 7. use appropriate vocabulary and sentence structure
_____ 8. pay attention to a story or lecture for 15 to 30 minutes
_____ 9. concentrate on an auditory task even when an auditory distraction is presented
_____ 10. identify and recall the sounds of individual letters
_____ 11. discriminate between/among words that sound alike
(e.g., "leaf" and "leave" or "cot" and "cat")
_____ 12. discriminate between/among letters that sound alike
(e.g., "sh" and "ch" or "a" and "o")
_____ 13. blend letters quickly to form words
_____ 14. sound out words and still retain the storyline

IDENTIFYING VISUAL STRENGTHS

11–13 = Excellent

8–10 = Good

5–7 = Moderate

0–4 = Poor to Fair

The student can:

_____ 1. follow a simple direction that is written and/or drawn
_____ 2. place four to six pictures in proper story sequence
_____ 3. recall a phone number after seeing it a few times

FIGURE 3-4. (*Continued*)

_____ 4. concentrate on a visual activity for 15 to 30 minutes
_____ 5. concentrate on a visual task when a visual distraction is presented
_____ 6. work on a visual task without looking away or rubbing his/her eyes
_____ 7. recall words after seeing them a few times
_____ 8. remember and understand words accompanied by a pictorial representation
_____ 9. read words without confusing the order of the letters (e.g., reading "spot" for "stop")
_____ 10. discriminate between/among letters that look alike (e.g., as "m" and "n" or "c," "e," and "o")
_____ 11. discriminate between/among words that look alike (e.g., "fill" and "full" or "that" and "what")

IDENTIFYING TACTILE STRENGTHS

11–13 = Excellent

8–10 = Good

5–7 = Moderate

0–4 = Poor to Fair

The student can:

_____ 1. draw and color pictures
_____ 2. perform crafts such as sewing, weaving, and/or making models
_____ 3. remember a phone number after dialing it a few times
_____ 4. concentrate on a tactile task for 15 to 30 minutes
_____ 5. hold a pen or pencil correctly
_____ 6. write legible letters of the alphabet appropriate in size for his/her age
_____ 7. write with correct spacing
_____ 8. recall words after tracing over clay or sandpaper letters that form the words
_____ 9. remember words after writing them a few times
_____ 10. recall words after playing a game containing those words, such as bingo or dominoes
_____ 11. recall the names of objects after touching them a few times
_____ 12. write words correctly after tracing over them with his/her finger
_____ 13. recall words after typing them a few times

FIGURE 3-4. (*Continued*)

IDENTIFYING KINESTHETIC STRENGTHS

10–12 = Excellent

7–9 = Good

4–6 = Moderate

0–3 = Poor to Fair

The student can:

_____ 1. run, walk, catch a ball, and so on, in a rhythmical, smooth fashion

_____ 2. concentrate for fifteen to thirty minutes during kinesthetic activities that require whole-body movement

_____ 3. recall dances, games, sports, and/or directions after performing them a few times

_____ 4. move his/her body easily and freely when acting in a play

_____ 5. remember words seen on posters and signs when on a trip

_____ 6. memorize a script more easily when actually performing in a play

_____ 7. understand concepts after "experiencing" them in some way (e.g., going on a trip, acting in a play, caring for pets, performing experiments, and so on)

_____ 8. remember words after "experiencing" them (e.g., looking at the word "apple" while eating an apple or pretending to be an elephant while learning the word "elephant")

_____ 9. recall words used in a floor game after playing the game a few times

_____ 10. remember facts, poetry, lines in a play more easily when he/she is walking and/or running, rather than standing still

_____ 11. recall a letter of the alphabet after forming it with his/her entire body

_____ 12. remember the "feeling" of a story better than the details

who are *both* highly global and highly analytic) appear to learn easily with virtually any reading method but that probably is the result of inadvertent matching.

Every reading method emphasizes either an essentially global or analytic approach to reading (Carbo, 1981, 1982b, 1983c, 1984a). To help students learn to read most easily and enjoyably, it is necessary to: (a) identify the existing global/analytic style of the child being taught (see the section that follows), (b) understand the global or analytic style required to succeed with each reading method and then, (c) use the reading method(s) that most closely match(es) the global/analytic style of the learner (see Chapter 4).

Identifying Global and Analytic Reading Styles

Some instruments identify global/analytic inclinations; they have not been verified as being either accurate or appropriate for very young children—those with whom we are most concerned when considering the identification of beginning reading approaches. For that reason, it is important that teachers recognize some of the more obvious behaviors that youngsters who are essentially analytic—or essentially global—tend to demonstrate. For example:

Analytic students often:

1. concentrate and learn when information is presented in small, logical steps
2. respond to appeals of logic
3. solve problems systematically
4. process information sequentially and logically
5. enjoy doing puzzles (e.g., crossword, jigsaw)
6. like putting things together by following specific directions (e.g., mechanical toys, objects with parts)
7. pay close attention to exact directions, such as measurements in a recipe or explanations for assembling an object
8. enjoy learning facts such as dates, names, and other specifics
9. learn phonics easily
10. understand and apply phonic rules
11. are critical and analytic when reading
12. can identify the details in a story

Global students often:

1. concentrate and learn when information is presented as a gestalt or whole
2. respond to emotional appeals
3. tend to like fantasy and humor
4. get "wrapped up" in a story and do not concentrate on the facts
5. process information subjectively and in patterns

6. easily can identify the main ideas in a story
7. dislike memorizing facts such as dates, names or specifics
8. learn easily through stories
9. use story context often to figure out unknown words

You can increase reading success substantially by matching analytic methods with analytic learners and global methods with global learners. To determine whether a youngster is global and/or analytic, use the global/analytic lists above, and match the students' style to the reading methods listed on the chart in Table 4-1. Global youngsters usually can learn to read words and sentences more quickly and easily than they can the sounds of isolated letters. Analytic learners frequently are content to begin by learning isolated letter sounds which they blend to form words and finally sentences (Carbo, 1983c). Youngsters who experience difficulty learning to read analytically with phonics, often can learn easily with global methods; those who have difficulty with global techniques may respond well to analytic approaches.

Most young children appear to be global. Not before the age of seven

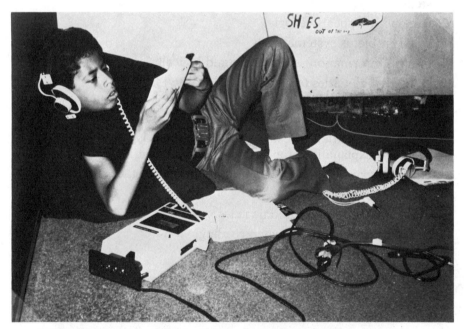

FIGURE 3-5. The strongly global students at the Key School have gained two to four years in reading comprehension in just one school year with the help of recorded, high-interest, well-written storybooks. See Chapter 6 for recording books. (Photograph by Helené Hodges, courtesy of the Key School, District 4, New York City.)

or eight do we find many analytic youngsters in school. Strongly analytic children learn well when information is presented sequentially and in segments, the way phonics is taught. In most primary classrooms, however, highly analytic youngsters are in the minority. When phonics is introduced too early, global children begin to perform poorly because they lack analytic abilities. Many students with reading problems tend to have a biased arousal of the right hemisphere (Oexle and Zenhausern, 1981), and need to learn with global—rather than analytic—reading methods and materials (see Table 4.2).

For parents and teachers who may be concerned about a youngster who does not become analytic, we want to stress that neither student— global or analytic—is more intelligent and/or capable of achieving than the other. Both types learn equally well when taught in ways that complement their styles. In fact, adults appear to be primarily global rather than analytic.

In the next chapter you will learn about 12 methods to teach reading, and how and when to select each, based on reading style diagnosis.

4

How to Match Reading
Methods to Individual
Reading Styles

Why and How to Match Reading Methods to Modality Strengths

Every reading method demands specific modality strengths and preferences of the learner. Students have such varied perceptual strengths and preferences, that no single reading approach can be effective for all. For example, youngsters with excellent auditory abilities can decode words easily and recall what they hear; such children tend to respond well to phonic and linguistic techniques. Visual students are able to remember a word after seeing it a few times; they generally learn well with whole-word and individualized methods.

On the other hand, language-experience approaches are appropriate for tactile youngsters who learn by writing, touching, and tracing over words. Some students, particularly the gifted, tend to learn to read with any method. But the reading method that most closely matches every reading style preference and strength of a student will be the most effective and enjoyable technique for that youngster.

Matching Reading Methods to Global/Analytic Styles

Many teachers know that there are different methods of teaching reading but often are unaware that each approach can be classified as being either analytic or global. Global reading methods are "holistic," that is, they begin with, and emphasize, the whole story and move from that whole to its parts (the skill work). Global approaches draw skill work from the characters, events, and vocabulary of the story (see Chapter 6 for examples of global skill materials). Analytic approaches begin with small bits of information—isolated letter sounds, letter blends, clusters of letters and rules—and then, gradually, that information is put together to form words, sentences, and thoughts.

Essentially analytic methods (sometimes called "synthetic"), include the phonic and linguistic methods; whereas, the whole-word, individualized, and language-experience methods are representative of predominantly global approaches (see Table 4-1) (Carbo, 1981, 1982a, 1983c).

To teach global learners well, *meaning* is the key. Global youngsters must be helped to learn with well-written stories because they can recall words presented within that context much more easily than through either a poorly conceived or written story, or out of context. They also are able to recall high-interest, dissimilar words (e.g., "elephant," "monster," "Charlie Brown") better than the low-interest, similar words commonly found in decoding materials (e.g., "jet," "met," "bet") (Burton, 1980).

Global learners tend to be extremely visual; they need to "draw" mental pictures to help them to remember. Their learning is hindered if the task cannot be visualized (Oexle and Zenhausern, 1981). Understandably, it is difficult for global students to recall "low-image-producing" verbalizations, such as isolated letter sounds or words with little meaning that are taken out of context (Carbo, 1983c, 1984).

To learn to read easily, global learners *must* have a visual image of the topic, an illustrative anecdote, and a reason for learning. Based on what we know about global youngsters, reading programs for young children should focus on high-interest stories, words learned in context, and reading skills that are drawn from the stories read (see Chapter 6).

Matching Reading Methods to Perceptual Strengths and Global/Analytic Styles

When a reading method is selected for a student, it should match both the youngster's perceptual strengths and global/analytic style. It is impossible to alter the perceptual abilities and global/analytic styles biologically imposed on each child. For example, by definition, phonics requires good auditory

TABLE 4-1. Two Basic Reading Approaches

Analytic Reading Methods
• phonic
• linguistic
• Orton-Gillingham (phonic method variation)
• Glass-Analysis (linguistic method variation)

Global Reading Methods
• whole-word
• individualized
• language-experience
• Fernald word-tracing (language-experience method variation)

skills and an analytic style; the student must learn isolated letter sounds, discriminate among those sounds, and then blend them to form words—all in a step-by-step, sequential manner. On the other hand, the individualized method requires good visual skills and a more global style, since the student must discriminate among and recall entire words and phrases without relying on phonic techniques.

Table 4-2 describes the perceptual strengths and global/analytic style needed to succeed with eight reading methods. The phonic, Orton-Gillingham, linguistic, and Glass-Analysis methods are best for auditory/analytic learners; whereas, the whole-word, language-experience, Fernald word-tracing and individualized approaches more closely match the reading styles of visual/global youngsters.

Note that the Orton-Gillingham and Fernald reading methods are recommended for students who have weak visual perception abilities. This is because the tactile reinforcement provided by the letter-tracing techniques of Orton and Gillingham or Fernald's word tracing program, is ideal for tactile learners who have difficulty recalling words through their visual sense. Tactile reinforcement aids both visual memory and discrimination; it helps youngsters who tend to reverse letters and words (e.g., "b" and "d," "saw" and "was"), confuse letters and words that look alike ("a" and "o," "hot" and "hat"), and/or transpose letters within a word ("blow" for "bowl").

Matching Reading Methods to Individual Reading Styles

Based on the reading style diagnosis of an individual child, the *Reading Style Inventory* (RSI) printouts itemize those methods that accommodate the

TABLE 4-2. Matching Reading Methods to Modality Strengths and Global/Analytic Styles

Method	Modality Strength/Weakness			Global/Analytic Style	
	Visual	*Auditory*	*Tactual*	*Global*	*Analytic*
Phonic		+			+
Orton-Gillingham	−	+	+		+
Linguistic		+			+
Glass-Analysis		+			+
Whole-Word	+			+	
Language-Experience	+		+	+	
Fernald Word Tracing	−		+	+	
Individualized	+			+	

KEY: − = Weakness, + = Strength.
(© Marie Carbo, 1981)

youngster's reading style, describe how each method should be modified to more closely match each student's reading style, and list the methods that are not recommended (see Chapter 2).

The following four analytic and four global reading methods are included in the RSI profiles. They are described in the next section and then matched to individual reading styles (see Table 4-3).

Each method has a checklist of required reading style preferences and strengths; critical elements are starred. If a student does not possess a starred element, then that method is an inappropriate choice for that youngster.

Matching Reading Methods and Reading Styles Checklist*

Analytic Reading Methods (Phonic, Linguistic, Orton-Gillingham, Glass-Analysis)

PHONIC METHOD

Instructional Procedures: Generally, the child is taught isolated letter sounds in a prescribed sequence. After a youngster has mastered the sounds of a few letters, those letters are blended to form words. Then the child learns additional letter sounds and learns to decode new and more complex words. That procedure continues until the student masters all the sounds of individual letters and some letter groups.

Beginning readers with a phonic emphasis have a controlled vocabulary that contains the sounds students have been taught in separate lessons; short, three- and four-letter-words are blended (in Chapter 5 see Figure 5-9); eventually students move on to longer and more difficult words.

Whole-class and small-group instruction often are used, especially when students begin learning to read. Instruction proceeds in small, discrete, sequential steps and youngsters are expected to keep pace with their group. During reading periods and when reading alone, students are encouraged to decode unknown words independently. The teacher's role is to introduce new material and to question, inform, and correct the students.

LINGUISTIC METHOD

Instructional Procedures: The linguistic method differs from phonics in that isolated letters are not stressed. Instead, letter clusters, patterns or "families" are taught (e.g., fat, mat, cat, bat). Word patterns are presented in a special sequence and students are encouraged to decode new words using their knowledge and understanding of those patterns (Bloomfield, 1942; Fries, 1962).

---

*This section is adapted from "Selecting Reading Methods That Accommodate Individual Reading Styles" by Marie Carbo in the *Reading Style Inventory Manual*, pp. 40–43, 1981a.

TABLE 4-3. Matching Conventional Reading Methods to Individual Reading Styles

Reading Method	Reading Style Stimuli				
	Environmental	Emotional	Sociological	Physical	Psychological
PHONIC *Isolated letter sounds are taught sequentially and blended to form words.*	• quiet • formal	• teacher-motivated • not/fairly persistent • not/fairly responsible • much structure	• read to a teacher • read w/teacher/ peers	• read at time of day lesson presented • little/no mobility *At least:* * good auditory strengths * fair visual strengths *Note:* Use Orton-Gillingham if student has * poor visual strengths	• reflective * strongly analytic
LINGUISTIC *Patterns of letters are taught and combined to form words.*					
ORTON-GILLINGHAM *Phonic method + student traces over letters w/his/her finger.*					
GLASS-ANALYSIS *Brief, linguistic exercises used as supplement to other methods.*					
WHOLE-WORD *Whole words, presented on flash cards and in sentences, precede the reading of a story.*	• quiet • formal	• teacher-motivated • not/fairly persistent • not/fairly responsible • much structure	• read to a teacher • read w/teacher and peers	• read at time of day lesson presented • little/no mobility *At least:* * good visual strengths * fair auditory strengths	• reflective * moderately global

Method					
INDIVIDUALIZED *Students read a large variety of printed material individually.*	● quiet or some talking ● formal or informal	● self-motivated ● responsible ● persistent ● little structure	● read alone ● read w/teacher and peers at times	● read at time of day reading is scheduled ● little/some mobility *At least:* * good visual strengths	● impulsive or reflective * moderately to strongly global
LANGUAGE-EXPERIENCE *Students read stories that they write.*	● some talking ● formal or informal	● self-motivated ● responsible ● persistent ● little structure	● read alone, read w/teacher, or peers	● write and read at time of day scheduled ● little to much mobility *At least:* * fair visual strengths moderate tactual preferences *Note:* Use Fernald method if student has poor visual strengths	● impulsive or reflective * moderately to strongly global
FERNALD *Language-experience method + student traces over new words.*					

(© Marie Carbo, 1983)

Linguistic readers and storybooks contain a highly controlled vocabulary with many words similar both in sound and configuration, as can be seen in this excerpt from a linguistic preprimer reader:

> The man can fan.
> I can fan the man.
> The man can fan Dan.
> I can fan Dan.
> (p. 3, Rasmussen and Goldberg, 1964)

Words that repeat particular letter clusters are selected for stories; story content is of secondary importance (see Figures 5-11 and 5-12 in Chapter 5).

Whole-class and small-group instruction often are used and each student is expected to keep pace with the group. As with the phonic method, the teacher's role is to introduce new material and question, inform, and correct the students.

Matching Individual Reading Styles with Phonic and Linguistic Methods

For a student to achieve well with the phonic and linguistic approaches to reading, his/her reading style should reflect the following specific characteristics (see Figure 4-1):

*1. The student has auditory strengths and can:
_____ associate printed letters with their corresponding sounds
_____ decode words and still retain the storyline
_____ recognize similarities and differences between/among the sounds of letters and letter groups
_____ blend letter sounds quickly to form words
_____ concentrate on an auditory task for 15 to 30 minutes

*2. The student is analytic and:
_____ learns in a sequential, step-by-step manner
_____ understands the rules of phonics
_____ can apply learned phonic rules to new words
_____ is motivated to read low-interest materials
_____ recalls words with ease regardless of their interest level

Additional reading style characteristics needed for success with the phonic and linguistic methods when used in a conventional classroom:

3. The student:
_____ prefers to read in a quiet environment
_____ prefers to read in a formal environment
_____ is adult-motivated
_____ is fairly persistent
_____ is fairly responsible

DATE OF PROFILE: 04/27/85   READING MATERIALS RECOMMENDATIONS   SC: 0855

STDNT NAME: MANTONE ROBERT   GRADE: 02 RL: 03.5 RM: PH WW DOB: 07/25/76 SEX: F STDNT ID:

HIGHLY RECOMMENDED
COMPUTERS WITH A VARIETY OF READING SOFTWARE

BASAL [...]
MODFCA [...]

GLASS-[...]

RECOMMEND[...]
GAMES: [...]
MULTIS[...]

TCHR-M[...]
GRADE [...]

RECOMMENDED
THE CARBO RE[...]
AND/OR RDG [...]

AUDIO--[...]
UNDER [...]

ACCEPTABL[...]
READIN[...]
TCHR-M[...]

SKILL [...]

INDIVI[...]
UNDER S[...]

USE LA[...]
EG., E[...]
P.50 R[...]
LANG--[...]

NOT RECOM[...]
BASAL [...]
(P.45 [...]

READING M[...]

FOR A DETAILE[...]
READING METHODS[...]

DATE OF PROFILE: 04/27/85   READING METHOD RECOMMENDATIONS   SC: 0855

STDNT NAME: MANTONE ROBERT   GRADE: 02 RL: 03.5 RM: PH WW DOB: 07/25/76 SEX: F STDNT ID:

HIGHLY RECOMMENDED
THE PHONIC METHOD AND THE LINGUISTIC METHOD ARE HIGHLY RECOMMENDED W/THE FOLLOWING MODFCATIONS:
-PRVIDE TAPE RECORDED LESSONS
-PRVIDE HI-INTEREST ASSGNMTS
-SCHDULE STDNT TO READ ALONE

DIAGNOSIS

THE LANGUAGE [...]
THE [...]

-PRVIDE QU[...]
-PRVIDE HI[...]
-DO NOT SC[...]
-SCHDULE S[...]

THE INDIVIDU[...]
-ENCOURAGE [...]
-PRVIDE FE[...]
-CHECK WOR[...]
-SCHDULE T[...]

THE WHOLE-WO[...]

THE FERNALD--[...]

THE ORTON-GI[...]

DATE OF PROFILE: 04/27/85   INDIVIDUAL READING STYLE PROFILE   SC: 0855

STDNT NAME: MANTONE ROBERT   GRADE: 02 RL: 03.5 RM: PH WW DOB: 07/25/76 SEX: F STDNT ID:

DIAGNOSIS	RECOMMENDED STRATEGIES FOR TEACHING READING	RSI MANUAL PAGE
PERCEPTUAL STRENGTHS/PREFERENCES		
EXCELLENT AUDITORY STRENGTHS	USE LISTENING ACTIVITIES; USE DECODING EXERCISES AS NEEDED	P. 21#27C
FAIR VISUAL STRENGTHS	LIMIT USE VISUAL AIDS; WORD FLASH CARDS, CHARTS, BOARD WORK	P. 22#28C
MODERATE TACTUAL PREFRNCES	USE TACTUAL ACTIVITIES WRITING, TYPING, MANIPULATIVES	P. 22#29B
MODERATE KINESTH PREFRNCES	COMBINE READG W/MAKING/BULDG/DOING; USE FLOOR GAMES	P. 23#30B
PREFERRED READING ENVIRONMENT		
QUIET (NO MUSIC)	PRVIDE QUIET AREAS, STUDY CARRELS, HEADSETS TO BLOCK NOISE	P. 15#1A
QUIET (NO TALKING)	PRVIDE QUIET AREAS, STUDY CARRELS, HEADSETS TO BLOCK NOISE	P. 15#2A
BRIGHTLY LIT OR DIMLY LIT	LIGHT IS NOT A FACTOR FOR THIS STDNT	P. 15#3C
COOL OR WARM TEMP	TEMPERATURE IS NOT A FACTOR FOR THIS STDNT	P. 16#4C
FORMAL DESIGN	PRVIDE HARD CHAIRS AT DESKS	P. 16#5A
HIGHLY ORGANIZED	PRVIDE READG MATERIALS THAT ARE COLOR-CODED, NUMBRD, LABLD	P. 16#6A
EMOTIONAL PROFILE		
THIS STUDENT IS:		
NOT PEER-MOTIVATED	DO NOT REQUIRE STDNT SHARE READG INTERESTS W/PEERS	P. 16#8B
ADULT-MOTIVATED	ENCOURAGE TO SHARE READG INTERESTS W/ADULTS	P. 17#9?
NOT SELF-MOTIVATED	PRVIDE MATERIALS BASED ON STDNT'S INTERESTS; PRAISE OFTEN	P. 17#10B
FAIRLY PERSISTENT	PRVIDE SHORT AND LONGER-TERM ASSGNMTS	P. 17#11B
FAIRLY RESPONSIBLE	GRADUALLY INCREASE NUMBER OF OBJECTIVES	
THIS STUDENT PREFERS:		
FEW/NO CHOICES	PRVIDE NARROW SELECTION HIGH-INTEREST MATERIALS	P. 18#12C
	SET CLEAR, SIMPL OBJECTIVES; TIME LIMITS, FEW OPTIONS	P. 18#13A
MUCH DIRECTION		
WORK CHKD IMMEDIATELY	PRVIDE BRIEF TASKS; CHECK AS COMPLETED	P. 19#14A
WORK CHKD BY ADULTS	CHECK WORK AT REGULAR INTERVALS; OFFER PRAISE/GUIDANCE	P. 19#15B
SOCIOLOGICAL PREFERENCES		
NOT TO READ TO A TCHR	DO NOT SCHDULE STDNT TO READ TO TCHR OFTEN	
NOT TO READ W/PEERS	DO NOT SCHDULE STDNT TO READ W/PEERS OFTEN	
TO READ ALONE	SCHDULE STDNT TO READ ALONE	P. 20#18
TO READ W/PEERS/TCHR	SCHDULE STDNT TO READ W/PEERS/TCHR	P. 20#19
NOT TO READ W/ONE PEER	DO NOT SCHDULE STDNT TO READ W/ONE PEER OFTEN	
PHYSICAL PREFERENCES		
NO INTAKE WHILE READG	STDNT DOES NOT REQUIRE FOOD/DRINK WHILE READG	
TO READ IN THE MORNING	SCHDULE READG WORK IN THE MORNING	P. 20#21B
TO READ EARLY NOON	SCHDULE READG WORK IN EARLY NOON	P. 20#22
NOT TO READ LATE NOON	DO NOT SCHDULE READG WORK IN LATE NOON OFTEN	P. 20#23
TO READ IN EVENING	DO NOT ASSIGN READG WORK TO BE DONE IN EVENING OFTEN	
LITTLE/NO MOBILITY	PRMIT STDNT TO READ FOR LONG PERIODS	P. 21#26C

FIGURE 4-1. RSI individual printout of a student whose reading style matches the phonic method. (See Chapter 2 for detailed information about the Reading Style Inventory [RSI].)

_____ prefers few or no choices of reading materials

_____ needs to work with highly structured reading materials

_____ needs a great deal of teacher direction

_____ needs specific time limits

_____ prefers reading work checked immediately by an adult

_____ enjoys reading with peers and a teacher

_____ is not embarrassed when answering or reading in front of a group

_____ can pay attention when group members are answering questions or reading aloud

_____ can learn well at the time of day the group meets

_____ does not require intake when learning to read

_____ does not require mobility when learning to read

VARIATION OF THE PHONIC METHOD: ORTON-GILLINGHAM METHOD

Instructional Procedures: The Orton-Gillingham method uses multi-sensory techniques to teach phonics. Both the sound and name of each letter are learned individually in a highly controlled, specified sequence. First the child sees the letter to be learned and hears the sound that it represents. Then the youngster traces over the letter with his/her finger and writes the letter (Gillingham and Stillman, 1968; Orton, 1937).

The reading style requirements of the Orton-Gillingham method are identical to those of the phonic method, except that the Orton-Gillingham approach is well-suited to youngsters with auditory/tactile/analytic strengths who have visual deficits.

VARIATION OF THE LINGUISTIC METHOD: GLASS-ANALYSIS METHOD

Instructional Procedures: With the Glass-Analysis method, clusters of sounds within words are taught. For example, the cluster sounds within the word lunch are "un" and "ch." Glass recommends specific perceptual conditioning techniques. First the child looks at and listens to the word, hears the cluster sounds within the word and then is asked to say the letters that make up those sounds. Next, the student is told the cluster sounds within the word and asked to pronounce their sounds (Glass, 1973; Glass and Burton, 1973).

One of the positive features of the Glass-Analysis method is that this decoding procedure is taught in brief, five- to ten-minute lessons as a supplementary technique. Therefore if Glass-Analysis matches a youngster's reading style, it easily can be used in addition to another reading method.

Global Reading Methods (Whole-word, Individualized, Language-Experience, Fernald Word-Tracing)

WHOLE-WORD METHOD

The whole-word method usually precedes a story in a basal reader. Before children read the story, their teacher introduces all the words believed to be unfamiliar to the students. Those words may be presented on flash cards, word lists, in the context of sentences, and so on. The students look at, listen to, and repeat the new words until they can read them quickly by sight. When reading a story, if a student cannot recognize a word instantly, he/she is encouraged to look at the word carefully, and to use accompanying pictures and sentence context as a clue to the word. Beginning readers using a whole-word approach tend to present and repeat more dissimilar words of varying shapes and lengths than are used in a phonic approach. In addition, new words are introduced in a specific sequence with the repetition of words highly controlled (see Figure 5-8 in Chapter 5).

As is generally true of the phonics method, the whole-word approach is used with either the entire class or small groups of students who read with the teacher. Youngsters are expected to maintain their group's pace. The teacher's role is to introduce new words and their meanings, to stimulate interest in the story, and to inform and correct students as they read.

Matching Individual Reading Styles with the Whole-Word Method
For a student to achieve well with the whole-word approach to reading, his/her reading style should reflect the following specific characteristics:

*1. The student has visual strengths and can:
_____ listen and attend to lessons presented primarily through the visual sense
_____ recall words presented visually
_____ discriminate between/among words and letters that look alike
_____ concentrate on a visual task for 15 to 30 minutes

*2. The student is global and:
_____ can use story context to decipher unknown words
_____ processes information subjectively and in patterns
_____ concentrates and learns when information is presented as a gestalt or whole
_____ enjoys reading stories with many illustrations
_____ uses pictures to enhance the meaning of the story

Additional reading style characteristics needed for success with the whole-word method when used in a conventional classroom include:

3. The student:
   _____ prefers to read in a quiet environment
   _____ prefers to read in a formal environment
   _____ is adult-motivated
   _____ is fairly persistent
   _____ is fairly responsible
   _____ prefers limited choices of reading materials
   _____ needs to work with structured reading materials
   _____ needs teacher direction
   _____ needs specific time limits
   _____ prefers reading work checked immediately by an adult
   _____ is not embarrassed when answering or reading in front of a group
   _____ pays attention when group members are answering questions or reading aloud
   _____ can learn well at the time of day the group meets
   _____ does not require intake when learning to read
   _____ does not require mobility when learning to read

INDIVIDUALIZED METHOD

Instructional Procedures: In this method students select from a large variety of high-interest, printed resources on many levels, such as magazines, books, filmstrips, and newspapers. Some students *become* motivated, persistent, and responsible because of the self-selection of resources based on their personal interests. Generally, youngsters read alone for approximately 15 to 60 minutes, depending on their age and ability. Emphasis is placed on silent reading skills, comprehension, and reading enjoyment. Therefore, children read with minimal interaction with peers and teachers. Those interactions do occur, but, for the most part, they do so either before or after the actual reading experience (see Figure 4-2) (Harris, 1962; Moore, 1979).

Because the individualized method is neither teacher nor group-centered, students need not sit quietly for long periods of time either listening to teacher's directions or to other group members' recitations. For those youngsters easily distracted by the movements and activities of others, it is possible to redesign the classroom so that those who cannot focus directly on their reading for lengthy periods are seated in sections away from others (see Figures 2-2a, b) (Dunn and Dunn, 1978).

There is no extensive teacher direction or structure; certainly some of both are provided but, essentially, the teacher serves as a resource by providing a stimulating reading environment, evaluating the student's comprehension and vocabulary skills during individual conferences, recommending further readings, and meeting with small groups of students to work on necessary reading skills.

(a)

(b)

FIGURE 4-2. Students in Butcher Lab School's individualized reading program are encouraged to select a comfortable spot for reading. Primary youngsters often enjoy sharing a story with a buddy and a student teacher (a), while intermediate youngsters tend to like to read alone (b). Research conducted at Butcher indicated that, regardless of past experience, most intermediate students preferred to read storybooks and their own stories ("Kansas Discovers . . . ," 1983). (Photographs by Michael Kasnic, courtesy of the Butcher Lab School, Emporia State University, Emporia, Kansas.)

Matching Individual Reading Styles with the Individualized Method

For a student to achieve well with the individualized approach to reading, his/her reading style should reflect the following specific characteristics (see Figure 4-3):

*1. The student has visual strengths and can:
_____ recall words presented visually
_____ discriminate between/among letters and words that look alike
_____ concentrate on a visual task for 15 to 30 minutes

*2. The student is global and:
_____ uses pictures to enhance the meaning of a story
_____ can use story context to decipher unknown words
_____ processes information subjectively and in patterns
_____ concentrates and learns when information is presented as a whole or gestalt
_____ enjoys reading stories with many illustrations
_____ recalls high-interest words more easily than low-interest words

Additional reading style characteristics needed for success with the individualized method when used in a conventional classroom:

3. The student:
_____ prefers to read in a quiet environment
_____ prefers to read in a formal or informal environment
_____ is self-motivated
_____ is persistent
_____ is responsible
_____ prefers many choices of reading materials
_____ prefers to read unstructured materials
_____ does not need a great deal of teacher direction
_____ does not need specific time limits when reading
_____ prefers reading work checked at long intervals
_____ prefers to self-check reading work
_____ can learn well at the time of day reading is scheduled
_____ prefers to read alone
_____ requires either no intake or some intake (either is acceptable)
_____ requires either no mobility or some mobility (either is acceptable)

LANGUAGE-EXPERIENCE METHOD

Instructional Procedures: During the reading readiness phase of this technique, students often draw pictures and tell their teacher a story about them. The teacher writes a few simple sentences dictated by the child onto the drawing. At this stage, youngsters are not expected to read what is written; the purpose is to help students to associate printed and spoken words. Later, as children share a common experience of interest—

DATE OF PROFILE:04/27/85   READING MATERIALS RECOMMENDATIONS   SC:0855

STDNT NAME:YARNOW JONATHAN   GRADE:08 RL:08.5 RM:MX   DOB:11/ 3/70 SEX:F STDNT ID:

HIGHLY RECOMMENDED
COMPUTERS WITH A VARIETY OF READING SOFTWARE.

AUDIO
UNDER

        DATE OF PROFILE:04/27/85   READING METHOD RECOMMENDATIONS   SC:0855
INDIV
UNDER   STDNT NAME:YARNOW JONATHAN   GRADE:08 RL:08.5 RM:MX   DOB:11/ 3/70 SEX:F STDNT ID:

TCHR
GRADE   DATE OF PROFILE:04/27/85   INDIVIDUAL READING STYLE PROFILE   SC:0855

HIGHLY RECOMMENDED
THE INDIVIDUALI
-DO NOT SCHDU   STDNT NAME:YARNOW JONATHAN   GRADE:08 RL:08.5 RM:MX   DOB:11/ 3/70 SEX:F STDNT ID:

RECOMMEN   DIAGNOSIS   RECOMMENDED STRATEGIES FOR TEACHING READING   RSI MANUAL PAGE
READI
TCHR   PERCEPTUAL STRENGTHS/PREFERENCES
              FAIR AUDITORY STRENGTHS   LIMIT LISTENING ACTIVITIES THAT FOCUS ON DECODING   P. 21#27C
GAMES   EXCELLENT VISUAL STRENGTHS   USE VISUAL AIDS:WORD FLASH CARDS:CHARTS:BOARD WORK   P. 22#28A
MULT   MILD TACTUAL PREFRNCES   LIMIT TACTUAL ACTIVITIES:WRITING:TYPING:MANIPULATIVES   P. 22#29C
RECOMMENDED   MODERATE KINESTH PREFRNCES   COMBINE READG W/MAKING/BUILDG/DOING:USE FLOOR GAMES   P. 23#30B
THE WHOLE-WORD
-PRVIDE LONG- PREFERRED READING ENVIRONMENT
-PRVIDE SOME   QUIET (NO MUSIC)   PRVIDE QUIET AREAS.STUDY CARRELS.HEADSETS TO BLOCK NOISE   P. 15#1A
-PRMIT STDNT   QUIET (NO TALKING)   PRVIDE QUIET AREAS.STUDY CARRELS.HEADSETS TO BLOCK NOISE   P. 15#2A
-SCHDULE STDN   BRIGHTLY LIT OR DIMLY LIT   LIGHT IS NOT A FACTOR FOR THIS STDNT   P. 15#3C
-PRVIDE SOME   COOL OR WARM TEMP   TEMPERATURE IS NOT A FACTOR FOR THIS STDNT   P. 16#4C
ACCEPTAB   FORMAL & INFORMAL DESIGN   HAV HARD CHAIRS AND SOFT CHAIRS AVAILABLE   P. 16#5C
SKILL   FAIRLY ORGANIZED   PRVIDE READG MATERIALS ORGANIZED BY INTEREST/SUBJECT LEVEL P. 16#6B

USE L   EMOTIONAL PROFILE
EG.   THIS STUDENT IS:
P. 50   NOT PEER-MOTIVATED   DO NOT REQUIRE STDNT SHARE READG INTERESTS W/PEERS   P. 16#9
LANG   NOT ADULT-MOTIVATED   DO NOT REQUIRE STDNT SHARE READG INTERESTS W/ADULTS   P. 17#10A
-DO NOT SCHDU SELF-MOTIVATED   PRVIDE STDNT WITH MANY OPPORTUNITIES TO READ   P. 17#11A
NOT RECO   HIGHLY PERSISTENT   PRVIDE LONG-TERM ASGNMNTS & CONTRACTS
BASAL   HIGHLY RESPONSIBLE   PRVIDE SOME SELF-SELECTION OF OBJECTIVES
THE PHONIC METH THIS STUDENT PREFERS:
GLASS   MANY CHOICES   PRVIDE LARGE VARIETY READG MATERIALS   P. 18#12A
THE FERNALD WOR LITTLE/NO DIRECTION   PRMIT MANY OPTIONS.FLEXIBLE TIME LIMITS   P. 19#13C
                WORK CHKD SELDOM   CHECK WORK ONLY AS NEEDED:MONITOR PROGRESS   P. 19#14C
THE ORTON-GILLI WORK CHKD BY SELF   PRVIDE SELF-CHKG MATERIALS:MONITOR PROGRESS   P. 19#15A

               SOCIOLOGICAL PREFERENCES
READING   NOT TO READ TO A TCHR   DO NOT SCHEDULE STDNT TO READ TO TCHR OFTEN
               NOT TO READ W/PEERS   DO NOT SCHEDULE STDNT TO READ W/PEERS OFTEN
               TO READ ALONE   SCHDULE STDNT TO READ ALONE   P. 20#18
               NOT TO READ W/PEERS/TCHR   DO NOT SCHEDULE STDNT TO READ W/PEERS/TCHR OFTEN
               NOT TO READ W/ONE PEER   DO NOT SCHDULE STDNT TO READ W/ONE PEER OFTEN

FOR A DETAILED DES PHYSICAL PREFERENCES
READING METHODS AR INTAKE SOMETIMES   PRMIT STDNT TO EAT/DRINK WHILE READG IF NEEDED   P. 20#21C
                    TO READ IN THE   SCHDULE READG WORK IN THE MORNING   P. 20#22
                    TO READ EARLY MORNING   SCHDULE READG WORK IN EARLY NOON   P. 20#23
                    TO READ LATE NOON   SCHDULE READG WORK IN LATE NOON   P. 20#24
                    TO READ IN EVENING   ASSIGN READG WORK TO BE DON IN EVENING   P. 21#25
                    SOME MOBILITY   PRMIT STDNT TO READ FOR SHORT PERIODS   P. 21#26B

FIGURE 4.3. RSI individual printout of a student whose reading style matches the individualized reading method. (See Chapter 2 for detailed information about the Reading Style Inventory [RSI].)

77

going on a field trip or caring for an animal—they dictate a story about their experience to their teacher who usually writes it on a large chart. As the story is being composed and written, the teacher may move his/her hand in a sweeping motion under the sentences and read them aloud so that the children learn that words proceed in stories from left to right. Sometimes the students join in and read the story along with the teacher as it is being written. Many stories are written this way and the teacher may accumulate the story charts into a book of stories created by the students.

After the students have composed a number of stories as a group and developed an initial sight vocabulary, they begin to write their own stories. Usually these are written daily on topics of interest provided either by the teacher or the students (see Figures 4-4 and 4-5). Words are controlled only by the student's own speaking vocabulary and writing interests (Ashton-Warner, 1963; Goodman and Goodman, 1979).

When a child cannot spell a word needed for a story, he/she may ask the teacher or a peer for help. Boxes containing words needed for writing, lists of words, and dictionaries usually are available for use; those that

FIGURE 4-4. The language-experience reading method is recommended on the RSI for tactile students who do not have severe visual perception problems. (Photograph by Ray Reynolds, courtesy Hillcrest Elementary School, Lake Stevens School District, Everett, Washington.)

FIGURE 4-5. The use of photographs to stimulate children's writing is particularly effective with students who have global/visual reading styles. (Photograph by Marie Carbo, courtesy of the Robert Carbonaro School, District 24, Valley Stream, New York.)

include many colorful pictures often are preferred for young children because they facilitate use, aid memory, and increase student interest.

Students work individually and in small groups. The teacher facilitates by establishing a stimulating writing environment, displaying the youngsters' stories, helping to develop their ideas, and meeting with small groups of students to improve their reading and writing skills (Stauffer, 1980).

Matching Individual Reading Styles with the Language-Experience Method

For a student to achieve well with the language-experience approach to reading, his/her reading style should reflect the following specific characteristics:

*1. The student has visual and tactual strengths and can:
  _____ hold a pen or pencil correctly
  _____ write with adequate control of the pen or pencil
  _____ recall words after writing them a few times

_____ discriminate between/among words and letters that look alike
after writing them

_____ concentrate on a visual/tactual task for 15 to 30 minutes

*2. The student is global and:

_____ can use story context to decipher unknown words

_____ processes information subjectively and in patterns

_____ concentrates and learns when information is presented as a
whole or gestalt

_____ enjoys writing his/her own stories

_____ enjoys reading his/her own stories

_____ recalls high-interest words more easily than low-interest words

Additional reading style characteristics needed for success with the
language-experience method when used in a conventional classroom:

3. The student:

_____ prefers to read in an environment with sound in the background

_____ prefers to read in either a formal or an informal environment

_____ is self-motivated and/or peer motivated

_____ is persistent

_____ is responsible

_____ prefers many choices of reading materials

_____ prefers to read unstructured materials

_____ needs little teacher direction

_____ needs few time limits to complete work

_____ prefers reading work checked at long intervals

_____ prefers either to self-check or have peers check reading work

_____ prefers to read and write alone and/or with peers

_____ can learn well at the time of day reading is scheduled

_____ requires either no, some, or much intake (any one is acceptable)

_____ requires either no, some, or much mobility (any one is
acceptable)

VARIATION OF THE LANGUAGE-EXPERIENCE METHOD: FERNALD WORD-TRACING METHOD

Instructional Procedures: The Fernald word-tracing method is similar to
the language-experience approach but provides additional tactual
reinforcement.

When a youngster cannot spell a word needed for a story he/she is
writing, the teacher writes the word on a large card by pressing down
hard with a crayon to form raised, waxy letter surfaces. After the teacher
writes the word, the student traces over it with his/her index finger a few
times while vocalizing the word; short words are vocalized in a natural
manner while long words are said in syllables (see Figure 4-6). Then the
youngster turns the card over and writes the word into the story from
memory. Fernald found that "the child stops tracing when he is able to

FIGURE 4-6. Tracing with her finger over words having raised letters (Fernald reading method) helps this little girl to compensate for her visual perception problem, and increases her word retention. (Photograph by Marie Carbo, courtesy of the Robert Carbonaro School, District 24, Valley Stream, New York.)

learn without it" (Fernald, 1943, p. 41). The use of cursive writing as early as possible was recommended by Fernald to help children experience tactually the flow of the complete word and to lessen "b" and "d" reversals.

After a story is written, the teacher types it and places the typed copy below the child's handwritten version. The student reads the typed copy within 24 hours of writing the story to help associate the typed words— that closely resemble the print found in books—with the child's own handwritten words.

The reading style requirements of the Fernald method are the same as those of the language-experience method, except that the process of tracing over raised letters helps increase the word retention of tactual learners who have difficulty learning words solely through their visual modality (see Figure 4-7).

Emerging Reading Methods That Respond to Individual Reading Styles and Interests

READING THROUGH THE ARTS

With this technique, students study a particular theme or subject through a variety of artistic experiences. Then they read and write about the theme. For example, a group of youngsters might learn about the

DATE OF PROFILE 04/27/85   READING MATERIALS RECOMMENDATIONS   SC: 0855

STDNT NAME ANDERSON MARGARET   GRADE 05   RL:02.4   RM:PH WW   DOB 04/11/73   SEX:F   STDNT ID:

HIGHLY RECOMMENDED
USE LANGUAGE-EXPER...
EG. ENCYC BRITANN) AL...
P.50 RSI MANUAL) AL...

RECOMMENDED
COMPUTERS WITH A V...

HIGHLY RECOMMENDED
THE FERNALD WORD-TRACING METHD IS HIGHLY RECOMMENDED W/NO MODFCATIONS

GAMES,EG.,DLM,CURRI...
MULTISENSORY INSTR...

RECOMMENDED

ACCEPTABL...
TCHR-M...
GRADE...

AUDIO-...

NOT RECOMM...
READIN...
TCHR-MA...

SKILL...

BASAL...

GLASS-...
BASAL...
(P.45...

INDIVI...
WORD-F...

READING M...

DATE OF PROFILE 04/27/85   READING METHOD RECOMMENDATIONS   SC: 0855

STDNT NAME: ANDERSON MARGARET   GRADE 05   RL:02.4   RM:PH WW   DOB 04/11/73   SEX:F   STDNT ID:

DATE OF PROFILE 04/27/85

STDNT NAME: ANDERSON MARGARET   INDIVIDUAL READING STYLE PROFILE   SC: 0855

GRADE 05   RL:02.4   RM:PH WW   DOB 04/11/73   SEX:F   STDNT ID:

DIAGNOSIS	RECOMMENDED STRATEGIES FOR TEACHING READING	RSI MANUAL PAGE
PERCEPTUAL STRENGTHS/PREFERENCES		
FAIR AUDITORY STRENGTHS	LIMIT LISTENING ACTIVITIES THAT FOCUS ON DECODING	P.21#27C
POOR VISUAL STRENGTHS	LIMIT USE VISUAL AIDS:WORD FLASH CARDS,CHARTS,BOARD WORK	P.22#28C
STRONG TACTUAL PREFRNCES	USE TACTUAL ACTIVITIES:WRITING,TYPING,MANIPULATIVES	P.22#29A
MODERATE KINESTH PREFRNCES	COMBINE READG W/MAKING/BUILDG/DOING:USE FLOOR GAMES	P.23#30B
PREFERRED READING ENVIRONMENT		
QUIET OR MUSIC	SOUND (MUSIC) IS NOT A FACTOR FOR THIS STDNT	P.15#1C
QUIET OR TALKING	SOUND (TALKING) IS NOT A FACTOR FOR THIS STDNT	P.15#2C
BRIGHTLY LIT OR DIMLY LIT	LIGHT IS NOT A FACTOR FOR THIS STDNT	P.15#3C
COOL OR WARM TEMP	TEMPERATURE IS NOT A FACTOR FOR THIS STDNT	P.16#4C
FORMAL & INFORMAL DESIGN	HAV HARD CHAIRS AND SOFT CHAIRS AVAILABLE	P.16#5C
FAIRLY ORGANIZED	PRVIDE READG MATERIALS ORGANIZED BY INTEREST/SUBJECT LEVEL	P.16#6B
EMOTIONAL PROFILE		
THIS STUDENT IS		
PEER-MOTIVATED	ENCOURAGE TO SHARE READG INTERESTS W/PEERS	P.16#7
NOT ADULT-MOTIVATED	DO NOT REQUIRE STDNT SHARE READG INTERESTS W/ADULTS	
SELF-MOTIVATED	PRVIDE STDNT WITH MANY OPPORTUNITIES TO READ	P.16#9
HIGHLY PERSISTENT	PRVIDE LONG-TERM ASSGNMNTS & CONTRACTS	P.17#10A
HIGHLY RESPONSIBLE	PRVIDE SOME SELF-SELECTION OF OBJECTIVES	P.17#11A
THIS STUDENT PREFERS:		
MANY CHOICES	PRVIDE LARGE VARIETY READG MATERIALS	P.18#12A
LITTLE/NO DIRECTION	PRMIT MANY OPTIONS,FLEXIBLE TIME LIMITS	P.19#13C
WORK CHKD SELDOM	CHECK WORK ONLY AS NEEDED:MONITOR PROGRESS	P.19#14C
WORK CHKD BY SELF	PRVIDE SELF-CHKG MATERIALS:MONITOR PROGRESS	P.19#15A
SOCIOLOGICAL PREFERENCES		
NOT TO READ TO A TCHR	DO NOT SCHEDULE STDNT TO READ TO TCHR OFTEN	
TO READ W/PEERS	SCHEDULE STDNT TO READ W/PEERS	P.20#17
TO READ ALONE	SCHEDULE STDNT TO READ ALONE	P.20#18
NOT TO READ W/PEERS/TCHR	DO NOT SCHEDULE STDNT TO READ W/PEERS/TCHR OFTEN	
TO READ W/ONE PEER	SCHEDULE STDNT TO READ W/ONE PEER	P.20#20
PHYSICAL PREFERENCES		
INTAKE SOMETIMES	PRMIT STDNT TO EAT/DRINK WHILE READG IF NEEDED	P.20#21C
TO READ IN THE MORNING	SCHEDULE READG WORK IN THE MORNING	P.20#22
TO READ EARLY NOON	SCHEDULE READG WORK IN EARLY NOON	P.20#23
TO READ LATE NOON	SCHEDULE READG WORK IN LATE NOON	P.20#24
TO READ IN EVENING	ASSIGN READG WORK TO BE DONE IN EVENING	P.21#25
SOME MOBILITY	PRMIT STDNT TO READ FOR SHORT PERIODS	P.21#26B

FIGURE 4-7. RSI individual printout of a youngster whose reading style matches Fernald reading method. (See Chapter 2 for detailed information about the Reading Style Inventory [RSI].)

Revolutionary War by drawing or painting scenes from descriptions of well-known battles, creating models of wagons of that period, making clay figures of famous revolutionaries, writing and acting in plays about the Revolution, performing dances of revolutionary times and, finally, writing stories and reading about the Revolutionary War (Jansson and Schillereff, 1981).

The reading through the arts method is compatible with global students who prefer either a formal or informal design, need mobility, require little or no structure, are teacher-motivated, peer-motivated or self-motivated, and who prefer to learn through their tactual, kinesthetic, and visual senses with peers, adults and/or alone (see Table 4-4).

THE CARBO RECORDED-BOOK METHOD

This method makes use of a large variety of high-interest storybooks that have been sequenced in order of difficulty and recorded in small sections (a few pages on each tape cassette side) (Carbo, 1978, 1985).

The recorded-book method is recommended for global, visual youngsters, who are unmotivated or adult-motivated, not necessarily persistent or responsible, and who may need structure and mobility. Chapter 6 provides an in-depth description of how to teach students to read with the Carbo recorded-book method.

NEUROLOGICAL IMPRESS METHOD

With the neurological impress method, both the teacher and student read simultaneously. The teacher sits behind the youngster and reads aloud near the student's ear. Either the teacher or student places his/her finger below the words as they are read. No preparations are necessary prior to reading. The objective is to read as much material as feasible in one sitting without tiring the student (Heckelman, 1969).

The neurological impress method is a whole-sentence approach that enables students to read high-interest books above their reading level. It accommodates the reading styles of global students who prefer either a formal or informal design, are adult-motivated, may be persistent or not, responsible or not, need a great deal of structure, prefer to read with an adult, can learn through their visual/auditory senses at the time of day the lesson is presented, and do not require intake or mobility while reading.

VISUAL LITERACY METHOD

The visual literacy method is used to stimulate student interest in and to develop the vocabulary related to a topic. It is a variation of the language-experience approach. Students look at and discuss visual media (paintings, photographs, movie films, filmstrips, and so on) to help them imagine and visualize an event, understand a sequence of ideas, and become familiar

TABLE 4-4. Matching Emerging Reading Methods to Individual Reading Styles

Reading Method	Reading Style Stimuli				
	Environmental	Emotional	Sociological	Physical	Psychological
VISUAL LITERACY *Students look at and discuss films and pictures to develop vocabulary. Then they write about the subject presented.*	• talking • formal or informal	• teacher-motivated • peer-motivated • self-motivated • persistent • responsible • little/some structure	• read w/teacher • read alone • read w/one peer	• no/some intake • no/some mobility *At least:* * fair visual strengths * moderate tactual preferences	• impulsive or reflective * moderately to strongly global
CARBO RECORDED BOOK *Students listen to brief recordings of portions of books 2/3 times and move finger under the words. Supplementary materials: writing activities & games.*	• quiet or talking • formal or informal	• teacher or peer-motivated • self or unmotivated • persistent or not • responsible or not • little to much structure	• read alone • read w/teacher and/or peers	• no/some intake • no to much mobility *At least:* * fair visual strengths	• impulsive or reflective * moderately to strongly global
READING THROUGH THE ARTS *Students have a variety of artistic experiences and then write and read about them.*	• talking • formal or informal	• teacher or peer-motivated • self-motivated • persistent • responsible • little/some structure	• read alone • read w/teacher and/or peers	• some/much intake • no to much mobility *At least:* * fair visual strengths * moderate tactual and kinesthetic preferences	• impulsive or reflective * moderately to strongly global
NEUROLOGICAL IMPRESS *Teacher and student read from a book simultaneously while one of them places finger under the words being read.*	• quiet • formal	• teacher-motivated • persistent or not • responsible or not • much structure	• read w/teacher	• no intake • no mobility *At least:* * fair visual strengths	• impulsive or reflective * moderately global

(© Marie Carbo, 1981)

TABLE 4.5. Individual Education Plan Accommodating James' Reading Style

James Greeley	Grade 7	DOB: 12/8/74	Reading Level: 3.2	September 1983

Reading Style Diagnosis	Complementary Reading Methods	Complementary Reading Resources
Preferred Reading Environment: • quiet • dim light • warm or cool • informal • highly organized Emotional Profile: • adult-motivated • not persistent • not responsible • needs structure Sociological Preferences: • to read to adults • to read alone Physical Needs: • tactual-kinesthetic learner with some visual strengths • poor auditory strengths • prefers reading in late morning • requires intake while reading • needs much mobility Psychological Profile: • global • right-hemisphere dominant • impulsive	• Fernald word-tracing method • Carbo recorded-book method • neurological impress method Special Modifications • Have Jimmy write in cursive to lessen his "b" & "d" reversals • Write directions for Jimmy to help him compensate for his weak auditory memory • Allow Jimmy to use an index card when reading to help him keep his place on the page • Do not have Jimmy sound out words while reading as this weakens his comprehension of the story	• Multisensory materials including skill games and book games, electroboards, learning circles, body games, multisensory instructional packages, sand-paper letters and words • writing activity cards • recorded filmstrips • recorded high-interest storybooks • high-interest storybooks • programmed learning sequences to practice comprehension and vocabulary (these should be brief) Special Equipment: • tape player and recorder • typewriter • card reader • filmstrip projector

Comments: Both the Fernald and Carbo reading methods will form the core of Jimmy's reading program, supplemented by many multisensory resources that primarily utilize his tactual-kinesthetic senses. Jimmy needs a great deal of mobility. His lessons will be brief (no more than five minutes) and interspersed with tactual-kinesthetic materials that allow him to move as he learns.

Jimmy works well in the magic carpet area which is quiet, dimly lit, warm and informal. His reading work will be scheduled in late morning and checked at short intervals by the teacher and parent aide. Jimmy responds well to honest praise and rewards from adults. These will be used and his work graphed so that he is aware of his progress. Healthy snacks will be provided throughout the reading period.

From the *Reading Style Inventory Manual* by Marie Carbo, 1983, p. 32.

with the language related to the media presented. Then the youngsters. write stories about the pictures and read them aloud (Sinatra and Stahl-Gemake, 1983).

This approach responds to the reading styles of global youngsters who are adult, self and/or peer-motivated, persistent and responsible, in need of some structure, like to read with peers, adults and/or alone, require little or some mobility, and prefer to learn through their visual and tactual senses at the time of day the lessons are scheduled.

Writing IEPs That Accommodate Individual Reading Styles

IEP (Individual Education Plan) writing is of growing importance because even parents of gifted and average youngsters are pressing school systems for IEPs for their children. By 1982, eight states had mandated IEPs for gifted students.

Both the Reading Style Inventory (RSI) and Learning Style Inventory (LSI) are invaluable for writing IEPs. The RSI computerized profiles identify a youngster's reading style and recommend complementary methods, resources, and teaching strategies. The LSI computerized profiles diagnose an individual's overall learning style and the *LSI Manual* suggests appropriate teaching procedures and materials that can be utilized in a general educational program.

Table 4-5 contains a portion of an IEP written for James Greeley, a seventh grade student who is reading on a third grade level. This particular section of James' IEP describes his reading style, how he will be taught to read, which reading resources will be utilized, what special modifications will be made to help him to compensate for his visual and auditory perception problems, and what teaching strategies will be used. All that information was provided by James' individual RSI printout.

How to Teach Students to Read through Their Individual Styles

The succeeding chapters will explain how to teach through each youngster's global/analytic reading style and perceptual strengths, and how to provide the kind of environment and degree of structure necessary for each of 30 or more children in a single classroom. If you are analytic, you may decide to proceed to the next chapter so that you do not miss anything in the book's sequence. If you are essentially global, you may choose to move to the second section in Chapter 5 that describes how to begin a reading program that complements individual reading and learning styles. Which do you choose to do?

Selecting and Adapting Reading Materials to Match Individual Reading Styles

Selecting Commercial Reading Materials That Match Reading Style Strengths

When reading materials are chosen, every reading style element deserves careful consideration, but it is essential to match both the kind of information (global and/or analytic) and the modality through which that information will be received. Many poor readers are right-brain preferenced learners (Oexle and Zenhausern, 1981; Maxwell and Zenhausern, 1982) who can learn to read well with reading methods and materials that complement their global/tactile/kinesthetic strengths (Carbo, 1982, 1983b,c; 1984b). Unfortunately, such youngsters often are taught to read through their weakest modalities (visually and auditorially), with sequential, step-by-step materials that are appropriate for analytic, left-brain preferenced students. The result is continued failure and/or disinterest in reading.

Matching Global/Analytic Styles

Most commercial reading materials use both global and analytic approaches but emphasize one more than the other. In Figure 5-1, vocabulary words are introduced globally, within the context of a high-interest story. The initial use of context helps the global learner to understand and then use the new words in sentences. The vocabulary exercise depicted in Figure 5-2 requires greater analytic strengths because new words are presented within an incomplete context and no visuals are included. Statements that test comprehension also can accommodate either a global or analytic style (see Figure 5-3).

Name _____

Which is your favorite comic strip? If you <u>selected</u> "Blondie," you chose the most <u>popular</u> comic strip of all time. "Blondie" is about a <u>foolish</u> husband, named Dagwood, who always gets into trouble. "Blondie" is the most <u>widely</u> <u>distributed</u> comic strip of all time. It is <u>published</u> in 1800 newspapers in 58 countries.

The longest-lasting comic strip in the world is called "The Katzenjammer Kids." The two boys in this comic strip are <u>mischievous</u> <u>youngsters</u> who are in trouble <u>constantly</u>. "The Katzenjammer Kids" was <u>originated</u> in 1897 by Rudolph Dirks.

CHOOSE THE BEST DEFINITIONS. SPELL THE SECRET WORDS.

1. youngsters __R__   (N) printed

2. mischievous __E__   ((N)) chose

3. popular __A__   (R) children

4. widely __D__   (I) all the time

5. constantly __I__   (U) begun

6. published __N__   (A) liked by many

7. distributed __G__   (G) given out

                          (D) over a large area

8. foolish __F__   (E) full of tricks

9. originated __U__   (F) silly

10. selected __N__

The secret words are _____ READING _____   FUN _____

FIGURE 5-1. This vocabulary exercise responds to a global reading style because words are introduced within the context of a high-interest story. The use of humor and strong visuals deepen the meaning of the passage. From *World Record Reading, Building Vocabulary* by Marie and Nick Carbo, Copyright 1980, World Record Publications. Reprinted by permission.

Detecting Clues

Be a word detective! Read the sentences below and use the clues to determine the meanings of the words in boldface. Then write a definition of each word on the line provided.

1. The rope holding the mountain climber was <u>taut</u>—it was drawn so tightly she couldn't fall.

   taut _____

2. The opponents stared at one another with <u>disdain</u>. These scornful looks made the whole audience feel uncomfortable.

   disdain _____

3. Tom is an extremely <u>sullen</u> person; that is, he never smiles or laughs.

   sullen _____

4. Many members of the basketball team are <u>lanky</u>; they are so tall and lean it looks as though they can just drop the ball through the hoop.

   lanky _____

5. Jenny is <u>apt</u> to blush when she is nervous, but she's not likely to blush when she's at ease.

   apt _____

6. The starving animal's stomach was <u>distended</u>; the swollen and bloated form it took upset the photographer.

   distended _____

7. Ms. Chi's <u>forte</u> has always been her ability to handle people. It has been her strong point for many years.

   forte _____

8. We were surprised by the <u>stark</u> appearance of Jerry's room. It was almost completely bare.

   stark _____

9. The campers found the beautiful blue water so <u>alluring</u> they dove right in!

   alluring _____

FIGURE 5-2. Compared to Figure 5-1, this vocabulary page requires a more analytic reading style because it begins with directions, there are no visuals, and new words are introduced in unrelated sentences. From Studybook for *Ride the Sunrise* of the *Ginn Reading Program* by Theodore Clymer and others. Copyright, 1982, by Ginn and Company (Xerox Corporation). Used by permission.

Name _____

Ah-choo! How many times have you sneezed without stopping? The world record for sneezing is <u>hard</u> to believe.

June Clark sneezed for a total of 155 days. She started to sneeze on January 4, 1966. Her sneezing didn't stop until June 8, 1966. June Clark must hate to catch colds.

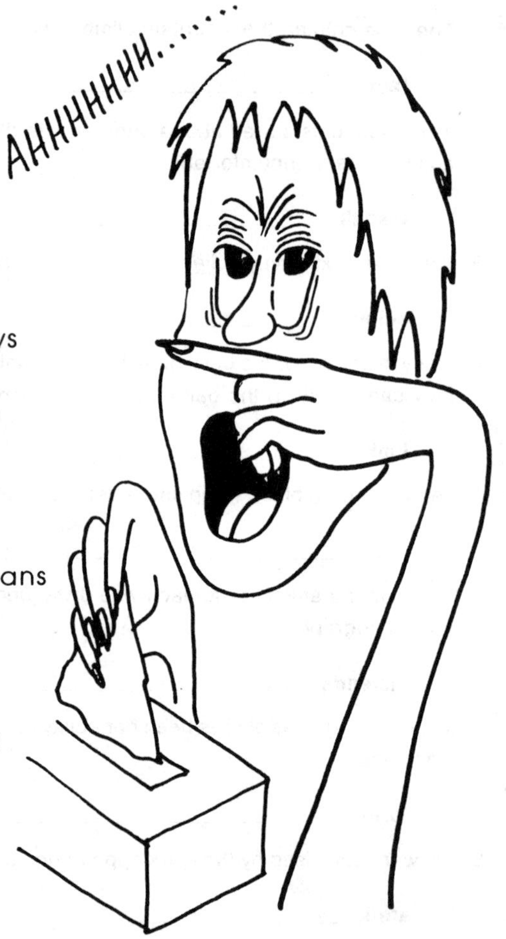

1. This story is mainly about
   (a) the sneezing world record
   b) the world record for colds
   c) how to stop sneezing
   d) catching colds

2. The story says that June Clark
   a) catches many colds
   b) has difficulty sneezing
   c) sneezed more than 155 days
   (d) must hate to catch colds

3. June Clark began sneezing on
   a) June 4, 1966
   b) January 4, 1976
   c) June 8, 1976
   (d) January 4, 1966

4. In this story the word <u>hard</u> means
   a) not possible
   b) sharp
   (c) difficult
   d) strong

5. When June Clark was sneezing she probably felt
   a) strong
   (b) tired
   c) happy
   d) friendly

AHHHHHHH........

Each of the above questions practices a specific reading skill.
1 = main idea   2, 3 = details   4 = vocabulary   5 = inference, conclusion

FIGURE 5-3. Item one (identifying the main idea) requires more global thinking strategies than items two, three (recalling details) and four (defining a word). From *World Record Reading, Reading Comprehension* by Marie and Nick Carbo. Copyright 1980, World Record Publications. Reprinted by permission.

Resources and tests that contain both analytic and global exercises are needed; but youngsters should be introduced to a *new* skill with commercial materials that complement their strengths. When new concepts are introduced analytically, with rules and detailed exercises, strongly global students who are not analytic often feel "lost" because facts without context are meaningless to them. Therefore, if you are not certain how to begin a skill lesson, start globally with visuals and anecdotes that develop relevant concepts, and provide many real experiences that deepen understandings, such as trips, interviews, and skits. After the context and importance of a skill is understood, most highly global youngsters will be ready to learn rules and perform exercises related to the skill.

Many of today's reading methods, materials, and tests are highly analytic, and, therefore unfairly penalize global students who are likely to have difficulty both learning analytically, and demonstrating what they know on analytic tests. For instance, resources and tests that require the learner to perform an exercise without the aid of a meaningful, complete context, are biased in favor of an analytic style. The cloze approach is an example; it closely matches an analytic reading style since the student is not shown a total context but must decipher meaning from incomplete sentences.

To match commercial reading materials to global/analytic styles: (a) use the *Reading Style Bias Inventory* (RSBI) (Figure 5-4) (Carbo, 1984a) to determine the extent a test or resource responds to global and/or analytic styles, (b) identify students' individual strengths with the global/analytic list in Chapter 3, and (c) select complementary reading resources.

Matching Modality Strengths

Reading programs must have a variety of reading resources that accommodate the diverse perceptual strengths of students. Visual youngsters need to learn with books, duplicating masters, films, filmstrips, computer software, and so on, whereas, tape recordings and resources that stimulate discussion are particularly appropriate for auditory students. The tactile/kinesthetic learners are the youngsters most in need of resources that are not sufficiently available in many classrooms. This group—which often has the greatest reading difficulties—needs to touch, feel, and experience what is being learned, through a wealth of tactile resources (task cards, games, learning circles, flip chutes, electroboards, sandpaper and clay words), and kinesthetic materials and experiences (floor games, multisensory instructional packages, going on trips, acting in plays).

READING STYLE BIAS INVENTORY (RSBI)

by Marie Carbo

The purpose of the RSBI is to help educators determine the extent to which a particular reading test or set of reading materials is biased in favor of a global or analytic reading style.

Directions: Place an "X" in the box that best describes the reading test or reading materials being evaluated.

Part I. Reading Comprehension

Never ... Always

1. Passages to be read are accompanied by visuals, such as photographs, drawings, or graphs.
2. The passages are high-interest, humorous, and/or exciting.
3. Storylines are presented in one continuous flow of thought.
4. Students are asked questions only after reading a complete story or description.
5. The reader's interest is captured almost immediately in every passage.
6. Passages contain rich and imaginative language.
7. The reader is likely to perceive immediately a clear purpose for reading.
8. Most passages appeal to the reader on an emotional level.
9. Many passages contain fantasy and humor.
10. Passages maintain student interest.

Always ... Never

11. There are missing words in passages.
12. Stories or descriptions are divided into small sections.
13. Students are required to answer questions before reading an entire story or description.
14. Most passages appeal to the reader on an intellectual level.

For each category, the value of the box at the extreme left = 1. The value of the box at the extreme right = 5. Add one to the value of each box as you count from left to right.
Scoring: Add the category values and divide the total by 14.

[| X | | |] = 2   [| | | | X |] = 5

Key:

RSBI Score		Reading Style Match
1.0-1.9	=	strongly analytic
2.0-2.7	=	analytic
2.8-3.3	=	global/analytic balance
3.4-4.0	=	global
4.1-5.0	=	strongly global

FIGURE 5-4. The Reading Style Bias Inventory (RSBI) can be used to identify reading tests and resources that accommodate global and/or analytic styles.

Part II.   **Skill Work and Types of Questions**

	Never				Always

1. Examples are provided before the student is required to perform the task.

2. Students are likely to understand the purpose of knowing the particular skill being tested.

3. Visuals are included to capture student interest, and/or clarify directions or the task.

4. Students are likely to feel that the skills being tested are important.

5. The directions are stated clearly, briefly and are understood easily.

6. Skill exercises relate to a meaningful context and rarely are presented in isolation.

7. Estimate the approximate percentage of questions that relate to:

   (a) identifying the main idea   [0% | | | 100%]

   (b) recalling facts that help students to understand important concepts or events   [0% | | | 100%]

   (c) recalling unimportant details   [100% | | | 0%]

   (d) sequencing events   [100% | | | 0%]

   (e) predicting events   [0% | | | 100%]

   (f) interpreting feelings   [0% | | | 100%]

   (g) identifying with a character   [0% | | | 100%]

8. Estimate the approximate percentage of questions that relate to:

   (a) decoding skills   [100% | | | 0%]

   (b) structural analysis   [100% | | | 0%]

   (c) comprehension   [0% | | | 100%]

Scoring: Count one point for each box. Add and divide by 16.

Key:	**RSBI Score**		**Reading Style Match**
	1.0-1.9	=	strongly analytic
	2.0-2.7	=	analytic
	2.8-3.3	=	global/analytic balance
	3.4-4.0	=	global
	4.1-5.0	=	strongly global

FIGURE 5-4. (*Continued*)

Matching Commercial Reading Materials to Reading Style Strengths*

In this section, the following reading resources are described and matched to individual reading styles (see Appendix C for addresses of publishers and suppliers).

I. Reading Programs
    A. Basal Reader Programs
        1. Whole-Word Emphasis in Beginning Readers
        2. Strong Phonic-Emphasis in Beginning Readers
        3. Strong Linguistic-Emphasis in Beginning Readers
    B. Language Experience Programs
    C. Individualized Programs
II. Supplementary Reading Materials
    A. Games
    B. Activity Cards
    C. Reading Kits
    D. Skill Development Books and Duplicating Masters
    E. Audio-Visual Materials
    F. Computer Software

Each reading resource complements certain reading styles and should be selected depending on the learner's unique characteristics (see Figure 5-5).

BASAL READER PROGRAMS

We do not recommend the use of only one basal reader series with every youngster in a class because that practice increases the likelihood that individual interests and styles will *not* be matched—particularly if every child is required to read the same stories and perform the same skill exercises. An extraordinary but accurate example of rigid adherence to one series, is a school district that adopted a linguistic basal and permitted youngsters to read a whole-word reader only if declared handicapped. Such uncompromising procedures cause youngsters to experience unnecessary reading difficulties. We strongly advise that many basal reader series be available and used when they match individual interests, abilities and styles.

Description of Basal Reader Programs

Typically, basal reader instruction is guided by a highly organized scope and sequence outline of skill development, which matches an extremely analytic style. Most teachers' manuals have either specific teaching procedures and suggestions, or an exact script for the teacher to follow.

---

*Adapted from "Selection Guide for Matching Reading Materials and Reading Styles," by Marie Carbo and Elizabeth H. Burton, in the *Reading Style Inventory Manual*, pp. 44–53.

Students usually read in groups with their teacher and peers, and then work independently in their workbooks. Some basal reader programs include placement and mastery tests as well as supplementary teaching materials that reinforce and/or extend reading skills, such as charts, flash cards, duplicating masters, tape recordings, and games.

Differences among Basal Reader Series

Every basal reader program we investigated incorporated some decoding skills both in the recommended teacher-directed lessons and in the students' workbooks; but phonic- and linguistic-emphasis series tended to stress those skills more. The greatest difference among basal reader programs is evident in the readers at the primary levels, most of which have a whole-word, phonic or linguistic emphasis (see Figures 5-6 to 5-12). At the intermediate and junior high levels, those differences become minimal.

At the first grade level, basal readers are seldom sufficiently interesting to global students (the majority of young children), because story content has been deemphasized so that students can practice and commit to memory individual letter sounds (phonic method), letter "families" (linguistic method), or particular words (whole-word method).

Matching Basal Reader Programs to Individual Reading Styles

Basal reader programs match the reading styles of students who are analytic, need a great deal of structure (i.e., few choices, much direction, work checked often by an adult), and prefer to learn primarily through their auditory (listening to lessons) and visual senses (looking at pictures and words). Whole-word emphasis programs complement the styles of visual youngsters with good auditory skills (needed to perform the decoding exercises in the teacher-directed lessons and workbook); while phonic and linguistic-emphasis programs match students with excellent auditory abilities. Generally, teacher-directed lessons and seatwork take place during a specific time—which may or may not coincide with an individual student's chronobiological preferences—in a quiet, formal environment that is appropriate for students who are not in need of mobility and intake. Such procedures are not as likely to benefit youngsters who are strongly global, tactile/kinesthetic, self-motivated, peer-motivated, persistent, have high mobility needs, and/or require little structure.

Poor readers and many youngsters at the initial stage of learning to read have styles that are not complemented by traditional basal reader techniques. Instead, they need to learn with more global resources of their choice—stories they create and well-written storybooks—with supplementary multisensory materials that utilize the tactile/kinesthetic modalities and allow mobility, intake and peer-interaction. When basal reader materials do not match a youngster's strengths and preferences, it is essential to adapt them (see the second half of this chapter) or, if that is not possible, to utilize different resources that *are* compatible.

Reading Program	Reading Style Stimuli				
	Environmental	Emotional	Sociological	Physical	Psychological
Basal Reader Programs: **WHOLE-WORD PROGRAMS** *At the beginning levels, readers tend to utilize more dissimilar words of varying shapes and lengths, and emphasize the development of an initial sight vocabulary more than phonic and linguistic readers. Accompanying workbooks usually stress decoding skills less than phonic and linguistic workbooks.*	• quiet • formal design	• teacher-motivated • not/fairly persistent • not/fairly responsible • much structure	• read w/teacher and peers in a group	• read at time of day lesson is presented • little/no mobility • little/no intake *At least:* * good visual strengths * fair auditory strengths	• reflective * moderately global * moderately analytic
PHONIC PROGRAMS *Students learn individual letter sounds and blend them to form words. First readers and workbooks provide highly structured practice of lettersounds that have been introduced.* **LINGUISTIC PROGRAMS** *Beginning readers and workbooks contain and practice words with similar patterns. Students are expected to decode new words based on their knowledge of spelling patterns.*	• quiet • formal design	• teacher-motivated • not/fairly persistent • not/fairly responsible • much structure	• read w/teachers and peers in a group	• read at time of day lesson is presented • little/no mobility • little/no intake *At least:* * good auditory strengths * fair visual strengths	• reflective * strongly analytic

Program	Description					
LANGUAGE-EXPERIENCE PROGRAMS	*Generally, there are two types of programs available, complete kits and teachers' manuals. Each contains ideas to stimulate children's writing.*	● music/talking ● formal or informal design	● self-motivated ● peer-motivated ● fairly/highly persistent ● fairly/highly responsible ● little/some structure	● read w/peers	● read at time of day reading is scheduled ● some/much mobility ● some/much intake *At least:* * fair visual strengths * moderate tactual preferences	● reflective or impulsive * moderately to strongly global
INDIVIDUALIZED PROGRAMS	*Collections of books, sometimes accompanied by tape recordings or supplemented with worksheets, activity cards, and/or games.*	● quiet or some talking ● formal or informal design	● self-motivated ● fairly/highly persistent ● fairly/highly responsible ● little/some structure	● read alone & at times w/tchr or peers	● read at time of day reading is scheduled ● little/some mobility *At least:* * good visual strengths	● impulsive or reflective * moderately to strongly global

(© Marie Carbo, 1981)

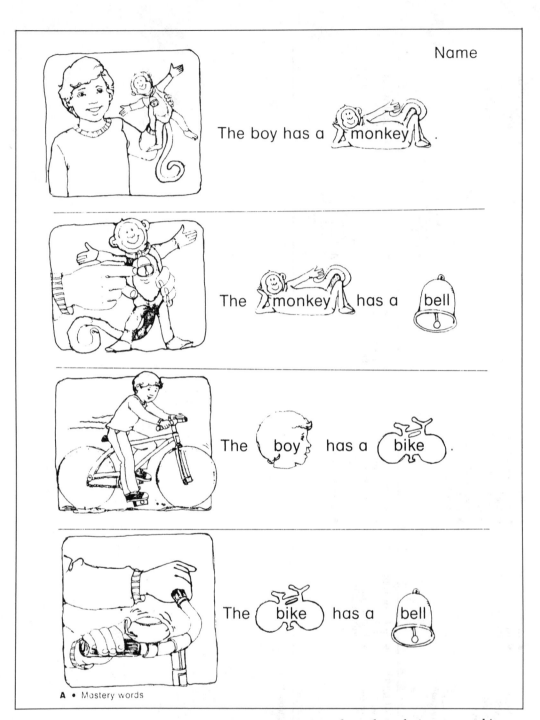

The boy has a monkey.

The monkey has a bell

The boy has a bike.

The bike has a bell

A • Mastery words

FIGURE 5-6. The excellent association of words and pictures on this workbook page helps global/visual youngsters retain the words being taught. From Scott, Foresman Reading (studybook for *Ride the Sunrise*, by Ira E. Aaron et al.). Copyright 1981, Scott, Foresman and Company. Reprinted by permission.

Each child will need a green, a blue, and an orange crayon.

The word *blue* appears in a later unit of *Skylights*.

You may wish to suggest that children say each word softly to themselves before they decide which color a space should be. Some children may find it easier to remember which color to use if, after reading the directions, they underline the word *hard* in green, the word *corn* in blue, and the word *first* in orange.

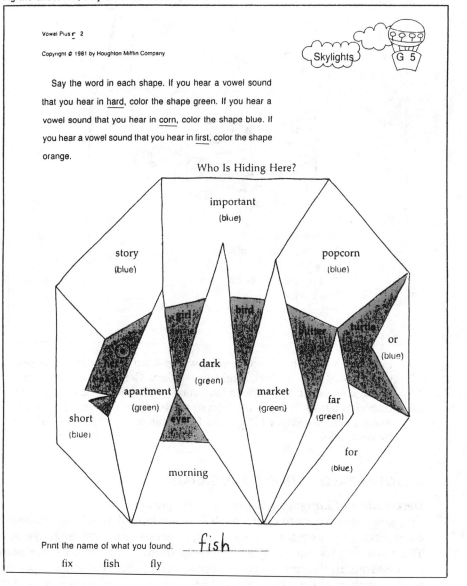

Vowel Plus r 2

Copyright © 1981 by Houghton Mifflin Company

Skylights

G 5

Say the word in each shape. If you hear a vowel sound that you hear in <u>hard</u>, color the shape green. If you hear a vowel sound that you hear in <u>corn</u>, color the shape blue. If you hear a vowel sound that you hear in <u>first</u>, color the shape orange.

Who Is Hiding Here?

important
(blue)

story
(blue)

popcorn
(blue)

girl

bird

butter

turtle

or
(blue)

dark
(green)

apartment
(green)

market
(green)

far
(green)

short
(blue)

ever

for
(blue)

morning

Print the name of what you found. __ f i s h __

fix   fish   fly

FIGURE 5-7. This workbook exercise requires strongly analytic/auditory abilities because students must understand and recall fairly complex directions, and discriminate among subtle differences in vowel sounds. From *Skylights* workbook, 1983, Houghton Mifflin Company. Reprinted with permission.

Now look at this ball.
Can a mouse and a bird have fun
with a ball?
They can play with the ball.
They can run with it.
They can have fun.

Bonus Unit   29

FIGURE 5-8. At beginning levels, whole-word basal readers repeat words to develop an initial sight vocabulary. Generally, these readers utilize somewhat more dissimilar words than phonic- and linguistic-emphasis basals. From Scott, Foresman Reading (*Taking Off*, by Ira E. Aaron et al.). Copyright 1981, Scott, Foresman and Company. Reprinted by permission.

LANGUAGE-EXPERIENCE PROGRAMS

Description of Language-Experience Programs

The language-experience approach is a method of teaching reading that capitalizes on youngsters' experiences, interests, and oral language ability. The materials for the program evolve primarily from the experiences of the children. In the first stage, students dictate their personal experiences to the teacher who records them. Later, students write their own stories. There is a great deal of reading and sharing, and often students' writings are transformed into an art form, such as a painting or drawing. Reading skills are not taught in isolation, but are related to and drawn from the content of the childrens' written material (Stauffer, 1980).

Gum is on the jug.
Gum is on the cup.
Val is mad at the pup.

FIGURE 5-9. Basal readers with a phonic-emphasis tend to repeat letter sounds and utilize words that are fairly similar in shape and length. This page provides practice in the sound of the short "u" (gum, jug, cup, pup). Reproduced from *Fun With Gum* by Janis Asad Raabe. Copyright Modern Curriculum Press, 1974. Reprinted with permission.

Generally, two kinds of programs are available: (a) complete kits containing pictures, stories and recordings and (b) teachers' manuals. Both have a large variety of suggested activities to stimulate original writing ideas, and to develop reading skills from the childrens' writing.

Matching Language-Experience Programs to Individual Reading Styles

Language-experience materials accommodate the global/analytic styles and modality strengths of many young children and poor readers. When students write stories about their own experiences, they are learning to read holistically (globally), through their visual/tactile senses. In addition, language-experience programs enable youngsters to work in a variety of sociological groupings, with mobility and intake needs easily satisfied.

Resources that stimulate youngsters to talk and write about themselves and their experiences, are ideal for students who are self-motivated, peer-motivated, persistent, responsible, and in need of little structure. They do not match the reading styles of students who are

FIGURE 5-10. The Distar phonic program alters letter size and shape, and uses special symbols to help children recall letter sounds. It matches strongly analytic/auditory reading styles. Page 122 from DISTAR® *Reading I* by Siegfried Engelmann and Elaine C. Bruner, copyright 1969, Science Research Associates, Inc. All rights reserved. Reprinted by permission of the publisher.

The man can fan.

I can fan the man.

The man can fan Dan.

I can fan Dan.

FIGURE 5-11. At beginning levels, linguistic-emphasis readers usually contain extremely similar words (same shape and length), and repeat clusters of letters (sometimes called "word families"). Page 3 from *A Pig Can Jig, Basic Reading Series,* copyright 1964, Donald Rasmussen and Lenina Goldberg. All rights reserved. Reprinted by permission of Science Research Associates, Inc.

strongly teacher-motivated, not persistent, not responsible, and/or in need of a great deal of structure. For such youngsters, teachers need to either (a) modify their language-experience program (provide additional structure—limit choices, give clear directions and time limits—and have peer volunteers and aides work with the youngsters), or (b) use other resources that more closely match the students' reading styles.

INDIVIDUALIZED PROGRAMS

Description of Individualized Programs

Collections of books that are likely to be of particular interest to a certain age group comprise the core of an individualized reading program. Some series represent a particular theme (American heroes, myths, detective stories), and may include tape recordings, skill worksheets, activity cards and games. Youngsters select books of their choice, or with some teacher guidance, and generally read them and work on the skill materials by themselves. Students have individual conferences with the teacher at specific intervals, usually once or twice weekly. At that time, the teacher

hat		Sam has on a hat. / ham.
h**at**		A cat is on the h___.
h**a**nds		Sam has a dish in his h__nds.
dish		A fish is in the __ish.
fan		That is a ship on the fan. / pan.
ship		The ___ip is tan.
p**an**		The p___ is on a mat.
no		Is the mat tan? yes / no

This is Sam's hand.

c**at**		This man has a hat and a c___.
h**and**		The hat is in his h_____. **143**

FIGURE 5-12. In this programmed reading exercise, students write in self-checking workbooks that present linguistic exercises in small, sequential steps. From *Programmed Reading* by Sullivan. Copyright 1963 by McGraw-Hill Book Company. Reprinted by permission.

may suggest additional readings, check the youngster's skill work, and determine if the student requires additional practice in a particular skill. Students are encouraged to share their reading interests with their peers through discussion, art projects, and writing.

Matching Individualized Programs to Individual Reading Styles

Research verifies that many students have specific reading interests and prefer to choose their own books (Carbo, 1983a; "Kansas Discovers . . . ," 1983; Moray, 1978; Stanchfield and Fraim, 1979). This is particularly true of youngsters in the intermediate grades and higher. Individualized programs usually allow youngsters a wide selection of books to read and, therefore, respond directly to individual preferences for choices and interests.

Individualized programs match the reading styles of students who are global, visual, self-motivated, somewhat peer-motivated, persistent, responsible, not in need of a great deal of structure or mobility, and who enjoy reading alone. When activity cards, games, filmstrips, and recordings are utilized as well, it is possible to accommodate many different styles. Those students who are strongly teacher-motivated, should read

FIGURE 5-13. Commercial games such as the task cards illustrated above, provide tactual reinforcement of reading skills and can be coordinated with an existing reading program. Step-by-step directions for designing effective originals are detailed in Chapter 7. From DLM *Language Arts*, Prefix Puzzles, copyright Developmental Learning Materials, a division of DLM, Inc., Allen TX 75002. Reprinted with permission.

with the teacher or an adult volunteer daily, either individually or as part of a group; youngsters who enjoy working with peers can read with a friend; students who need to move can be permitted that mobility (getting a snack, reading in an informal area), and those who require structure and are not persistent and responsible, should be given brief assignments that are checked frequently.

SUPPLEMENTARY READING MATERIALS

Supplementary reading materials should be an integral part of every reading program because they provide practice in many different reading skills, can be coordinated with most reading programs, and enable teachers to match individual styles—particularly modality strengths. Such materials include games, activity cards, reading kits, skill development books, duplicating masters, audio-visual materials, and computer software (see Figures 5-13 and 5-14).

Adapting Commercial Reading Materials to Match Individual Reading Styles*

First Accommodate Students' Environmental, Sociological, and Physical Preferences

Permit youngsters to read with the amount of sound, light, heat and degree of informality desired, because environmental preferences have significantly increased reading achievement and improved attitudes. Follow these four steps: (a) encourage students to use headphones to block out unwanted noise or listen to music while reading; (b) turn off half the lights in the classroom so that children can read in the amount of light preferred; (c) allow youngsters to read in the area of the room that most closely matches their temperature preferences; and (d) create an informal area with a rug, pillows and/or comfortable chairs for those who need informality while reading.

In many schools, students are directed to do worksheets alone, and to read with their teacher and peers in a reading group. But many primary children prefer to read in pairs while older students like to read alone (Carbo, 1983a). Students' sociological preferences are not difficult to accommodate. Allow youngsters to decide with whom they want to read and be certain that they understand that they are responsible for achieving the objectives they have been assigned.

---

*This section is adapted from, "How to Start a Super Reading Styles Program," by Marie Carbo, in *Early Years K/8*, Vol. 15, No. 2, 1984.

Whales live in the sea. But they are not fish. They are warm-blooded animals. Whales live in warm seas and in cold seas. They cannot live in fresh water. They can be found in all of the world's ____

1. a. lakes   c. ponds
   b. rivers   d. streams
              e. oceans

TYPE THE LETTER OF THE BEST CHOICE.
OR, PRESS SPACE FOR CLUES.

(a)

(b)

FIGURE 5-14. Commercial reading programs for computers (a) match the reading styles of visual/tactile youngsters who prefer structure and enjoy learning alone. From *Cloze Plus*. Reprinted with permission of Milliken Publishing Company, St. Louis, Missouri. Computer-like devices, like "Charlie" (b), have accompanying reading software and can be programmed easily by teachers. From Educational Insights.

Schedule reading at the time of day students—particularly poor readers—are most alert. For many poor readers, late morning or early afternoon would be a better choice. Provide snacks for those who require intake. That will help them to feel relaxed and concentrate better while reading.

Adapting Commercial Reading Materials to Students' Emotional Needs

Vary the Length of Assignments and Provide Feedback.   Students who are self-motivated, persistent, and responsible usually are capable of performing lengthy tasks and checking their own work. For unmotivated youngsters who are not persistent and responsible, divide skill exercises and stories into small sections that can be completed in a few minutes; assign only certain portions, and provide immediate feedback.

Here are some specific procedures to use with unmotivated students. As youngsters are working, mark only those items that are correct. Give students time to find their own errors, and then help them to correct their work. Essentially, that is what many computer programs do. Another technique is to post, or place onto cards, the answers to an exercise. If all answers are provided, then students can check themselves; when only some are, they can self-check those and their teacher can evaluate the remainder. Placing answers in a special section of the room allows students to walk to that area and satisfy their mobility needs without disrupting others.

Tactile/kinesthetic resources (described in detail in Chapter 7), enable students to correct their own work. In addition, computer-like machines permit self-checking reading exercises to be programmed; those can be highly motivating and particularly ideal for tactile/visual students who enjoy working alone.

Have Students Keep a Record of Their Progress and Completed Work. Poor readers often are neither persistent nor responsible when reading. They need praise, encouragement, and evidence that they have completed their work well. Figure 5-15 shows five ways to record a student's work: tally sheets, sign-in sheets, and record cards indicate finished tasks; individual graphs and work folders help youngsters to become aware of their progress.

Provide Choices of Reading Materials.   Most students have specific reading interests and like to select their own materials. That preference is stronger for good rather than poor readers, but even those with reading difficulties like to choose their materials some or most of the time. Therefore, classrooms should have a large selection of interesting resources. Children who have difficulty making a choice, can be given guidance and a limited selection on topics they enjoy.

If a basal reader is used, choices can be provided to spur interest. For example, primary youngsters could read Story One and Two with their

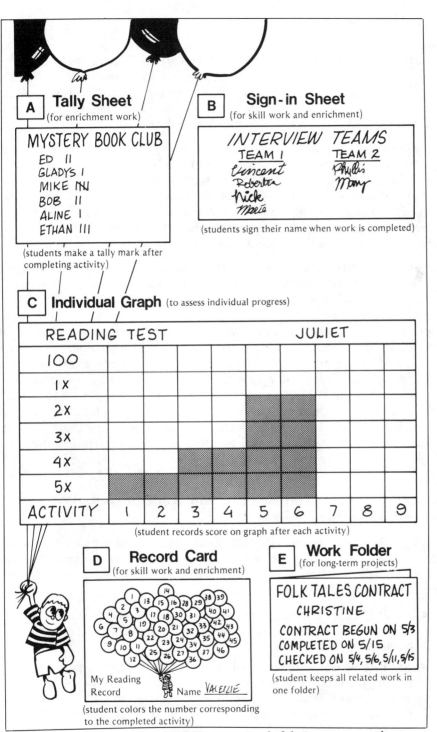

A **Tally Sheet** (for enrichment work)

MYSTERY BOOK CLUB
ED   II
GLADYS I
MIKE   IIII
BOB   II
ALINE I
ETHAN III

(students make a tally mark after completing activity)

B **Sign-in Sheet** (for skill work and enrichment)

INTERVIEW TEAMS
TEAM I   TEAM 2
Vincent   Phyllis
Roberta   Mary
Nick
Maria

(students sign their name when work is completed)

C **Individual Graph** (to assess individual progress)

READING TEST					JULIET			
100								
1X								
2X					▓	▓		
3X					▓	▓		
4X			▓	▓	▓	▓		
5X	▓	▓	▓	▓	▓	▓		
ACTIVITY	1	2	3	4	5	6	7	8	9

(student records score on graph after each activity)

D **Record Card** (for skill work and enrichment)

My Reading Record   Name VALERIE

(student colors the number corresponding to the completed activity)

E **Work Folder** (for long-term projects)

FOLK TALES CONTRACT
CHRISTINE
CONTRACT BEGUN ON 5/3
COMPLETED ON 5/15
CHECKED ON 5/4, 5/6, 5/11, 5/15

(student keeps all related work in one folder)

FIGURE 5-15. Students should keep a record of their progress and completed work. From *Practical Ideas for Using Activity Cards* by Marie Carbo, copyright World Record Publications, 1976. Used with permission.

group, and then choose to read either Story Three or Four alone. The teacher then would meet with the groups, depending upon the story selected. By the intermediate levels, many students have definite reading preferences and need a wider range of reading materials (trade books, newspapers, magazines, their own stories) than basals alone can provide.

Vary Time Limits and Objectives.   Highly persistent and responsible youngsters may enjoy long-term assignments because they can plan their time; those who are not, however, usually can handle just one or two objectives and short work periods. Generally, begin with one or two objectives and a brief amount of time; praise youngsters as their work is completed. Gradually, increase the number of objectives and give longer-term assignments as the student proves capable of handling them.

Organize Reading Materials so that Students can Use Them Independently.   Organized resources free the teacher to teach and enable students to find, use, and return materials without assistance. Most reading resources can be organized by: (a) reading level, (b) skill, or (c) topic. A simple procedure is to label boxes, folders, or bulletin boards and place materials related to a topic or skill in a central location.

Color-coding and numbering are useful when there are many items to be organized. Color-coding can be utilized to organize resources that are related to one subject (reading = red, math = yellow), or to teach a skill (purple = reading comprehension materials; purple, items 1–10 = main idea; purple, 11–20 = vocabulary). Teachers of young children often code with symbols that do not require any reading (faces, dots, triangles, stars).

Adapting Commercial Reading Materials to Global Styles and Modality Strengths

1. Begin Reading Lessons Globally; Draw Skills from the Characters and Events of Stories Read.   For optimum progress, global youngsters should practice needed reading skills within familiar, meaningful contexts. Here is a three-step process we recommend.

- STEP I. First, a high-interest story should be read, discussed, and understood so that global youngsters comprehend the context of the lessons that follow.

- STEP II. Next, students should practice specific skills with exercises drawn from the characters, vocabulary, and events of the story. When appropriate, these should be presented in either a game-like format (see Chapter 6 for examples) or through tactile/kinesthetic materials (see Chapter 7 for examples).

Steps I and II will assure that most primary youngsters and poor readers learn new skills through what is likely to be their cognitive style (global) and their modality strengths (tactile/kinesthetic).

- STEP III. When the skill is mastered at STEP II then—and only then—global students should be given out-of-context practice, such as a workbook page.

EXAMPLE OF A READING UNIT PRESENTED GLOBALLY

Mr. Ramos is starting the seventh day of a reading unit on fairy tales. On each of the first three days of the unit, his students read a different fairy tale in their basal reader. Then they received a fairy tale Contract Activity Package. This was one of the objectives: *Create an original fairy tale that has: (a) a hero or heroine with a problem; (b) a magical solution to the problem; and (c) a happy ending.*

For a few days, the students worked on their fairy tale contract; they read more books and filmstrips about fairy tales, listened to recordings of fairy tales, and created and shared their own. Today the youngsters are going to play a game to help them understand the concept of "cause and effect," using the events and characters of the first three fairy tales they read, "Beauty and the Beast," "Cinderella," and "Snow White." Figure 5-16 shows a portion of that game.

Next the youngsters will use their original fairy tales to design cause and effect materials that all their classmates can use for additional skill practice (e.g., games, electroboards, duplicating masters, task cards, and so on). Finally, the children will do the pages on cause and effect in their reading workbook.

Why is this a global reading approach? Because the teacher began with a whole concept—fairy tales—and provided examples of many fairy tales (the three fairy tales in the basal reader and the supplementary materials). The students were given time to explore and develop familiarity with the idea of fairy tales by creating and sharing their own. Only after many experiences with fairy tales, did the youngsters begin any detailed skill work. Their first encounter with the concept of cause and effect was not within an unknown, isolated context but, rather, was drawn from the fairy tales they had all read and enjoyed. After this initial, global exposure, the children were allowed an important discovery period when they applied what they had learned (making their own cause/effect games). Only after these in depth understandings were established did the youngsters do the workbook pages. School districts that are committed to basal reader instruction should incorporate into their reading program language-experience and individualized materials and techniques, and tactile/kinesthetic resources (as described previously).

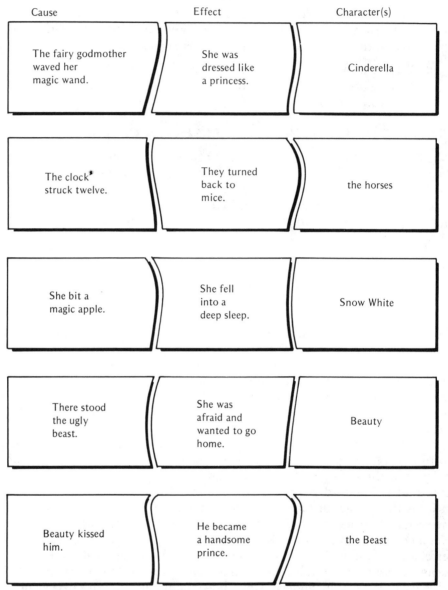

FIGURE 5-16. Global students should practice specific skills (e.g., identifying cause and effect) with exercises drawn from the characters, vocabulary, and events of the story.

2. Exclude Poorly Written and/or Dull Stories. Evaluate the stories contained in your basal reader series, individualized reading program, computer software, and so on. Omit those that are poorly written and/or do not hold the interest of the reader (see Chapter 6 for identification criteria).

3. Provide Tape Recordings of Stories.   Global students benefit greatly from hearing a story in its entirety. Stories can be tape recorded with special techniques that enable youngsters to associate the spoken and printed words (see Chapter 6). Establish a listening center where students can listen to a tape recording of a storybook or a story in their basal reader before any discussion or group work is to take place.

4. Simplify Directions and Provide Concrete Examples.   Skill exercises with unclear and/or lengthy directions can be especially difficult for youngsters whose auditory memory is not strong. By the time some students read the second sentence in a paragraph, they have forgotten the first. If the exercise itself is well-done and important for a youngster, provide many examples before discussing the directions to help globally inclined youngsters; afterward discuss a simplified, shortened version of the directions.

5. For Global Students, Deemphasize Reading Skills That Require a Highly Analytic Reading Style.   A good reading program should enable students to: (a) comprehend the printed page on many levels; (b) develop a sensitivity and appreciation for good writing; and last, (but certainly not least), (c) enjoy reading. Many publishers of reading materials and reading tests have identified reading subskills that are inappropriate and/or unnecessary for global youngsters.

The scope and sequence charts that are the foundation of many reading programs and describe hundreds of skills to be mastered by every child, make sense only for those youngsters who are highly analytic, have the auditory or visual abilities to perform the exercises, and need all the skills listed to become good readers. If students can read fluently and comprehend what they read, but cannot perform reading skills well, it means that for those youngsters, the particular skills being tested or taught are unnecessary and invalid and, therefore, should be discarded.

Decoding skills are tested most extensively at the primary level, while reading comprehension is stressed for intermediate students. Since young children tend to be more global and less auditory than intermediate students, exactly the reverse emphasis should be made; primary level tests should contain many comprehension and vocabulary exercises and very little decoding. The latter (decoding activities) should be reserved for youngsters who are sufficiently auditory and analytic to perform phonic exercises easily, and who need phonics to improve their reading. Because some parents believe that phonics is a necessary ingredient for every good primary reading program, it is important to provide parents with information about students' individual reading styles.

6. When Appropriate, Eliminate/Abbreviate Skill Work.   If a student dislikes or is having difficulty with a certain task, first decide the all-important question—will mastery of the task help the youngster to become a better reader? If the answer is no, eliminate the drudgery and move on to experiences that will help the child; if the answer is yes, try decreasing the amount of work. Sometimes students are bored or cannot perform well because a task is too repetitive or just too long to hold their interest. Experiment with assigning less work by dividing pages into sections, skipping some parts, and assigning fewer pages.

7. Locate and Coordinate the Reading Materials You Have. Most teachers store and save a great many resources. Before deciding which new items need to be ordered or created, reading materials should be displayed and coordinated by skill, topic, and/or reading level. Include school media because much of it will relate to student-developed stories, storybooks, and basal readers (see the text extenders, available from Scholastic Book Services, Appendix D). Many types of resources should be available to teach every reading skill so that youngsters' reading style strengths and preferences can be matched.

8. Order, Design and Create Needed Materials. To determine the kind and quantity of reading materials needed, administer the *Reading Style*

FIGURE 5-17

FIGURES 5-17 through 5-19. Some students listen to recordings of stories in their basal reader (Figure 5-17), while others read near a friend (Figure 5-18). Students said that it was "easy" and "fun" to learn how to sequence the events of a story with a game designed by their teacher (Figure 5-19). (Photographs by David Adams, courtesy of Juanita Elementary School, Lake Washington School District, Kirkland, Washington.)

Inventory (RSI) to students, and compare the materials recommendations on the group profile to those that are available. For example, games, audio-visual materials, and computer software often are highly recommended for many students, but few of those resources may be on hand. In that case, they will need to be ordered and/or created.

Excellent techniques were developed at Juanita Elementary School, (Lake Washington School District, Washington State) for adapting a basal series to individual reading styles, designing global reading materials, and enlisting parents and aides to create reading resources.

Principal Dave Adams, and Juanita's faculty evaluated their basal reader series and found that: (a) many stories were not well-written and interesting, (b) the skill objectives for each grade level were cumbersome—most seemed irrelevant, and (c) the workbook exercises did not always teach a skill well and seldom related to the stories in the basal reader. They decided to: (a) eliminate stories that were poorly written and dull, (b) focus on a few important reading skills at each grade level, (c) emphasize reading comprehension, (d) tape record stories in the basal reader in small sections, (e) use the vocabulary, characters and plot of the stories to teach reading skills, and (f) order and/or design resources that would enable youngsters to learn reading skills through their strongest modalities (see Figures 5-17 to 5-19).

To help facilitate the creation of materials, teachers displayed their best resources in one area of the school and requested those they wanted. Parents, aides and students made duplicates. After four months of

FIGURE 5-18

FIGURE 5-19

implementation, Juanita's students enjoyed reading more and scored significantly higher in reading comprehension and vocabulary than previously (see Appendix B).

Subsequent chapters of this book will show *how* to select and tape record high-interest storybooks, basal readers, and children's stories, and how to design a multitude of reading resources that accommodate individual reading styles—tactile/kinesthetic materials, Contract Activity Packages, Programmed Learning Sequences (PLSs) and Multisensory Instructional Packages (MIPs)—all of which will make reading interesting, easy and fun for many students who previously experienced unnecessary difficulties.

The Carbo Recorded Book Method: Matching Global/Visual Reading Styles*

The Carbo recorded book method is a special way of recording books in small, sequential portions so that the printed and spoken words are synchronized for the reader. By regulating four, distinct variables when recording—pace, phrasing, expression, and amount recorded—this approach integrates the rate, rhythm, and natural flow of language so necessary for good comprehension and enables many youngsters to read books well above their reading level.

What It Does . . .

Originally, the recorded book method was developed for a group of elementary level poor readers who had severe auditory perception problems. Before learning to read with recorded books, those youngsters perceived a page of print as hundreds of individual letters which had to be decoded, remembered, and then blended in the correct sequence to form words—an impossible task for them. By using books specially recorded for each youngster, instantaneous, dramatic improvement in the students' oral reading occurred.

> Instead of their previous slow, hesitant, labored reading, they now read with enthusiasm and expression, appropriately altering their voice and pacing to suit the mood of the passage. (Carbo, 1978b, p. 271)

After two months of working with recorded books, that group advanced an average of eight months in reading, with the greatest gain (1½ years!) made by a sixth grader.

Davis (1983) noted similar results. After using tape recorded books for just a few days, she found that her meek, fearful students became proud of their ability to read fluently:

---

*Chapter 6 is adapted from the following articles by Marie Carbo, "Recorded Books = Remarkable Reading Gains," in *Early Years K/8*, Vol. 15, No. 3, 1984, and "Advanced Book Recording: Turning it Around for Poor Readers," in *Early Years K/8*, Vol. 15, No. 5, 1985.

They come in each morning clamoring for their turn at the tape
recorder! . . . The most exciting part to me was the immediately
noticeable improvement in their reading ability. The boys also enjoy
sharing a page or two . . . after every listening they're showing off their
skill! They're so proud.

Using tape recorded books with handicapped students for just a
few months, LaShell (1983) reported that poor readers had become excited
about reading and many were gaining rapidly in reading ability:

As it is, I can't keep up with the recordings. The kids go faster than
I—they are becoming more and more excited about 'how many' books
they can read and some are moving way ahead in jumps.

Why It Works . . .

For many young children and poor readers there is a substantial time lag
between when they see and say a word. That lag produces slow, laborious
reading. It is simply difficult for students to recall what a passage is about
when so much effort is required to figure out each word. Specially
recorded books are crucial for youngsters who do not read fluently,
because the recording enables them to see and hear words simultaneously
within natural, high-interest context. In effect, the recording does what
the child is not yet able to do naturally; it verbalizes the printed words
with the correct pace, phrasing and expression. Failure and frustration
are minimized because recorded books provide a correct reading model
for students to imitate. As a result, they make fewer reading errors and
are less likely to form incorrect reading patterns.

Book tapes also help most youngsters to develop a sight vocabulary
rapidly and to gain confidence in their ability to read because each
student decides the number of times to listen to a recording and when to
read aloud. Thus, the child has a sense of control over his/her own
learning.

Recorded books seem to become the raw material—the data—from
which the brain can extract the patterns of printed language (Hart, 1983);
that knowledge also appears to be applied to new words without any
apparent effort on the part of the child. Thus, many youngsters learn to
read with recorded books as easily and naturally as they acquire aural/
oral skills in their own language (see Figures 6-1 and 6-2) (Carbo, 1982).

The reading styles of many primary youngsters and poor readers
respond to the recorded book method because it is intended for global
students who need to discover phonic patterns naturally, within a
comprehensible context, and without the imposition of phonic rules. After
global youngsters have read many high-interest books, enjoyed them, and
can recognize a few hundred words on sight, decoding work can be
started—providing the student will derive benefit from that type of skill
exercise.

FIGURE 6-1. A story recorded by his teacher, Donna Michel, holds this student spellbound. (Photograph by Kay Johnson, courtesy of Northfield Elementary School, Howard County, Maryland.)

Reading styles are extremely diverse and no one reading approach is appropriate for all youngsters. The recorded books are not recommended as the primary technique for children with severe visual discrimination and/or directionality problems. Those students need a highly tactile method, such as Orton-Gillingham for analytic youngsters, or Fernald for global children (see Chapter 4).

Selecting Books to Record for Students

No one loves to read just for the sake of reading. We may "love to settle down with a good book"—one that we enjoy—but no one wants to read a dull, poorly written book. Most of the time, we adults simply can set aside an uninteresting book and choose something else to read. Students seldom have that option. They *must* read what is assigned. Too often youngsters who are learning to read are given poorly written books far below their spoken language comprehension level. The simple sentences and words that predominate low-level reading materials often result in stilted, lifeless, dull stories. That is exactly what young children and poor readers—who tend to be strongly global—neither need nor want. To make the best progress and to become lifelong readers, global learners must be given well-written books that interest them.

FIGURE 6-2. At the Hamblen School, Charlotte Johnson found that using the Carbo method to record stories greatly improved her students' reading fluency and reading comprehension. (Photograph by Bill Benish, courtesy of the Hamblen School, District 81, Spokane, Washington.)

Love of reading is always dependent on two important factors. First, the process must be sufficiently effortless so that the individual can concentrate on what he/she is reading. Second, the material must be of great interest to the reader. With the recorded book method, books that are near, on, or even somewhat above the child's language-comprehension level can be recorded so that youngsters can read them easily.

Four Factors That Should Affect Book Selection

When recording books for a youngster, these four factors should affect your choice of books (Carbo, 1984):

1. the quality of the writing,
2. the student's interests,
3. the student's language comprehension level, and
4. the student's reading level.

QUALITY OF THE WRITING

To select children's books that are well-written, consult both a librarian and lists of award-winning books (e.g., Newberry Medal, William Allen White List, Caldecott Award). If a book seems interesting, read a portion and check the following:

INDICATORS OF GOOD WRITING

_____ 1. Does the author capture the interest of the reader almost immediately?

_____ 2. Will the reader want to read on? Is there a clear purpose for reading?

_____ 3. If the book is fictional, does it create an air of expectancy, suspense, mystery?

_____ 4. Is the book *at least* one of these: (a) entertaining, (b) informative, (c) exciting, (d) humorous?

_____ 5. Is rich and imaginative language used?

_____ 6. Does the writer have a good command of the language?

_____ 7. Do the sentences vary in structure and length?

_____ 8. Is original and evocative imagery used?

THE STUDENT'S INTERESTS

During seven years of experimentation with the recorded book method, Carbo noted that: (a) youngsters made the slowest progress in basal readers, particularly at the primer and preprimer levels; (b) as soon as students began to listen to high-interest, recorded storybooks, their word retention improved dramatically in direct proportion to their interest in the book; and (c) after the development of an initial sight vocabulary, youngsters made the most rapid gains with books close to their language comprehension level, which usually was far above their reading level.

High-interest reading materials are a crucial ingredient of the recorded book method because most students learn and retain words within such contexts more easily and permanently than they learn either isolated words or words presented within dull contexts. Recent theories about how the brain learns indicate that the central function of the human brain is to construct meaning. In fact, the "process of extracting meaningful patterns from confusion, is now recognized by investigators of the brain as one of its essential functions" (Hart, 1983, p. 7).

THE STUDENT'S LANGUAGE-COMPREHENSION AND READING LEVELS

Most young children and poor readers are assigned so-called "high-interest," low-readability materials. Seldom is the student's language-comprehension level considered although it is a powerful factor. When selecting books to record, consider both the student's reading level and language comprehension level.

For example, suppose you were selecting books to record for two average youngsters—Joe, a fourth grader, and Tom who is in the sixth grade. Both have a third grade reading level, but their language-comprehension levels differ markedly. A more difficult book should be recorded for Tom who is likely to feel insulted by low-level books. Tom is interested in, and probably capable of understanding, sixth-grade-level vocabulary and concepts. On the other hand, his third grade reading level probably would make it unwise to start with a sixth-grade book. Because Tom's language comprehension level is three years higher than his reading level, it would be advisable to begin recording fourth or fifth-grade level books for him. In Joe's case, books about six months above his reading level should be recorded.

Use these three rules as a guide for book selection.

Guide for Selecting Books to Record

1. Students Who Have Attained at Least a Second-Grade Reading Level

If the child's language-comprehension level is about two or more years higher than his/her reading level, try recording books that are one to 1½ years *above* the youngster's reading level. If there is less than a two year difference, or the levels are approximately similar, record books that are about six months above the student's reading level.

2. Students Who Read Below a Second-Grade Level

For such youngsters, record books that are about six months above their reading level, provided their language-comprehension level is at least as high as the book. If not, record books that are just a few months above their reading level.

3. Nonreaders

Begin with stories created by the children. Either have them dictate short paragraphs and then make recordings of them or ask the youngsters to talk directly into a tape recorder and later write what was spoken. To store children's recordings and make them easily accessible, tape or paste a youngster's story and drawing inside a folder. Both the folder and accompanying tape cassette should have the same design or number (see how to code below). Also record simple storybooks that have: (a) descriptive pictures, (b) about five to ten words on each page, and (c) words repeated sufficiently so that the youngster can commit them to memory.

To help young children read a storybook with ease, each of the following four, specific linguistic patterns used in folk tales was recommended by Lauritzen (1980):

1. *Repeated Wording*, which uses sets of words like a chorus:

   Hundreds of cats
   Thousands of cats
   Millions and billions
   and trillions of cats.
   > (Gag, 1929)

2. *Repeated Syntax Patterns*, in which new words are inserted into a syntactic structure that is repeated many times:

   I was walking down the road
   Then I saw a little toad
   I caught it
   I picked it up
   I put it in a cage.

   I was looking at the sky.
   Then I saw a butterfly.
   I caught it.
   I picked it up.
   I put it in a cage.
   > (Barchas, 1975)

3. *Link Wording*, which repeats words or phrases at the end of a sentence:

   Obadiah jumped in a FIRE.
   The FIRE was so hot, he jumped in a POT.
   The POT was so black, he jumped in a
       CRACK.
   The CRACK was so high, he jumped to the
       SKY.

   and

4. *Cumulative Structure*, which adds episodes, such as *The Farmer in the Dell*.

Students should not be able to read selected books fluently. That is exactly what the book tapes will enable them to do if they are recorded correctly.

How to Record Books to Produce the Greatest Reading Gains

If you have observed slow readers listening to a commercially recorded read-along book, you probably have noticed that their eyes usually wander to everything except the print on the page. Sometimes, after spending an inordinate amount of time on one—they frantically turn pages trying to find their place in the story. Clearly, those youngsters are not associating the printed and spoken words. Although some researchers (Chomsky, 1976) have reported reading progress using commercially recorded books with slow readers, for most youngsters commercial recordings are too fast, and have too few or unclear page cues and distracting sound effects. Most of those problems can be removed by using the special recording procedures that follow.

To be most effective, recorded books should be above the student's reading level and on, close to, or even somewhat higher than the youngster's language comprehension level. The difference between the reading level of the student and the level of the book being recorded can be closed by altering these four variables: (a) the amount recorded; and the recorder's: (b) pace; (c) phrasing; and (d) expression. The simple key is this:

If the gap between the book level and the student's reading level is small, record approximately four or five minutes of a story on one tape side at a fairly normal pace, with natural expression and phrasing. If the gap is large, use a slower pace, fewer words to a phrase, exaggerate your expression, and record much less—about two minutes (p. 46, Carbo, 1984).

Books should be recorded in very small segments because most youngsters will need to listen to a tape side more than once to be able to read the portion back fluently. That is why only about one to five minutes should be recorded on each tape side. Therefore, a 15-page picture storybook might require four tape sides, while a longer book might take ten (see Figure 6-3).

Recording at a slow pace enables the listener to absorb the words seen and heard. The short, natural phrases translate the printed page into meaningful segments; the pauses help to increase both comprehension and word recognition. Vernon (1962) explained the importance of pauses in the reading process:

In reading the eyes do not move smoothly and regularly along the line of print. . . . they move in a succession of short jerks, stopping at one point or another along the line; and perception takes place only during the pauses, not during the movements. At each pause, which lasts only a fraction of a second, not more than two or three words can be perceived directly. (p. 110)

An increase in the amount of expression also seems to aid memory, perhaps because both speech stimuli (King and Kimura, 1972)—moaning, crying, coughing, laughing—and the melody or inflection of the voice (Kimura, 1964) stimulate the right hemisphere of the brain.

FIGURE 6-3. Record small amounts on each tape side. Number the spine of the tapes so that students can locate them easily.

Step-By-Step: How to Record the Books

Record each book using these procedures (Carbo, 1985).

1. Set aside a block of quiet time to record. If necessary, let others know that you are recording and need quiet.

2. Decide on the book you will record and code the tapes accordingly (see coding techniques below).

3. Speak into the microphone from a distance of approximately eight inches. If you hear little "explosions" on your recording when you pronounce an "f," or "p," then you are speaking too close to the microphone. On the other hand, you may be too far away if your voice sounds too soft when you play the tape back.

4. In general, use the same naturally expressive voice you would use if you were reading to one child. Above all, sound natural and relaxed. If you are recording a book well above a youngster's or a group's reading level, exaggerate your expression somewhat.

5. Convey your interest in the book through your voice. Let the child feel your enthusiasm.

6. Begin by reading the story title, pausing, and then telling students the

page to which they should turn. Always pause long enough so that the youngster has ample time to turn pages and look at pictures.

7. End each tape with, "That ends this recording. Please rewind the tape for the next listener." Without that important cue, some youngsters may listen to the blank tape for a while without realizing that the recording is finished.

8. Tell the student when to turn the page. As you begin each story, say, "Turn to page ____." Slowly reduce the cues until you need only pause, state the page number, and pause again. It is important to work up to omitting the words "Turn to page ____," because this interruption tends to distract the listener from the story.

9. Since it is the story that is all important, your voice should be softer when giving cues to the student than it is when you are reading.

10. Phrasing is extremely important. Read the story in logical sections. It is the way you phrase that will help youngsters understand the passage and increase their reading comprehension.

11. If you think a word may be unfamiliar to students, isolate it by pausing slightly before and after saying it. That will give youngsters more time to look at, absorb, and retain the word.

12. Read slowly so that students can visually track the words they hear, but not so slowly that they become bored.

13. Teach students with visual perception problems who lose their place easily on the page, to follow the recording by placing a finger under the words they hear; show them how to use an index card to keep their place.

After recording one story, allow a few students to listen to your tape. Check to see if your directions are followed easily, if interest is maintained, and if the youngsters have time to turn pages, look at pictures, and track the printed material visually. You may want to practice reading each book aloud before actually recording it.

SAMPLE RECORDING

The following excerpt is part of an actual book tape recorded for a first grade class. The curved lines indicate the phrasing used on the recording. Students read from the actual book and did not see the curved lines.

> Book 16, Side 1 (pause)
> *The Story About Ping* (pause)
> This is a story about a little lost
> duck who tries to find his way back
> to his family.

Please turn to page 3. (long pause)
That's the page with the little
yellow duck on the stone. (pause)
Once upon a time
there was a beautiful young duck
named Ping.
Page 4 (pause)
Ping lived with his mother
and his father
5 (pause)
(Flack, 1966, pp. 3–4)

Notice that there was a long pause after the student was told to turn to page three. That allowed the youngster to turn to the title page, look at the pictures, and find page three. The page cues are consistently reduced until only the page number is stated.

ANSWERS TO FOUR COMMONLY ASKED QUESTIONS

1. *How Do You Know If a Book is the Correct Level for a Student?* The youngster should be able to read back the taped portion fluently with no more than two or three errors after listening to the recording approximately two or three times.

2. *What Should be Done if the Student Does Not Require Any Repetition of the Recording?* If no repetitions are needed, or the youngster can read the book fluently without the recording, assign a more difficult book unless the youngster wants to listen to the tape for reinforcement. In that case, allow it, but also encourage the student to move on to higher level books.

3. *When Should Students be Told to Decode Unfamiliar Words?* The purpose of the Carbo method is to eliminate the need for youngsters to sound out words and to increase reading comprehension and fluency. If a student has trouble decoding a word it is permissible to help. If more than three words are missed, follow the suggestions in number 4 below. If the youngster has the auditory and analytic abilities to decode, and wants to, encourage it if—and only if—the student has difficulty with just a few words when reading the content after hearing the tape recording two or three times.

4. *What Should be Done if a Youngster Needs More Than Three Repetitions of a Tape?* Either the book was not recorded correctly for that student, or it is too difficult. If the child is highly motivated to read the book, make a special recording of a small portion using

shorter phrases and a slower pace. If the youngster can read that portion back after three repetitions, continue to record the book. If not, assign an easier book and, at the same time, allow the child to listen to the difficult tape for enjoyment, but do not require a readback of it. Another possibility is to allow the youngster to listen once to an entire recording of a section of a difficult book, and then to the first paragraph or so another two times. Ask the youngster to read back just the beginning portion. Since every rule has its exceptions, there may be some strongly motivated students who will make excellent progress after four repetitions.

HOW TO RECORD FOR ONE STUDENT

The recorded book method has produced the highest gains when special recordings were made for individual students, with some advancing a few years in reading ability in several months. If a student is a poor reader and does not have severe visual perception problems, ideally, that youngster should be assigned individualized tape recordings for about two to six months. After that period, most will make remarkable progress, and will be ready for book tapes recorded for a group (see directions below for recording for a group).

A recording is just right for a youngster if he or she can read the recorded section back fluently with no more than two or three errors. If the reading is halting, or many mistakes are made, then there may be a problem with the recording. Ask the youngster how it can be improved and try recording again. If the student still has difficulty, try an easier book.

The students described below have very different interests, reading levels, and language comprehension levels. Most read below grade level, some are near grade level, and one reads above grade level. The recording procedures, of course, vary, depending upon the youngster (Carbo, 1985).

Note: RL = Reading Level; LCL = Language Comprehension Level; Gap = difference between RL of book and RL of student; WPM = words per minute.

How to Record for Joan: Grade 7

Joan is in seventh grade and has attended remedial reading classes for most of her school career. She has been reading on a third-grade level for nearly five years, and just about has lost hope of ever learning to read well. Joan has the verbal ability, experience, and intelligence to understand sixth-grade vocabulary and concepts that are well above her reading ability. This is how her first book should be recorded.

Joan: Grade 7; RL: 3.7; LCL: Below-Average

Book: *Charlotte's Web,* Estimated RL: 5.0

Gap: One year, three months

How to Record: PACE: Slow, about 75 WPM

                   PHRASING: about 2–4 words per phrase

                   EXPRESSION: exaggerated

                   LENGTH: about 2 minutes

> On foggy mornings, Charlotte's web was truly
> a thing of beauty. This morning each thin strand
> was decorated with dozens of tiny beads of water.
> The web glistened and made a pattern of loveliness
> and mystery, like a delicate veil.
>
>   (White, 1952, p. 77)

How to Record for Carlos: Grade 4

Carlos is a fourth grader reading slightly *above* grade level. Like Joan, he probably would be able to read *Charlotte's Web* easily with the aid of a book tape. Because the gap between Carlos' reading level and that of the book is small, the recording should be made for him in this way.

Carlos: Grade 4; RL: 4.5; LCL: Average

Book: *Charlotte's Web,* Estimated RL: 5.0

Gap: ½ year

How to Record: PACE: almost normal, about 95 WPM

                   PHRASING: 4–8 words per phrase

                   EXPRESSION: normal

                   LENGTH: about 4–5 minutes

> Wilbur never forgot Charlotte. Although he
> loved her children and grandchildren dearly,
> none of the new spiders ever quite took her place
> in his heart. She was in a class by herself.
> It is not often that someone comes along who is a
> true friend and a good writer. Charlotte was both.
>
>   (White, 1952, p. 184)

How to Record for Mike: Grade 5

Mike is a bright, highly verbal, fifth grader reading on a second-grade level. His first recorded book should be approximately one to 1½ years above his reading level. But Mike is extremely interested in a fifth-grade-level book about gerbils. His ability and strong motivation increase the likelihood that he will do very well with the book of his choice, *Gerbils*.

Mike: Grade 5; RL: 2.7; LCL: Superior

Book: *Gerbils*; Approximate RL: 5.0

Gap: 2.3 years

How to Record: PACE: very slow, about 70 WPM

PHRASING: 2–4 words per phrase

EXPRESSION: exaggerated

LENGTH: about 1½ minutes

Captive gerbils will even thrive on a regular diet
of birdseed. The easiest way to feed them, though,
is with packaged foods that are prepared for hamsters,
mice, and other rodents. These are balanced to provide
the best nutrients a gerbil needs—a mixture of corn,
wheat, barley, and various seeds.

(Dobrin, 1971, p. 23)

How to Record for William: Grade 2

William is a second grader reading about a year below grade level; he has average verbal abilities. He needs to read many recorded books just a few months above his reading level to build his sight vocabulary. This is a portion of William's first recorded book.

William: Grade 2; RL: 1.2; LCL: Average

Book: *The Happy Egg*; Estimated RL: 1.4

Gap: Two Months

How to Record: PACE: very slow, about 60 WPM

PHRASING: about 2–3 words per phrase

EXPRESSION: exaggerated

LENGTH: about 2 minutes

There was a little little bird.
It was just born.
It still was an egg.

It couldn't walk.
It couldn't sing.
It couldn't fly.
(Krauss, 1967)

As William's reading improves, books slightly above his reading level should be read at a faster pace, and in longer phrases of about 3–5 words to improve his fluency and confidence. In a few months, he should be able to read taped books that are ½ year above his reading level.

In summary, recording books for each student does take time, but has produced remarkable reading gains of a few years in just a few months' time. Parents and students can be trained to make the recordings. The following should be considered when recording a book for a student: (a) the youngster's interest in the book; (b) the maximum phrase length the student can assimilate; (c) the highest reading rate the youngster can follow comfortably; (d) the amount of expression required to maintain interest and increase word retention; and (e) the amount of material that should be recorded.

HOW TO RECORD FOR A GROUP

Most groups will have a wide range of reading abilities. When recording for a group of students, add about half a year to the lowest reading level in the group and at least 1½ years to the highest level. Then record books within that range. For example, suppose a fifth grade class has reading levels from 3.0 to 6.8. Then books ranging from a 3.5 level to about an 8.2 level should be recorded for the youngsters in the group. For reinforcement purposes, a few 3.0 level books also might be recorded. (See Figure 6-4.)

Since poor readers may want to sample some books three and four years above their reading level, the pace should be somewhat slow and the recordings brief (four to six minutes). In that way, poor readers can attempt some difficult books, and good readers can complete more than one tape at a sitting if they are able.

Getting Organized: How to Code and Store the Books and Tapes

Let's assume that you are ready to record. Here is the procedure you would use if you were going to begin by recording eight books for a group of students.

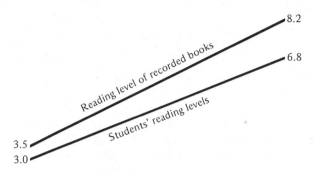

FIGURE 6-4. Record a wide range of books for a group.

Nine Organizational Steps

1. *Select the Books.* Choose the eight books you will record based on the quality of the writing and the students' interests, reading levels, and language comprehension levels.

2. *Number the Pages.* Be certain that the pages in each book are numbered consecutively. If they are not, paginate them. The numbers will enable you to give the listener page cues as you record, and will help the student to keep his/her place in the story.

3. *Code the Books.* Number the books in order of difficulty. Write the number with an indelible marker on a sticker and place it onto the upper left-hand corner of the book cover (see Figure 6-5).

   If most youngsters have difficulty with higher numbered books than those at the beginning levels, renumber the books and tape cassettes. Peel off the number of the book and replace it. Remove the indelible marker on the tape cassette (duplicating master fluid or nail polish remover work well), and renumber it.

4. *Decide the Amount to be Recorded on Each Tape Side.* Plan exactly how much you will record on each tape side. For example, if a simple storybook has 21 pages and you decide to record about three minutes on each tape side, first, read aloud for three minutes at the

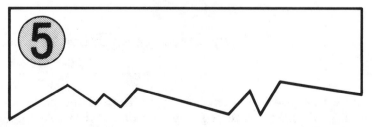

FIGURE 6-5. Code each book with a numbered peel-off sticker.

same pace you plan to record. If you have read four pages, you would then divide the book into three to five-page sections, depending upon the amount of print on each page and whether the section ends in a logical place (see Figure 6-6).

5. *Monitor Your Recordings.* Try recording only the first tape of each book and ask for comments from your students. Do they like the books? Are they able to follow your recording? Is there sufficient time for them to turn pages, look at the pictures, and find the first line of print on each page? Can most of them read the pages fluently after two or three repetitions? Is your pace, phrasing, and expression appropriate? Is the length of the recording too long, too short, or just right?

6. *Adjust Your Recordings.* Based on student recommendations, adjust the pace, phrasing, expression, and amount recorded. If necessary, recalculate the number of pages you will record on each tape side.

7. *Make a Chart of the Book Coding.* This will serve as a guide for coding the tapes *and* can be used to keep a record of each student's progress. Just duplicate the chart, and place a copy in each child's folder (see Figure 6-7).

   Note that the books are listed down the left-hand column and a place is provided to indicate the date the book was begun and completed by the student. The pages to be recorded on each tape side are listed across the chart. For example, the first book, *The Monkeys and the Water Monster,* has pages 44 to 48 recorded on tape side 8, and the third book on the list, *Pandas,* has pages 2 to 8 recorded on the first tape side.

8. *Code the Tapes.* Using a fine-tipped, indelible magic marker, write the number of the book and the numbers of the tape sides on the spine

Book 3:   Side 1 - pages 2-8
          Side 2 - pages 9-17
          Side 3 - pages 18-23
          Side 4 - pages 24-29

FIGURE 6-6. Before recording, plan which pages you will record on each side of tape.

Book No.	Date(s)	Book title and author	TAPE SIDE AND PAGES									
			1	2	3	4	5	6	7	8	9	10
1		Monkeys & Water Monster by B. Chardier	7-11	12-15	16-23	24-27	28-32	33-38	39-43	44-48		
2		Bigger Giant by N. Green	3-9	10-17	18-23	24-30	24-29					
3		Pandas by R. L. Gross	2-8	9-17	18-23	24-29						

FIGURE 6-7. A chart placed in each child's folder makes record keeping easy.

of the cassette. For the first book in the series above, Figure 6-8 shows the way the tapes would be coded.

9. *Store the Books and Tapes.* Place the numbered books in sequential order into a bookcase so that each book cover and its number can be seen easily by students. After recording, the tape cassettes should be stored vertically with the labeled spines facing the youngsters (see Figure 6-9).

How to Color-Code the Books and Tape Cassettes

An effective way to organize the materials is to color-code the books and tapes. The time expended will be rewarded in time saved because the reading materials will be less likely to be misplaced. To color-code the books, either buy colored paste-on stickers or color white tape with a

Book No.	Date(s)	Book title and author	TAPE SIDE AND PAGES									
			1	2	3	4	5	6	7	8	9	10
1		Monkeys & Water Monster by B. Chardier	7-11	12-15	16-23	24-27	28-32	33-38	39-43	44-48		

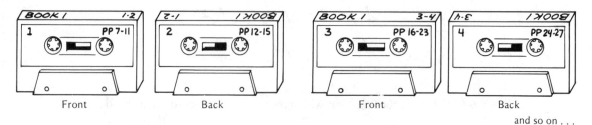

Front   Back   Front   Back

and so on . . .

FIGURE 6-8. Code the tapes with an indelible marker.

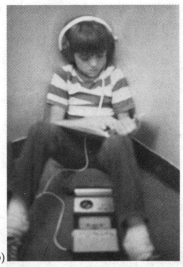
(a)   (b)

FIGURE 6-9. (a) Book tapes should be labelled on their spine and stored vertically in a box, near the books. (b) A variety of reading areas should be available nearby. (Photographs by Marie Carbo, courtesy of the Robert Carbonaro School, District 24, Valley Stream, New York.)

marker. Place the stickers onto the books according to the level, subject, or whichever system you used to organize the resources. The spines of the tape cassettes also can be color-coded so that each corresponds to the number of its companion book. Do this before writing the number of the book onto the cassette spine. (See Figure 6-10.)

Designing Resources to Supplement the Tape Recordings*

Some youngsters need only the recorded books to make excellent progress in reading. Others benefit greatly from resources that provide: (a) additional practice of the vocabulary presented on the recording and/or (b) specific skill work which uses the characters, events, and vocabulary of the recorded story. Four global, multisensory resources that have been very successful are audio cards, tactile/kinesthetic materials, skillsheets, and writing activity cards.

Audio Cards

For those students who need additional vocabulary reinforcement after reading back the recorded portion of their story, audio cards are ideal. Blank audio cards usually are available from manufacturers of card readers. Each card has a tape band on the bottom that enables the

*The audio cards, tactile/kinesthetic materials, skillsheet, and writing activity card in Chapter 6 were created by Marie Carbo.

FIGURE 6-10. When designing the recorded book method, Carbo sequenced these 135 storybooks, and color-coded them according to grade level. Within each color, each book was numbered in order of difficulty. Last, the books were recorded. (Courtesy of Robert Carbonaro School, District 24, Valley Stream, New York.)

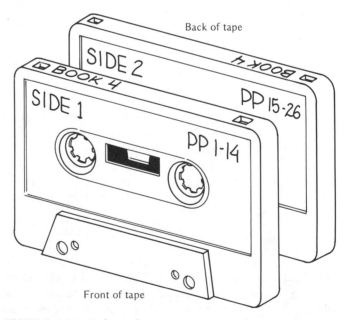

FIGURE 6-11. Code each tape on its spine, front, and back.

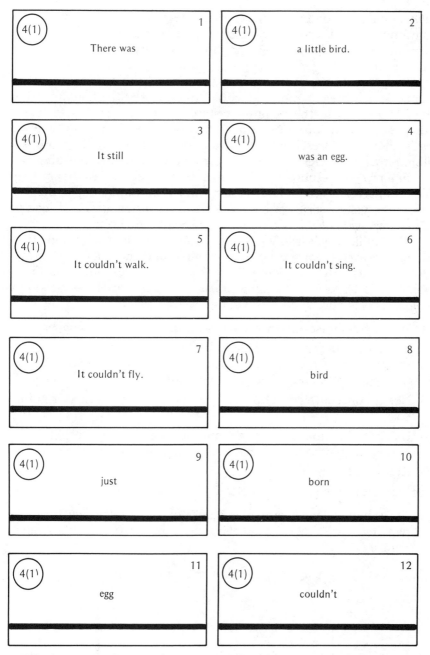

FIGURE 6-12. These audio cards reinforce the vocabulary on tape side 1 of *The Happy Egg*.

teacher and the student to make separate recordings. By placing each programmed card into the card reader, students can see and hear the words on the card, record them, and then compare their recording to that of the teacher's.

Recorded books are a highly global approach to teaching reading because words are encountered within the context of high-interest stories. The second step in the beginning stage of this process is to help the youngster to focus on phrases and then words from the story. Isolated words should be presented *after* the global child can read those words within phrases. The technique can best be understood with examples.

In a previous section, we described how to record *The Happy Egg* for William in second grade. Let's assume that *The Happy Egg* is the fourth book in the yellow series of books. William has listened to and read back the first tape side of the book which is shown in Figure 6-11.

The audio cards shown in Figure 6-12 would enable him first to practice phrases from the book in context, and then new words in isolation. He has just completed the first tape side of the book (Yellow, Book 4, Side 1). Now he is going to use the audio cards that accompany his tape. This is how to code the audio cards.

1. Write the phrases and words to be practiced on scrap paper.
2. On color-coded stickers (yellow, in the case of *The Happy Egg*), write the number of the book and tape side (4-1). Place a coded sticker in the upper-left-hand corner of each audio card needed.
3. Next, consecutively number the cards in the upper-right-hand corner.
4. Using a fine-tipped, indelible marking pen, write the phrases and words written on scrap paper, onto the coded audio cards.
5. Record each card.
6. Last, store the cards in a color-coded box.

When William completes Side 2 of *The Happy Egg*, the accompanying cards begin again with the number one, as illustrated in Figure 6-13.

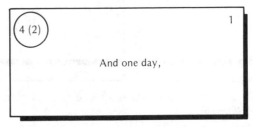

FIGURE 6-13. The first card for Book 4, tape side 2. For each tape side, code consecutive numbers in the upper right-hand corner. Write the book number and the tape side in the upper left-hand corner.

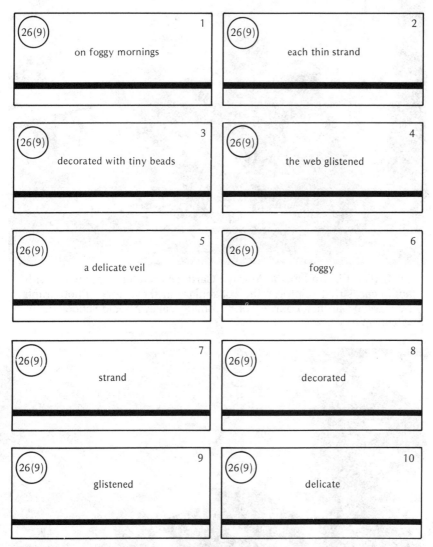

FIGURE 6-14. For more difficult books like *Charlotte's Web*, list phrases and words from the recorded passage.

Audio cards for books above a second-grade level should not be programmed in the same way, because each tape side could require hundreds of cards. For books on a second-grade level and above, select from the story particularly difficult phrases and words that students should practice. For instance, the cards shown in Figure 6-14 would probably help Joan, the seventh grader for whom *Charlotte's Web* was recorded. These audio cards supplement tape side 9 of *Charlotte's Web*, which is book number 26 in the white series. Most students no longer need

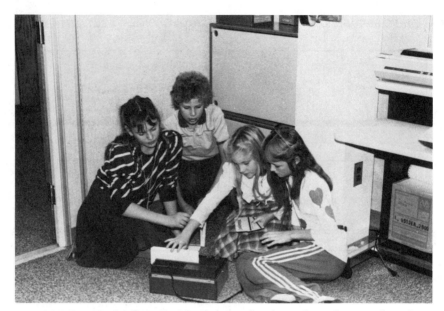

FIGURE 6-15. Students in Marilyn Gardner's reading class work with audio cards that reinforce the vocabulary in their story. (Photograph by Marilyn Gardner, courtesy of Lycoming Valley Middle School, Pennsylvania.)

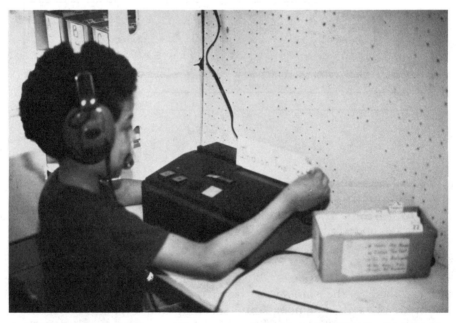

FIGURE 6-16. In the reading program developed by Marie Carbo, phrases from recorded stories placed on audio cards helped students to retain the vocabulary encountered initially in their recorded storybooks. (Photograph by Marie Carbo courtesy of the Robert Carbonaro School, District 24, Valley Stream, New York.)

THE
HAPPY
EGG

pages 1-21

Write T if the sentence is true.
Write F if the sentence is false.

____ 1. The little bird was just born.
____ 2. The little bird was in the egg.
____ 3. The egg could sing.
____ 4. The little bird could sing.
____ 5. The egg sat on the bird.
____ 6. The egg got sat on and sat on.
____ 7. One day a cat came out of the egg.
____ 8. The little bird could fly.
____ 9. It could sit on other happy eggs.

FIGURE 6-17. Skillsheet for *The Happy Egg.*

to work with audio cards once they can read comfortably at a fourth grade level.

Skillsheets

Skillsheets can be used to reinforce the vocabulary in a recorded book and to introduce or review a reading skill. Exercises that relate to book recordings can be stored in folders and reproduced for individual students or groups. To create a permanent system for an individualized program, tape each worksheet onto construction paper; color-code, number and laminate each one, and store it upright in a box so that the numbers are easily seen. The skillsheet shown in Figure 6-17, which accompanies the first tape side of *The Happy Egg*, has been coded and laminated.

Tactile/Kinesthetic Resources

These materials are important for youngsters who learn easily through their tactile/kinesthetic senses, particularly young boys, who tend to have more reading problems and are more tactile/kinesthetic than girls. Tactile/kinesthetic resources are multisensory, allow mobility and peer interaction, and help youngsters to relax while learning so that they absorb and retain better.

Figure 6-19 shows samples of different tactile/kinesthetic resources from storybooks. Chapter 7 has detailed directions for their construction. Each of the items can be color-coded and numbered to match the book it accompanies.

(a)   (b)

FIGURE 6-18. Following a recorded story, a high-interest reading skill game based on their book is enjoyed by Donna Michel's students (a) and Marilyn Gardner's (b). (a) Photograph by Kay Johnson, courtesy of Northfield Elementary School, Howard County, Maryland. (b) Photograph by Marilyn Gardner, courtesy of Lycoming Valley Middle School, Pennsylvania.

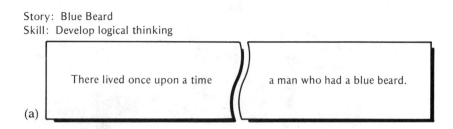

Story: Blue Beard
Skill: Develop logical thinking

(a)

There lived once upon a time | a man who had a blue beard.

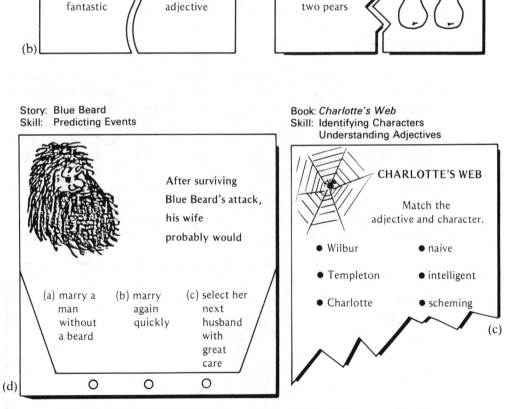

Book: Star Wars
Skill: Understanding adjectives

(b)

fantastic | adjective

Book: The Very Hungry Caterpillar
Skill: Developing sight vocabulary

two pears

Story: Blue Beard
Skill: Predicting Events

(d)

After surviving
Blue Beard's attack,
his wife
probably would

(a) marry a man without a beard   (b) marry again quickly   (c) select her next husband with great care

Book: *Charlotte's Web*
Skill: Identifying Characters
        Understanding Adjectives

(c)

CHARLOTTE'S WEB

Match the
adjective and character.

● Wilbur   ● naive

● Templeton   ● intelligent

● Charlotte   ● scheming

FIGURE 6-19. Global/tactile/kinesthetic students learn easily when reading skills are taught within the context of the characters, events and vocabulary of a story read, with tactile/kinesthetic materials, such as: task cards (a and b), electroboards (c), and pik-a-hole games (d). See Chapter 7 for construction directions.

FIGURE 6-20. Books, book tapes, skill cards, games and activity cards can be color-coded and numbered so that they are easily accessible to the students. (Photograph by Marie Carbo, courtesy of the Robert Carbonaro School, District 24, Valley Stream, New York.)

Activity Cards

To make an activity card which complements a book, design the activity on scrap paper. Then select pictures from the book to accompany it. These can be drawn, or taken from an extra copy of the book. Paste or tape the illustration onto a large activity card (preferably the same color as the book is coded), write the activity on it, place the book number onto the upper-right-hand corner, and store the card in an index card box (Carbo, 1976) (see Figure 6-21).

All the materials outlined in this chapter—recorded stories, audio cards, skillsheets, tactile/kinesthetic materials and activity cards—can be created to complement any story (see Chapter 7). They help global students learn to read naturally, easily and, best of all, with enthusiasm!

FIGURE 6-21.

7

Teaching Children to Read through Tactile and Kinesthetic Resources

Most learning in the early years after birth is a result of touching, feeling, moving, and experiencing. Indeed, many students do not develop full visual acuity until third grade and full auditory acuity until fifth grade (Restak, 1979). Yet, initial reading instruction often is based solely on either auditory or visual approaches.

Tactile and kinesthetic resources should be developed and incorporated into regular instruction for those who are having difficulty learning to read. In addition to that central use of tactile/kinesthetic materials, they are desired by gifted students at more sophisticated levels and provide variety and options for all.

Learning Style Characteristics Responsive to Tactile and Kinesthetic Resources

Tactile and kinesthetic materials may be used anywhere in the instructional environment, provided space is available. They respond to individual preferences for quiet or sound, low or bright light, an informal or formal design, and warmth or cool, while learning. In fact, because they may be moved easily from one section of the room to another, children who require variety may alternate how they use such resources.

Because of their gamelike qualities, these resources tend to be motivating to students who previously have been unsuccessful academically. The gifted also enjoy them but tend to want to create their own after only limited experiences with those designed by their teachers. They should be encouraged to do so, because learning occurs rapidly when information is understood, absorbed, translated into another form, and then applied. It is important that the youngsters to whom tactile and kinesthetic resources are assigned are positive about them and, therefore, are willing to follow directions for their use, care, and replacement. If they then begin to enjoy learning through a hands-on approach, they will become persistent and will continue using the materials until they have achieved the stated goals or objectives outlined for them.

All the materials are self-corrective. If youngsters experience difficulties while using them, they can manipulate the parts to find correct answers. Nevertheless, the motivation for using these resources is necessary if students are to become responsible for them—for the parts and sections of each set must be kept intact, returned to holders and boxes, and maintained in good condition. However, it has been our observation that previously apathetic or negative children often become highly motivated because of their interest in and enjoyment with learning circles, task cards, electroboards, pic-a-holes, and flip-chutes. Once they realize that they *can* learn well through such materials and are successful, motivation increases to the point where children often beg for tests to permit them to demonstrate their newly acquired knowledge or skills.

Tactile and kinesthetic resources respond to individuals' sociological preferences because they may be used alone, in pairs, with a group, and either near or away from the teacher. Youngsters who need variety may alter the devices they use on a daily basis; those who feel more comfortable with routines and patterns may study a complete unit through identical materials.

Perceptual preferences are complemented because the materials are: (a) tactile (they are touched, manipulated, and moved); (b) visual (the same information is seen in several different forms and is repeated); (c) kinesthetic (body games or out-of-seat activities may be included); and, (d) auditory (resources may be accompanied by an explanatory tape). These activities may be assigned in a sequence that initially responds to each youngster's strongest perception, reinforces through a secondary modality, capitalizes on a tertiary modality, and reviews through a fourth sense. Thus, youngsters can be exposed to the same concepts or skills through many different, interesting resources with which they are actively, rather than passively, engaged.

These suggested resources may be used at any time of day or evening, for they may be taken home, used in a classroom, Interest or Learning Center, library, or special Resource Room. They respond to mobility needs because students may work as long as they are able to, may stop, and then return to the resources as their energy is revitalized. Because the materials are so motivating, youngster's inclinations are to use—rather than to avoid using—them. Certainly, children may snack while using tactile/kinesthetic resources since chewing sounds will not interfere with the concentration of either their teachers or classmates, because the youngsters can work away from others, with those whose learning styles are similar, or engage in intake at appropriate moments when others are not near.

Finally, tactile and kinesthetic materials appeal to children whose arousal systems are both Left or Right; what determines student success with them is perceptual strengths rather than hemispheric inclinations. The materials can be designed so that they are analytic (sequential, providing small amounts of information in tiny steps that build up to understanding) or global (holistic, providing an overview and understanding and then analyzing the details).

Materials and Equipment

If you are willing to experiment with several of the following suggested tactile and kinesthetic (T/K) resources, Figure 7-1 illustrates the items that can be used. If inservice workshops are planned for a group of teachers, parents,

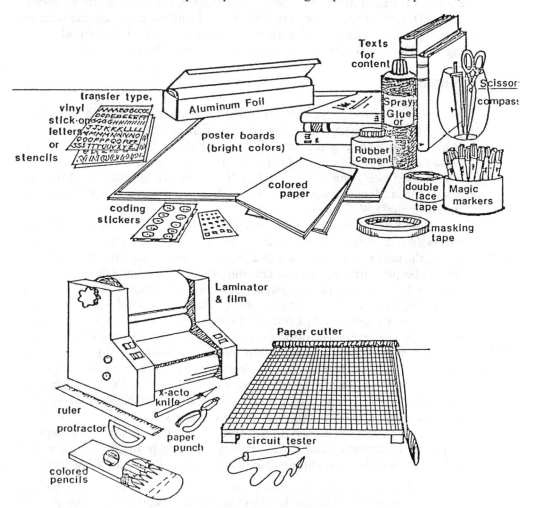

FIGURE 7-1. Materials and Equipment. Designed by Dr. Angela Bruno for Lamtex, Incorporated, Canton, Ohio.

or aides, all the materials would be useful. This diagram provides a global overview of what is needed. However, should you choose to experiment with only selected items, each of the following sections provides information concerning what is needed to produce each resource.

T/K Resource #1: Learning Circles

Teachers use many different methods to teach children to read; they read to them and let them hear and see words and sentences simultaneously; they explain how to combine the sounds of letters to form words; they describe how different groups of letters form word families; and they use familiar, real experiences that are described verbally as the basis for initial decoding experiences. Another way is to use Learning Circles.

Situation

You plan to introduce a unit on folktales. For the tactile and kinesthetic youngsters who usually are less motivated than their classmates and are unable to absorb a great deal of meaning solely from verbal or printed explanations, you develop a Learning Circle to explain the new terms that will be used (see Figures 7-2 and 7-3). If the student is global, read folktales first; if the student is analytic, you may introduce the unit either through the stories or the T/K resources.

Note that the Learning Circle is a large round; in this case it is divided into eight triangular sectors. Each of the eight sectors has an explanation of one of the unit's unique terms and a picture representing the concept. Notice the clothespins attached to the Learning Circle; each has one of the terms described on the face of the Learning Circle printed neatly on it. Figure 7-3 shows the back of the Learning Circle. The rear side of each triangular sector has a shape on it. Look at the rear of the clothespins; each has one of the same shapes found on the back of the Learning Circle. When a student places the clothespins with the correct answer onto the matching triangular sector on the front of the learning circle, the shape on the back of the clothespin and the shape on the back of the Learning Circle match; if the clothespin is placed onto the incorrect sector, the back shapes do *not* match. Thus, students know whether they are correct or not.

If the youngster does not read well, a tape can describe the steps for using the Learning Circle. If the printing on each triangular shape is in a different color, the tape can describe what each section states: For example:

> Hold the Learning Circle so that the section with the *red* printing is at the top. Notice the picture of the knight on the horse in that same triangle. The printing says: "A character admired for his actions is the _____ ."
> When we read folktales, we read of many persons who are admired for

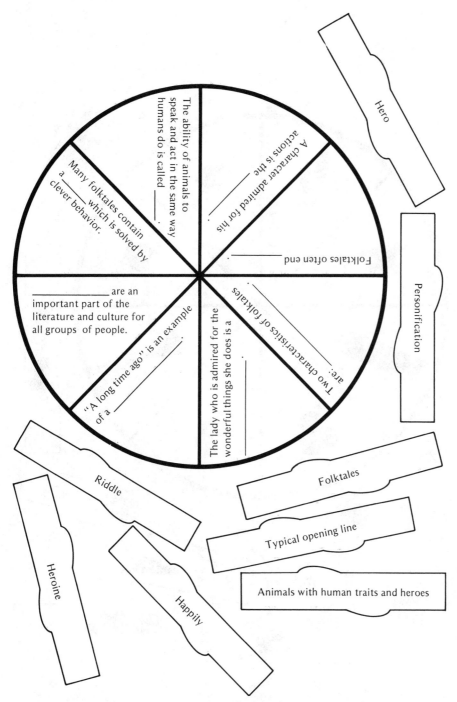

The ability of animals to speak and act in the same way humans do is called _____.

A character admired for his _____ actions is the _____.

Folktales often end _____.

Two characteristics of folktales are: _____.

The lady who is admired for the wonderful things she does is a _____.

"A long time ago" is an example of a _____.

_____ are an important part of the literature and culture for all groups of people.

Many folktales contain a _____ which is solved by clever behavior.

Hero

Personification

Folktales

Typical opening line

Animals with human traits and heroes

Riddle

Heroine

Happily

FIGURE 7-2. Front of Learning Circle on Folktales. This Learning Circle was designed by Jeanette Bauer and Mary Dauber, St. John's University graduate students who also are certified New York State teachers.

FIGURE 7-3. Back of Learning Circle on Folktales.

their courage, strength, and actions. We call those people _____. Can you guess? You can learn that answer by using this Learning Circle! Let's turn the Circle to the right. If you are seated, facing the teacher's desk, turn the Circle toward the classroom door. If you turn it toward the right, the triangular section with the *blue* printing will be at the top. Notice the picture of the frog and the prince on the blue section. The words on that section say: "The ability of animals to speak and act in the same way humans do." We use a special word to describe what we call it when animals or things behave like people. Turn the Circle to the right again. Remember, you are turning it toward the door if you are facing the teacher's desk. If your back is to the teacher's desk, turn the Circle toward the window.

The first time you introduce any tactile resource, show the children how to use it, take care of it, return it to where it was before they took it, and to handle its tape correctly. If your students can read fairly well, they may prefer to use the resource in either a pair or team; in that way, they may not need the cassette.

Situation

You introduced long and short A sounds to selected youngsters that seemed ready to tackle the concept. Now, six weeks later, several children who were *not* taught the skills of recognizing words with either short or long A sounds have become interested in the concept because of their classmates' involvement. They have begun to ask questions about how to know which words have which sounds. As an introduction, you encourage them to begin with the Learning Circle and obtain assistance, if necessary, from either children who have mastered the concept, or from the accompanying cassette.

In addition, two children who previously appeared to have mastered these sounds, now are evidencing an inability to indicate which words have long or short As. Suggest that they work with the Learning Circle to refresh their memories (see Figures 7-4 and 7-5).

Situation

Your advanced students have learned about antonyms. As a homework assignment, you require that each design one Learning Circle on antonyms that later can be used by tactile students who also need/want to develop that skill.

Directions for Constructing a Learning Circle

1. Cut either oaktag or poster board into circles (see Figure 7-6) or any shape related to the information being taught. For example, if the unit is concerned with using a computer, the Learning Circle may be

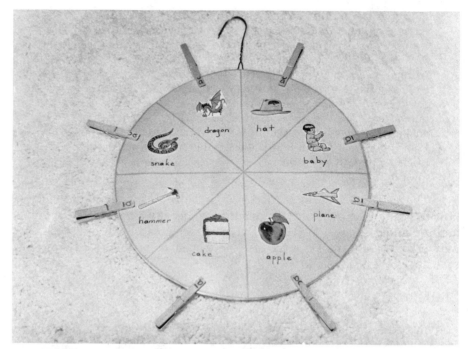

FIGURE 7-4. Front of Learning Circle on The Long And The Short Of The Letter A. This Learning Circle was designed by Jean Erle, Mary Ellen Foye, and Mary Ann Liddy, New York teachers and graduate students of St. John's University.

in the form of a computer. The Learning Circle on folktales could be in the shape of a castle; the one on government could be an outline of the White House; the one on the vocabulary for a specific story might represent either a character or item from it (see Figure 7-7).

2. Boldly print task content on the front side of the card and self-corrective (color-code, picture-code, shape-code or answer-code) answers on the back side of the card.

3. Laminate before cutting each card into the parts which separate the task from the answer.

4. Package, organize and label card set for storage.

If storage is a problem, a wire hanger can be attached to the back of the Learning Circle and a separate, matched-in-size-and-shape backing can be *glued* on top of the hanger. In that way, many Learning Circles can be suspended over a doorknob, a hook, or a hardware arm.

If you prefer to avoid making another Learning Circle every time you want to teach tactile children a new skill or concept, cut out a large,

(front)

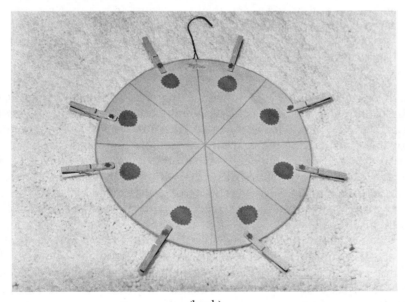

(back)

FIGURE 7-5. Learning Circle on The Long And The Short Of The Letter A. This Learning Circle was designed by Jean Erle, Mary Ann Liddy, and Mary Ellen Foye, graduate students, St. John's University, New York.

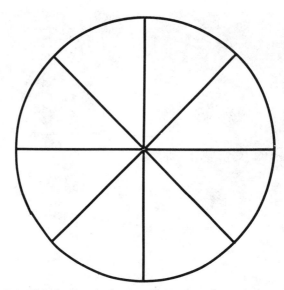

FIGURE 7-6. This basic circle may be xeroxed, copied, or otherwise duplicated to provide an easy model for constructing Learning Circles for your classroom. Add content related to your students' needs, color and laminate the model, and then cut it out. Add clothespins with answers that correspond to the questions printed on the face of the Learning Circle, and you will have an easily made tactile resource (Bruno and Jessie, 1983, page 5).

18-inch oaktag round, cover it with a matched-in-size-and-shape clear plastic round, and sew along the diagonal lines of each of the triangular sectors, being certain to leave the outer rim of the Circle open. Then make removable construction paper triangular sectors that can be inserted into and withdrawn from the pockets—which the sewn sectors have become. Whenever students experience difficulty with what needs to be mastered, you quickly can make new insertions for the Learning Circle. You also can have tactile youngsters construct the information triangular insertions themselves!

Because they are self-corrective, Learning Circles can be used in ways that are most responsive to varied learning styles—alone, with a friend or two, in a team, or with the teacher, and wherever in the class, library, or Resource Room the students feel most comfortable. This visual/tactile approach to learning facilitates remembering, and when added either to a Programmed Learning Sequence, a Contract Activity Package, or a Multisensory Instructional Package, this resource provides excellent introductory *and* reinforcement experiences. (See Chapters 8, 9, and 10.)

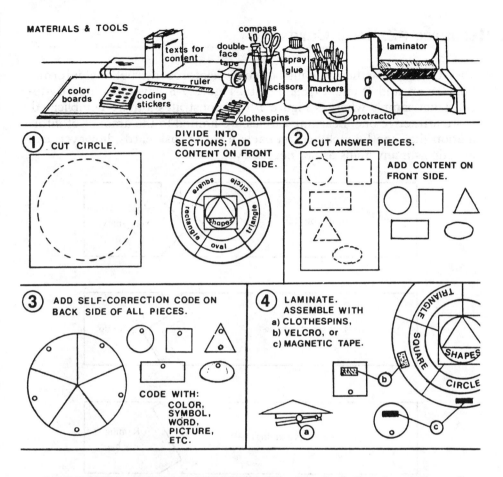

LEARNING CIRCLE EXAMPLES—Varied Content Levels

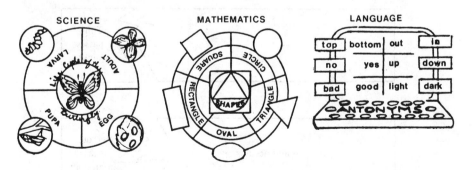

FIGURE 7-7. Basic Learning Circle Construction. Designed by Dr. Angela Bruno for Lamtex, Incorporated, Canton, Ohio.

T/K Resource #2: Task Cards

Task Cards too, either may introduce or reinforce instructional information (Dunn and Dunn, 1978a, 1978b). Figure 7-8 illustrates an easy-to-construct sample whereas Figure 7-9 demonstrates a more complicated, more attractive one. Learning Circles are limited to the amount of information that can be included on each; a set of task cards, however, can include as many items as are necessary.

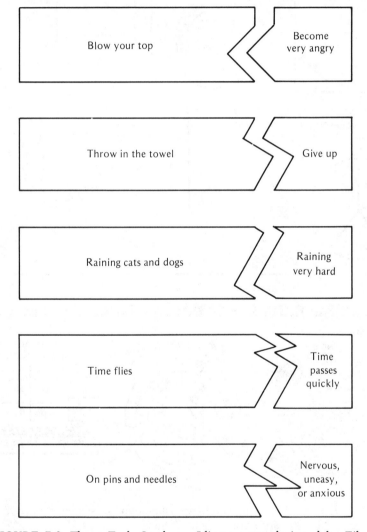

FIGURE 7-8. These Task Cards on Idioms were designed by Eileen O'Keefe, teacher, American Martyrs School, Bayside, New York.

FIGURE 7-9. Designed by Jeanette Bauer and Mary Dauber, graduate students, St. John's University.

These five sample Task Cards represent only a few in the series on Idioms. Students may be introduced to a concept with a limited number of Cards, and then, as knowledge is acquired, additional sections may be added to the set until, eventually 30 or 40 idioms and their meanings are included. Children shuffle the Task Cards and try to match the two parts that go together. In the beginning, the cards are easy to combine correctly because they are shape-coded. After a while, the same information can be placed on identically shaped cards; students must turn them over to learn whether they have been matched correctly. The cards can be picture-, sign-, or color-coded to indicate correct pairs.

The attractive task cards depicted in Figure 7-9 are used to introduce folktales to the tactile student and serve as a reinforcement activity for auditory students.

Situation

The results of a reading achievement test indicate that your students need to learn how to sequence events in the correct order. One of their favorite books is *Dr. Jekyl and Mr. Hyde*, and you create a task card game that provides the needed practice. After the students have mastered the skill with many highly global book games, most or all will be ready for more analytic resources, such as worksheets (see Figure 7-10).

Situation

A group of your students has difficulty recalling the details of stories they read. Recently those youngsters finished reading *Dick Whittington and His Cat*. You know they are strongly tactile/kinesthetic—but not auditory, and decide to devise a simple task card game in which they will match the characters and specific events of the story. In effect, you have structured the task so that the youngsters will touch, move, see, and discuss the details.

Directions for Constructing Task Cards

1. Cut either oaktag or poster board into rectangles—or any other shape you creatively decide to use. Sets in varied shapes seem to attract student interest.
2. Divide the shape into two or more sections. We suggest that you introduce students to two-part Task Cards initially; as they develop an understanding of, and sophistication with, this resource, gradually increase the number of parts for each card. For an example, see the multisectioned Task Cards in Figure 7-10.

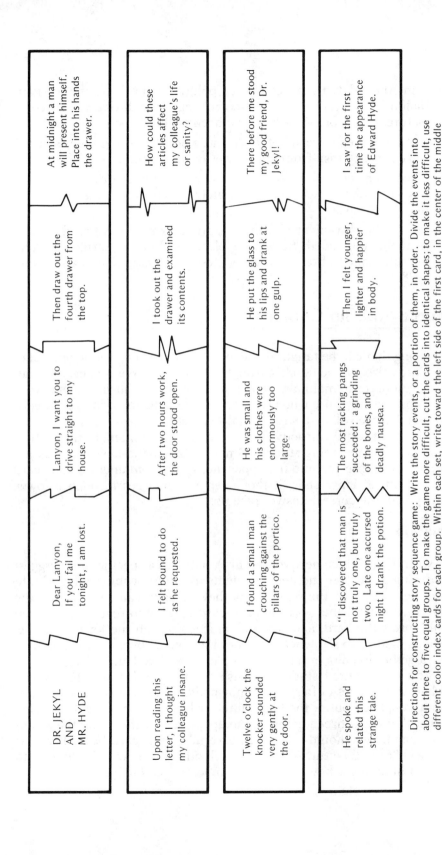

Directions for constructing story sequence game: Write the story events, or a portion of them, in order. Divide the events into about three to five equal groups. To make the game more difficult, cut the cards into identical shapes; to make it less difficult, use different color index cards for each group. Within each set, write toward the left side of the first card, in the center of the middle cards, and toward the right of the last card so you have the proper space needed to cut out the cards which will form the attached sequence. Students sequence the cards within each group, and then place the groups into the correct order.

FIGURE 7-10. This set of task cards was designed by Marie Carbo from the book, *Dr. Jekyl and Mr. Hyde* by Robert Louis Stevenson.

3. Print the related subject matter boldly on the face of the shape (half on each section). Add self-correcting codes through either color, picture, shape, or symbols on the back of the shape.

4. Laminate the entire set of Task Cards before cutting them apart to separate each task from the answer or match to it.

5. Place each set into either a plastic bag, an envelope, or an attractive box—the label of which appropriately indicates the tasks related to that set of cards.

6. Store in a convenient place where students may have ready access to them as needed. Suggested places include a learning station, interest center, library corner, or Resource Room (Dunn and Dunn, 1978a).

T/K Resource #3: Flip Chutes

Everything that can be taught through either a Learning Circle or a set of Task Cards also can be taught through a Flip Chute. We suggest alternating the resources to maintain student interest and enthusiasm when variety is required; for those who prefer to use the same materials repeatedly, this single device will be a strong reinforcement.

Flip Chutes are attractively decorated milk containers that reflect the subject matter being studied. Small question-and-answer cards are designed to be inserted into the upper face of the container. As each card descends on an inner slide, it flips over and emerges through a lower opening with the correct answer face up.

Situation

You wish to introduce new vocabulary related to a specific unit. Suggest that during a few free moments students use the Vocabulary Flip Chute to see how many of the new words they actually can read. Direct the children to look at the word on each card and try to read it. They then should insert the card, and when it returns through the lower opening, check its picture to see whether or not they were correct. Students may work together in pairs or a small group of three (see Figure 7-11).

You've permitted students to use a set of Task Cards to become familiar with a series of fairly well-known idioms. For homework you give them a sample cutout of the Flip Chute cards and direct them to develop a series of at least three idioms on the upper face of the cards; the meaning of each idiom should be printed carefully on its card back. The next day the children take turns inserting each others' Homework Idioms into the Flip Chute to see how many they can learn (see Figure 7-12).

FIGURE 7-11. Sample Flip Chute developed by Barbara Gardiner, New York City teacher and consultant, National Learning Styles Network, St. John's University, New York.

FIGURE 7-12. This Flip Chute was made by an elementary student in the Hewlett-Woodmere Public School System, New York, in conjunction with a project required by her teacher, Janet Perrin.

Situation

You have been given a home computer for your classroom. It is difficult to demonstrate how to operate it with the entire class at once, and yet everyone is so eager that you do not wish to choose only a few while the others remain uninvolved. You develop a Flip Chute with pictures of the parts of the computer on the top of each of its cards and the name of each part on their flip sides. You challenge the children to learn all the parts, and as that is accomplished, you will demonstrate how to operate the machine on a first-learned, first-taught basis (see Figure 7-13).

Situation

You wish to have your students become familiar with analogies. You use a regular, standard Flip Chute which is appropriate for any topic, but

FIGURE 7-13. This Computer Flip Chute was designed by Barbara Gardiner, New York City teacher, for exactly the situation described.

develop a series of Flip Chute cards, each having an analogy on the card's top face and the answer on the flip side. Suggest that students use the cards to learn what analogies are. For homework they have a choice from among three options: they may: (a) make a set of illustrated Flip Chute cards that include at least five analogies different from those on the sets you designed (see Figure 7-14); (b) write at least five new analogies on a

Father is to mother as
sister is to _____ .

brother.

Knife is to fork as
cup is to _____ .

saucer.

Track is to train as
highway is to ____ .

car.

Hot is to cold as
thin is to ____ .

fat.

Lunch is to noon as
breakfast is to ____ .

morning.

FIGURE 7-14. These sample Analogy Flip Chute cards demonstrate the types of questions and answers that lend themselves to this format.

sheet of paper and illustrate each; or (c) make a set of new Analogy Task Cards that they should try with at least two other classmates.

Directions for Constructing Flip Chutes

1. Pull open the top of a half-gallon milk or juice container.
2. Cut the side folds of the top portion down to the top of the container.

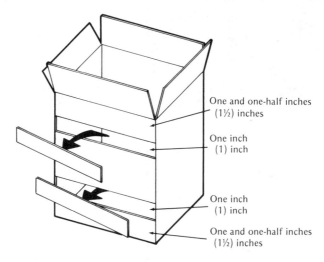

One and one-half inches (1½) inches

One inch (1) inch

One inch (1) inch

One and one-half inches (1½) inches

3. On the front edge, measure down both: (a) 1-½ inches, and (b) 2-½ inches. Draw lines across the container. Remove that space.
4. Mark up from the bottom: (a) 1-½ inches, and (b) 2-½ inches. Draw lines across the container. Remove that space.
5. Cut one 5 × 8 index card to measure 6-½ inches by 3-½ inches.
6. Cut a second index card to measure 7-½ inches by 3-½ inches.
7. Fold down ½ inch at *both* ends of the smaller strip. Fold down ½ inch at *one* end of the longer strip.

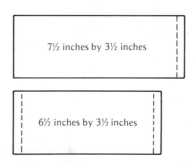

7½ inches by 3½ inches

6½ inches by 3½ inches

Flip Chute directions were developed by Barbara Gardiner (1983).

8. Insert the smaller strip into the bottom opening with the folded edge resting on the upper portion of the bottom opening. Attach it with masking tape.

9. Bring the upper part of the smaller strip out through the upper opening with the folded part going down over the center section of the carton. Attach it with masking tape.

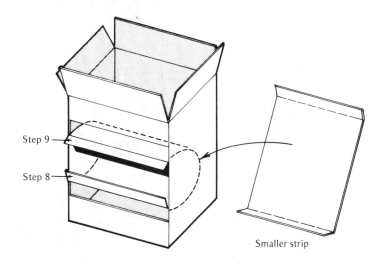

Step 9

Step 8

Smaller strip

10. Working with the longer strip, one end is folded down, and the other end is unfolded. Insert the unfolded end of the longer strip into the bottom opening of the container. Be certain that the strip goes up along the back of the container. Push it into the container until the folded part rests on the bottom part of the container. Attach it with masking tape.

11. Attach the upper edge of the longer strip to the back of the container creating a slide. Secure it with masking tape. Follow the next illustration.

12. Fold down the top flaps of the container and tape them in place, forming a rectangular box.

13. Use small, 3 × 5 index cards, cut into halves, to write the question on one side and the answer on the flip side.

If you want to make the Flip Chute reflect a particular theme or area of study, add a rounded section at the top to represent a head, arms, or other "special effects." Paint, color, or cover with colored Contact™ or vinyl wall covering and add lettering describing this particular Flip Chute's purpose. When completed, an everyday sample should look similar to the one in Figure 7-15.

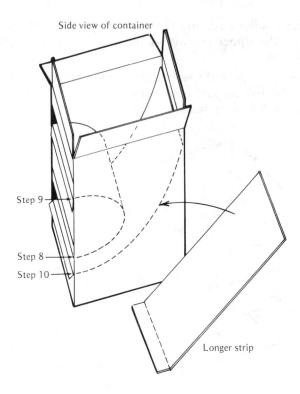

Side view of container

Step 9

Step 8

Step 10

Longer strip

T/K Resource #4: Pic-A-Holes

Pic-A-Holes are more of an *introductory*, rather than a *reinforcement* type of resource. A Pic-A-Hole offers choices from among three options, and should a youngster's first—or even second—choice be incorrect, the self-corrective feature of the device ensures eventual success in a private, nonthreatening environment.

Similar to a series of cards with printed questions, students consider answers and look at three possible options at the bottom. With a tied-on golf tee, they place the point directly below the option they believe to be correct and then attempt to lift the question card. If the answer selected is correct, the card lifts easily and can be removed; should it be incorrect, the card will not budge. (See Figure 7-16.)

Situation

You've been working on long and short A sounds with certain children. You develop a Pic-A-Hole series so that they can test themselves to see whether they really can recognize the difference between the two A sounds (see Figure 7-17).

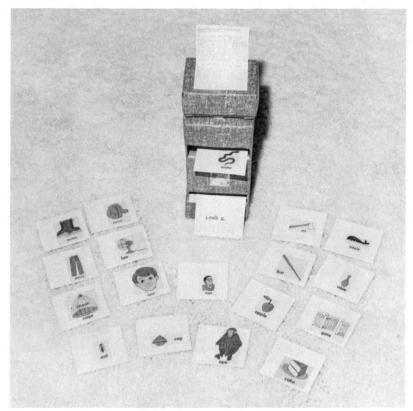

FIGURE 7-15. Sample completed Flip Chute to use with new vocabulary.

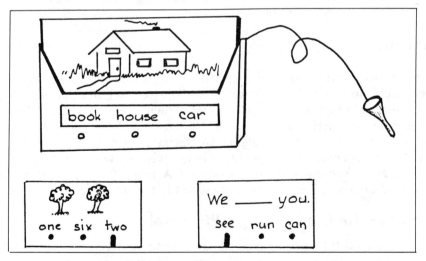

FIGURE 7-16. This illustration of a Pic-A-Hole was created by Barbara Gardiner, New York City teacher and consultant, National Learning Styles Network, St. John's University.

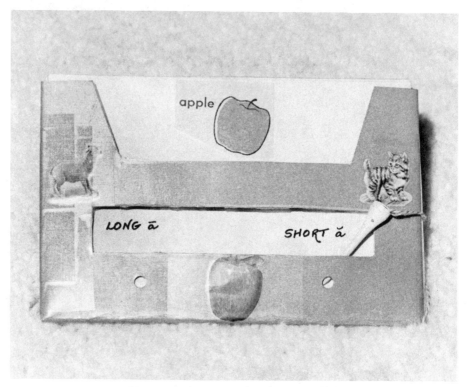

FIGURE 7-17. This sample Pic-A-Hole on Long and Short A was created by Jean Erle, Mary Ann Liddy, and Mary Ellen Foye, St. John's University graduate students.

Situation

Your students are interested in learning about the difference between their mind and their brain. Your Pic-A-Hole set includes cards such as those shown in Figure 7-18. The samples shown in Figure 7-18 are from a Pic-A-Hole card series on Getting It All Together: Your Mind and Your Brain and are part of a set designed by Barbara Gardiner, New York City teacher and consultant, National Learning Styles Network, St. John's University, New York, based on a Contract Activity Package and a Programmed Learning Sequence designed by Cindy Gaharis for the Network.

Directions for Constructing a Pic-A-Hole

1. Cut a colorful piece of cardboard or posterboard 24-⅜ inches by 6-½ inches.

Pic-A-Hole directions were developed by Barbara Gardiner (1983).

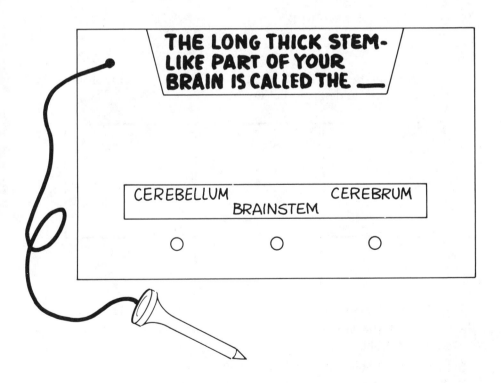

FIGURE 7-18. Sample Pic-A-Hole.

2. Following the guide below, measure and mark the cardboard (on the wrong side) to the dimensions given. Use a ball point pen and score the lines heavily.

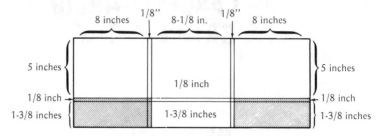

3. Remove the shaded areas. Use a ruler and a razor or exacto knife to get a straight edge. The piece of posterboard then should look like the illustration below.

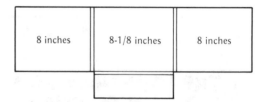

4. Working on the wrong side of the center section only, follow the measurement guide given below.

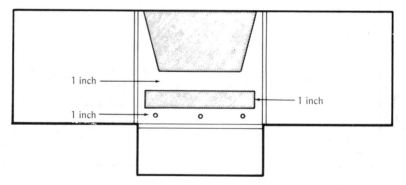

5. Remove the shaded areas with a ruler and razor or exacto knife.

6. Fold on all the drawn lines using a ruler as a guide to obtain sharp, straight fold lines.

7. Punch three holes as shown in the diagram.

8. Place an index card under the center section. Trace the openings onto the card. Remove the same areas from the index card. This will

serve as a guide for placement of questions and answers which can be written on 5 × 8 index cards in appropriate places. Punch the holes.

9. Using 5 × 8 index cards, mark holes and punch them out. Use the guide for the placement of information.

10. Fold over the first side under the center section; then fold up the bottom flap; now fold over the last side. Paste or staple them together, being certain that the bottom flap is in between.

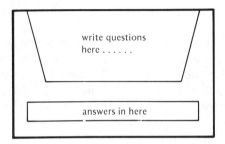

T/K Resource #5: Electroboards

Although most youngsters pay rapt attention to what they are trying to decipher when the tactile component is added, Electroboards may be the single resource that consistently holds their attention. They appear to be less tactile than Learning Circles, where clothespin answers must be sought, handled, and attached to their matching questions; they require less handling than Task Cards which merely need to be shuffled, examined, and then placed side by side with their correct half. Indeed, Electroboards certainly require no more tactile involvement than do Flip Chutes where an answer, once selected, is placed into the upper slot and caught as it emerges from the bottom opening; and, the Pic-A-Hole, if anything, is *more* tactile, for students must choose the correct answer and then insert the golf tee into the correct hole, attempt to pull out the card, place it onto a nearby surface, and then reach for the cards and tee again.

Electroboards, however, have a bulb that lights up whenever the chosen answer is correct, and similar to a slot machine, or a computer, that facet appears to mesmerize children because the lighted bulb is immediate visual feedback of the student's success. These resources take longer to make, but once completed will be worth every moment devoted to them.

Generally speaking, questions are listed on one side of the resource while answers are listed on the opposite side—but out of order so that they do not match correctly. Students hold a two-part continuity or battery tester in their hands. They attach one prong to the question they are try-ing to answer, and after reading the list of possible answers on the oppo-site side of the board, touch what they believe is the correct answer with the second prong. If they are correct, the bulb lights; in some instances a bell rings—but that sound often is disconcerting to others.

Electroboards and any other tactile resource are particularly delight-ful when their outer shapes are in harmony with the subject matter they are trying to teach. The following situation is an example.

Situation

You are introducing the concept of fruits to primary children. You design the Electroboard in the shape of a fruit, and down the right side you list as many fruits and other objects as fit. On the left side you have only two possibilities: FRUIT and NOT A FRUIT. Children use the continuity tester to indicate whether or not each item on the list is, or is not, a fruit. (See Figure 7-19.)

Continuing Situation

An alternative Electroboard would list the names of the fruits on the left side and their matching pictures pasted in a scattered fashion on the right side. The continuity tester is used to correctly match the picture with its name.

Situation

To increase vocabulary or to approach the concept of synonyms, you might develop an Electroboard similar to one suggested by Bruno and Jessie (1983, p. 10) in Figure 7-20.

Directions for Constructing Electroboards

Creatively vary the outer dimension of each Electroboard so that it reflects the theme or unit being studied and is easy for the children to locate without assistance. For example, they will learn that when looking for an Electroboard dealing with a unit on Transportation, the likelihood is that its outline will be in the form of a car, a train, a plane, or so on. Thus, when focusing on a specific theme, the tactile resources for that theme should each have the same shape. A unit on the New England states might, thus, all be in the shape of a map of the northeastern section of the United States; a unit on Community Workers might have a Learn-ing Circle, a set of Task Cards, a Flip Chute, a Pic-A-Hole, and an Electro-board all in the shape of a fireman's or policeman's hat (Dunn and Bruno, 1983).

FIGURE 7-19. Sample of a Fruit Electroboard.

1. Begin with two pieces of either posterboard or oaktag cut into exactly the same size and shape.

2. List the exact questions you want the Electroboard to ask; then list their answers. Count the number of questions and divide the face of the left side of the Electroboard into evenly divided spaces so that the questions all fit on the left side.

3. Use a paper hole puncher to make one hole on the left side of the face of the Electroboard for each question you developed. Then punch corresponding holes *on the same horizontal level as the beginning of each question*—but on the *right* side; those holes are for the answers to the questions.

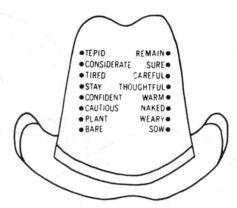

FIGURE 7-20. Sample Electroboard for either increasing vocabulary or the concept of synonyms. Notice the interesting shape of the resource to set it apart from other Electroboards being used in that classroom.

4. Print the questions and each answer separately in large, black, capital letters either directly on the oaktag or posterboard, or to secure very neat, attractive lines, onto *double* line (26" × 8") strips of Dennison PRES-a-ply™ correction tape. The Dennison tape can be obtained in most large stationery stores or directly from the Dennison Manufacturing Company, Framingham, Massachusetts 10701. When you are satisfied with the printing of the questions and their corresponding answers, peel the correction tape from its base and carefully place each question next to one of the prepunched holes on the left side of the developing Electroboard's face. Be certain that each is placed horizontal to the other and leaves even spaces between. Then peel off and place the answers onto the right side of the Electroboard near the other prepunched holes, but *be certain to randomize the answers so that none are on the same horizontal level as its matched question.*

5. Turn the oaktag or posterboard face over, and on its back create circuits made with aluminum foil strips and masking tape. Lay strips of aluminum foil "connecting" each question and its correct answer. Then use masking tape that is wider than the foil strips to cover each foil strip. Be certain to press both the foil and the masking tape cover so that they: (a) completely cover the punched holes and (b) remain permanently fixed.

6. Note the positions of each question and its answer so that you have a self-corrective guide in case one is necessary for substitute teachers or aides. Write the name and number (assuming you have several) of the Electroboard at the top of the code. Place into a secure place where access is available when necessary.

7. Using a continuity tester, which can be purchased in any hardware store, check every circuit to be certain that each is working. Do that by touching each question with one prong of the circuit tester and its related answer with the other prong. If the circuits were put together correctly, the tester's bulb should light. Experiment with touching several questions and *incorrect* answers (one at a time) to be certain that the bulb does *not* light.

8. Next tape the second, identically shaped and sized piece of oaktag or posterboard to the *back* of the first piece on which you have been doing all this tactile work; the second piece will serve as a cover to conceal the circuits so that your students do not know which questions are paired with which answers. Then tape the entire perimeter of both cards together, or as Bruno and Jessie suggest (1983, p. 3), "connect the cards using double-faced tape."

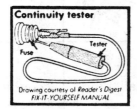

Continuity tester

Drawing courtesy of *Reader's Digest*
FIX-IT-YOURSELF MANUAL

T/K Resource #6: Book Games

You were introduced to book games in Chapter 5 in a description of a sample global reading lesson and again in Chapter 6. Practicing reading skills by using the context of a story through games is important because such materials have been extremely successful with youngsters with a global/tactual/kinesthetic reading style. It is the use of story context that increases meaning and makes certain resources more global than analytic (Carbo, 1979; 1982).

Before working with a book game, children should be familiar with the story; they can read it, listen to the tape, see a filmstrip or a movie, or listen to it being read. The purpose of the book game is to develop particular reading skills using the characters, events and vocabulary of a story. Most youngsters enjoy games and will practice a skill sufficiently so that mastery occurs.

Situation

You notice that a group of students needs to be able to read words more quickly on sight. When reading *The Five Chinese Brothers* many of them miss the same words. Within only 45 minutes, you create a bingo game (Figure 7-21) containing the most difficult words in that story. The chil-

extraordinary	desperate	indefinitely	algae
crest	promptly	presently	assembled
consented		exactly	burst
condemned	delighted	condition	execution

Directions for constructing bingo book game: Select from a story those words or phrases that you want your students to practice. For primary youngsters, approximately eight to sixteen items are appropriate; most older students are capable of playing bingo games with sixteen to twenty-five choices. Draw lines on the index cards to form one box for each item. Write the words and/or phrases in different locations on each card. Cut out the words on one card to form the calling cards for the game.

FIGURE 7-21. The Five Chinese Brothers Bingo Game designed by Marie Carbo

dren are delighted to encounter words taken from a tale they enjoyed so thoroughly; they play the game a few times, and become extremely proficient in the book's vocabulary. During the school year, some youngsters will replay *The Five Chinese Brothers* bingo game for a review.

Situation

Your students need practice with rhyming words. Book games containing rhymes are ideally suited for your purpose. After reading a portion of a book with many rhymes to a group of youngsters, you begin to pause just before a rhyming word, allowing the youngsters to verbalize it. Most become expectant and quite involved in the activity. For further practice,

Directions for constructing a book-card game. Choose 15 pairs of rhyming words from the book. Write the phrase from the story containing the rhyming word at the bottom of each card. Cut out, draw, or trace pictures from the book that match the selected phrases. Write the title of the book on one card. The card game can be played by two to five players. First, all the cards are dealt. Then each player in turn selects one card from the player on his right. If a player matches a rhyming word, he/she places the pair down and reads the words and the sentence. When all (but one) cards are discarded, the player with the title card is the winner.

FIGURE 7-22. Book Card Game designed by Marie Carbo.

you construct a domino game from the rhyming words in the book *I Was Walking Down the Road* and a card game for the story "My Box and String" (Figure 7-22). These provide hours of enjoyable practice of the rhymes your students heard when you read the books to them.

Summary

Young children, just learning to read, often delight in the T/K process—particularly if it provides successful outcomes. Tactile/kinesthetic materials make learning fun and provide an easy-to-see and understand overview of small amounts of information at a time.

When students experience difficulty with reading, the opportunity to work with the resources described in this chapter often facilitates their understanding and skill development. Because most primary youngsters learn more easily through a hands-on approach than they do by listening or watching, these materials should prove to be extremely valuable to any beginning reading program. They will prove effective with advanced students as well, for once a problem arises, repetition through the same method will not break the barrier to internalized comprehension—except with a great deal of unnecessary tedium and pain.

We encourage readers to experiment with the resources described herein and request feedback on whether, or how well, they helped your students learn.

8

Teaching Children to Read through Programmed Learning Sequences

Programmed instruction represents a viable alternative for average and above average students who do not respond adequately to conventional approaches used in developmental reading programs. This type of student requires structure and sequence in an orderly step-by-step approach to reading objectives. Such procedures are not appropriate for all but should be prescribed for youngsters who exhibit the specific learning style characteristics described in the next section.

Programmed Learning Sequences provide flexibility to teachers who are concerned with individuals who are not progressing as well as they should. Such youngsters can work alone without the direct supervision of the teacher and on appropriate objectives in areas of interest to them. They can learn as slowly or as quickly as they need and in any location where they feel comfortable as long as they do not impede the progress of others.

Learning Style Characteristics Responsive to Programmed Learning Sequences (PLS)

Environmental

Sound. The pupil using a PLS can control all of the environmental elements with some guidance from the teacher. He or she can complete a sequence in a quiet corner using earplugs, if necessary, or earphones and music if preferred and essential to better performance.

Light. Low or bright light can be selected, adjusted, and regulated by the student through location, switches, lamps, sunglasses, and so forth.

Temperature. Modifications to work in an optimum learning climate for the individual include types and amount of clothing, location, thermostats, air conditioning, sunlight through windows, and other arrangements.

Design

Permitting choices among formal and informal designs such as desks, tables, chairs, arm-tablet desks, couches, beanbag seats, or carpeting will aid students who have strong productivity preferences for one or another situation.

Emotional

Motivation, persistence and responsibility. Because programmed materials usually are used independently (alone), it is important that those students to whom this resource is assigned are motivated to learn the contents of the package. They should also be persistent, suggesting that they normally would continue using the materials until the program has been completed. Should they experience difficulty, they either will review the previous frames and continue to try to progress, or they will seek assistance from appropriate persons. Programmed instruction also requires responsibility from students; should they daydream or neglect to work toward completion of the materials, they will be wasting valuable instructional time.

Obviously, motivation (and persistence and responsibility) will be enhanced if sequences are developed on topics of high student interest. Specific reading skills and developmental objectives can be designed around themes of intense concern to individuals at different ages, intellectuality, and emotional development. Current television, film, and media heroes, animals, space creatures, and others can offer an attractive framework for specific objectives. Often the content itself, given a global introduction, will spark sufficient enthusiasm.

Success and immediate feedback also promote motivation, persistence and responsibility. Initially, teachers should guide students to an appropriate PLS for their continued achievement and progress through a continuum of developmental objectives.

Structure

By organizing everything that should be learned so that only one item at a time is presented, the sequenced materials in each program provide a great deal of structure. A student cannot proceed until what must be achieved at each stage has been fully understood, as demonstrated through a short quiz at the end of each frame or page. Youngsters who prefer to be directed and told exactly what to do will feel at ease with programmed packages, while creative students may find them boring and, thus, irritating.

Sociological

Programmed instruction is ideally suited to youngsters who *prefer to work alone* and to avoid the sounds, movement, and interaction of classmates. In actual practice, students are each given a program for which they are responsible, and as the various objectives and their related tests are completed, gradual progress is made toward completing the material. Unless learners need and seek assistance, they may be virtually isolated for long periods of instructional time. It is also possible for them to engage in hours of study without benefitting from either adult or peer interaction. There are youngsters who prefer to work alone; but the Scribner and Durell studies conducted at Boston University (1975) and the Poirier methods instituted at the University of California (1970) verify that for many students, retention is increased after peer discussions of what is being learned. A teacher who chooses to use programmed materials for students who are peer-oriented may overcome the isolation factor, however, by incorporating selected small-group techniques into the programs—such as team learning, circle of knowledge, group analysis, case study, simulations, and brainstorming (Dunn and Dunn, 1978); also see Chapter 9.

Physical

Perceptual Strengths.   Programmed Learning Sequences provide a perfect match for students who learn best by seeing and for those who need to read, and, perhaps, reread materials before they can be absorbed. For auditory youngsters, a teacher should add a tape that repeats orally what the text teaches visually. When students are either tactual or kinesthetic learners, the teacher should add games that introduce the program's objectives through those senses. For students who learn slowly or with difficulty, it is wise to supplement a visual programmed sequence with three other types of perceptual resources—auditory, tactual, and kinesthetic. Pictures, graphs, drawings and symbols should be added for interest and reinforcement, and for those whose initial visual strength is pictorial.

Intake, Time, and Mobility

A student may snack or not as he or she works, may use a PLS at any time of day that is preferred and most productive, and may take a "break," stroll around, and return to the learning sequence if mobility is necessary.

Psychological

Programmed Learning Sequences usually are analytic in design. Each frame is part of a tightly organized structure which builds knowledge or skills step-by-step in related, simple, overlapping stages. Each bit of knowledge is prerequisite to the next.

Left brain initiators or sequential processors respond well to these word oriented, step-by-step programs. Reflective students, rather than impulsive ones, tend to perform better work with them. For those who require a global, motivating section, a short story introduction should be utilized to build interest and envelop the reader in the basic content of the material at the beginning.

Basic Principles of Programmed Instruction

Programmed Learning Sequences are designed on the basis of several important principles that tend to facilitate academic achievement for students with the previously described learning style patterns. All programs tend to follow a similar pattern, which includes each of the following characteristics:

1. Only one item is presented at a time.   A single concept or skill that should be mastered is introduced through a simple written statement. After reading the material, the learner is required to answer a question or two to demonstrate that what has been introduced by that frame (page, section) has been understood. This procedure prevents the lesson from advancing faster than the student, and it does not permit the student to fall behind. The youngster may learn as quickly as he or she is capable of comprehending the material, or as slowly and with as much repetition as may be needed. No one may continue into a subsequent frame or phase of the program until each previous one has been mastered.

Presenting one item at a time is effective for the youngster who wants to learn (is motivated), who will continue trying (is persistent), and who wants to do what is required (is responsible). For students in need of structure, being exposed to one item at a time breaks the content into small phases and the process into short steps that can be mastered gradually. Understandably, this process is not effective for the student who needs to be exposed to a gestalt of the information, who, rather than piecing a totality together bit by bit, prefers to develop an overall view of the end product. It is also inappropriate for those who cannot continue to work with the same set of materials for any continuing amount of time and who need diversity and variety. In addition, it appears to be a method that does not attract and hold creative students who want to add their own knowledge and special talents to what is being learned before they have accomplished the entire task.

2. The student is required to be an active, rather than a passive, learner.   Unlike large-group instruction, where a student may merely sit and appear to be listening, programming requires that a response be made to questions related to each introduced item. Youngsters cannot progress through the program without responding, and only accurate answers permit continuation of this learning process.

3. The student is immediately informed of the correctness of each response.   As soon as a youngster has read the frame, he or she is required to answer a question based on the material that has just been read. The moment that the student's response has been recorded, the youngster may turn to a section in the program (usually the back of each frame) where the correct answer is stated. The student, therefore, is immediately made aware of the accuracy or inaccuracy of the response. This technique of immediate reinforcement is a highly effective teaching strategy with most learners.

4. The student may not continue into the next phase of a program until each previous phase has been understood and mastered. When the program reveals that a student's responses to the questions related to each frame are correct, the student is directed to continue into the next section (frame, page, or phase). When students' responses are not correct, they are directed either to restudy the previously read frames or to turn to another section of the program that will explain in a different way the material that has not been understood. Because each phase of the program must be mastered before students are permitted to continue into the next phase, learners do not move ahead aimlessly while grasping only parts of a concept or topic. Their base of knowledge is solid and complete before they are exposed to either new ideas or related ones.

5. The student is exposed to material that gradually progresses from the easy to the more difficult. Frames are written so that the first few in a series introduce what should be learned in an uncomplicated, direct manner. Gradually, as the student's correct answers demonstrate his or her increasing understanding of what is being taught, more difficult aspects of the topic are introduced. Through this technique, students are made to feel both comfortable and successful with the beginning phases of each program and their confidence in their own ability to succeed is bolstered. Youngsters who find themselves achieving are likely to continue in the learning process.

6. As the student proceeds in the program, fewer hints and crutches are provided. Programming uses a system of fading, or gradually withdrawing easy questions or hints (repeated expressions, illustrations, color-coding, and similar crutches) so that the student's developing knowledge is tested precisely. This technique enables the teacher to accurately assess the youngster's progress and mastery of the material.

Step-by-Step Guide to Designing a Programmed Learning Sequence

Developing a program is not difficult, but it does require that you organize the topic that will be taught in a logical, easy-to-follow sequence. Begin with Step 1 and gradually move through each of the remaining steps until you have completed your first program. Each consecutive program will become easier and easier to design. By their questions and responses, students will provide direct feedback on how to revise and improve your initial efforts. Subsequent programs will require fewer revisions.

Step 1

Begin by identifying a reading topic, concept, or skill that you want to teach. A good choice would be something that most youngsters in your classes need to learn. Since all students are not capable of learning at the same time, in the same way, and with the same speed, a program is one way of permitting individuals to self-pace themselves with materials whenever they are ready to achieve. Thus, some youngsters may use this program early in the semester while others will use it later. Some will use it to learn before the remainder of the class is exposed to a new idea, and others will use it to reinforce an idea that you have already taught—but which they did not master.

Step 2

Write the name of the reading topic, concept, or skill that you have decided to teach as a heading at the top of a blank sheet of paper.

Step 3

Translate the heading that you have written at the top of the sheet into an introductory sentence that explains to the youngsters using the program exactly what they should be able to do after they have mastered what the materials are designed to teach.

Examples

- By the time you finish this program, you will be able to recognize *adjectives* and identify the *nouns* that each of the adjectives modifies.
- This program will teach you to recognize exceptions to at least four basic spelling rules.
- I am so pleased that you are going to work with this program, because it will teach you how to:
  1. Punctuate a sentence correctly, and
  2. Write a series of correctly punctuated sentences to form a paragraph.

Step 4

List all the prerequisites for using the program effectively.

Examples

- Before you use this program, you should be familiar with the meanings of each of the following words: desert, nomad, oasis, arid, mirage.

• Be certain that you begin using this program either on or near a large table so that you will have ample room to use these materials and the tape recorder at the same time.

Since you may recognize that certain knowledges or skills are, indeed, prerequisite after you have moved beyond Step 4, leave space on your paper so that you may insert additions as they come to mind.

Step 5

Decide which of the two basic types of programming you will use.

*TYPE 1: LINEAR PROGRAMMING**

This type of programming presents material in a highly structured sequence. Each part of the sequence is called a frame, and each frame builds upon the one immediately preceding it. Each frame ends with an item that requires an answer—either in completion or multiple choice formats. Prior to the introduction of each subsequent frame, the answer to the previous frame is supplied. Program efficiency increases when the correct answer is accompanied by an explanation. Additional comprehension is developed when the incorrect answers also are accompanied by explanations.

Example

FRAME 1

Read the paragraph below. Then write the correct answer on the line at the end of the paragraph.

A computer is an electronic machine that enables information to be processed very quickly. Computers rapidly store, relate, and provide feedback on the knowledge put into them. Thus, computers enable information to be _____ very quickly.

---

*The authors suggest that you begin with linear programming. After designing several successful linear Programmed Learning Sequences, you may wish to develop some intrinsic programmed sequences.

BACK OF FRAME 1

ANSWER: processed

The paragraph tells us that computers store, relate, and give information feed-back rapidly. That is called processing.

FRAME 2

Write the correct answer on the line at the end of the paragraph.

Input is all the information that someone puts into the computer. That is done by typing onto a keyboard.

1. People type on a _____ to feed information to the computer.

2. The information given to a computer is called _____ .

BACK OF FRAME 2

ANSWERS: (1) keyboard
(2) input

You get input into a computer by typing on a keyboard.

TYPE 2: INTRINSIC PROGRAMMING

Intrinsic programming also presents material in a highly structured sequence, but the major difference between linear and intrinsic types is that the intrinsic does not require that each student should complete every frame. Intrinsic programming recognizes that some youngsters can move through learning experiences faster than others can, and it permits those who score correct answers to skip over some of the reinforcement frames.

When students may bypass frames that teach the same aspect of a subject, the system is called branching. Branching, in effect, permits a faster rate of self-pacing.

When a student answers a question incorrectly, he must continue from one frame to the next, to the next, and so on until every frame in the entire program has been completed. When a student studies several introductory frames and then answers the questions correctly, he may branch over additional reinforcement frames if the program is an intrinsic one.

Example

FRAME 1

An adverb is a word that describes how something is done. When we say, "Jim drives well," the word "well" describes how Jim drives. The word "well" is an

_____ .

(circle one)

adverb   noun   adjective

BACK OF FRAME 1

ANSWER: (adverb)

Any word that describes how something is done, is an adverb.

FRAME 2

Mary smiles sweetly. The adverb in the sentence, "Mary smiles sweetly," is

_____ .

(underline one)

Mary   smiles   sweetly

BACK OF FRAME 2

ANSWER: sweetly

"Sweetly" tells how Mary smiles. Mary is a girl's name. Mary is a noun. "Smile" is what Mary does. Smile is a verb. If you wrote that "sweetly" is an adverb, you understand how to recognize some words that are adverbs.

Turn to Frame 5. You may skip Frames 3 and 4. If you did not write that "sweetly" is an adverb, turn to Frame 3 for more practice in recognizing adverbs.

FRAME 3

John walks quickly.

Circle the adverb in the sentence above.

BACK OF FRAME 3

ANSWER: (quickly)

"Quickly" tells how John walks.
"John" is the boy's name. "John" is a noun.
"Walks" is what John does. "Walks" is a verb.

FRAME 4

Susan plays quietly.

Write the adverb in the above sentence on this line. _____

BACK OF FRAME 4

<u>ANSWER:</u> quietly

"Quietly" explains how Susan plays.
"Susan" is a noun. It is a girl's name.
"Plays" is a verb. It describes what Susan does.

FRAME 5

Circle the two adverbs in the next sentence.

The boys were playing quietly and nicely.

BACK OF FRAME 5

<u>ANSWERS:</u> (quietly) and (nicely)

"The" is an article.
"Boys" is a noun.
"Were" and "playing" are verbs. They tell what the boys were doing.
"And" is a conjunction.

If you had both answers correct, turn to Frame 8. If you did not have both "quietly" and "nicely" correct, turn to Frame 6.

Step 6

Outline how you plan to teach the topic. Use short, simple sentences, if possible.

Most people have two different vocabularies: one is used for speaking, the other for writing. When you begin to outline your program, make believe that you are speaking to the student who will have the most trouble learning this material. Use simple words and sentences. Then write exactly the words that you use when you act out the way you would teach this material if you were actually talking to that youngster. In other words, use your speaking vocabulary rather than your professional writing vocabulary to develop the program.

Step 7

Divide the sentences in your outline into frames. Frames are small sections of the topic that teach part of the idea, skill, or information. After listing the sentences that teach, ask a question that relates to the material. The student's answer will demonstrate his or her growing understanding of the subject. Think small! Most people who begin to write programs try to cover too much in a frame. Keep each frame simple. It should contain a small portion of the total knowledge represented by your instructional objectives. In some cases you may wish to start with a simple generalization and move to specific examples and applications.

Pose fairly easy-to-answer questions in the first two or three frames to:

- build a student's self-confidence
- demonstrate to the student that he or she can learn independently through the program
- provide the student with a couple of successful experiences by using the process of programmed learning.

Example

FRAME 1

Today we are going to take a close look at something. When we look closely at something, our action is known as OBSERVATION. When you have completed this program, you will know how to make:

Check one: _____ Summarizations
                _____ Observations
                _____ Outlines

Vary the way you ask students to respond to the questions on each frame. Sometimes require *fill-in* answers; sometimes have students *match* possible responses; at other times; have them *circle* or *underline* correct items.

Step 8

Using a 5 × 7 index card to represent each frame, develop a sequence that teaches a subject and, simultaneously, tests the student's growing knowledge of it.

Step 9

Refine each index card frame.

1. Review the sequence to be certain that it is logical and does not teach too much on each frame.
2. Check the spelling, grammar, and punctuation of each frame.
3. Examine the vocabulary to be certain that it is understandable by the slowest youngsters that may use the program. Avoid colloquialisms that are acceptable in conversation but are less than professional in written form. But remember to use good oral language as opposed to good written language.
4. Reread the entire series to be certain that each frame leads to the next one, and so on.

Step 10

When you are satisfied with the content, sequence, and questions on the frames, add colorful illustrations to clarify the main point on each index card.

If you do not draw, use magazine cutouts or gift wrapping paper to graphically supplement the most important sections of the text.

Step 11

Read the written material on each frame onto a cassette so that poor readers may use the program by listening to the frames being read to them as they simultaneously read along. (See Chapter 10 for directions on making a tape.)

Step 12

Ask three or four of your students to try the program, one at a time.

Observe each youngster using the material and try to identify whether any errors, omissions, or areas of difficulty exist. Correct anything that requires improvement. If necessary, revise the program based on your observations of student usage.

Step 13

Laminate each of the index cards that comprise the program or cover them with clear Contact™. Student use will cause the index cards to deteriorate unless they are protected by a covering. Laminated programs have lasted for years and can be cleaned with warm water and soap. They can be written on with grease pencils and then erased for use by another youngster.

Step 14

Add a tactile activity in game form for reinforcement of the most important information in the program. (See Chapter 7.) The program, as designed through Step 14, will respond only to youngsters who learn through either their visual or auditory senses. If you can add tactile reinforcement through materials such as task cards, learning circles, or an electroboard, you will be providing youngsters who need to learn through their sense of touch with a method appropriate for them. You thus will be adding to the effectiveness of the program and increasing the number of students who can learn successfully through it. Make the tactile supplements small enough to fit onto a frame or into an envelope that can be laminated or attached securely to a program frame.

Step 15

Ask additional students to use the program.

Step 16

Add an introduction, directions, specific vocabulary if required, and a short global story or description to spark interest in those who would profit from a PLS but who tend to be simultaneous processors (right brained, holistic, global) in their initial approach to learning.

Step 17

When you are satisfied that all the "bugs" have been eliminated, add a front and back cover. Place the title of the program on the front cover which, if possible, should be shaped in the form of the topic and illustrated attractively.

Example
A PLS on *CLOUDS* can be cut and shaped like a large, oblong cumulous cloud and colored accordingly. Another on *VOWELS* could be presented

as A E I O U in raised letters with edges of the cover cut away to emphasize the letter outlines.

Use heavy oaktag or cardboard for the cover and laminate it for durability. Some teachers have used wood or thick plastic for covers. Bind the covers to the index card frames. You may use notebook rings, colored yarn, or any other substance to fasten the frames and their supplementary tactile reinforcements together.

Step 18

Design a record-keeping form so that you know which students are using— and have used—the program and how much of it they have completed successfully (see Figure 8-1).

Reading Programs Completed

Student	Adjectives	Test Score	Adverbs	Test Score	Pronouns	Test Score	Recommended Prescriptions
Adams, William	3/17	87	3/25	88	3/29	90	Continue Programs.
Altman, Susan	3/9	94	3/10	93	3/15	98	Continue Programs; try a Contract.
Baron, Mary	3/15	82	3/21	80	3/10	85	Supplement adverbs Program with games.
Brice, Amy	3/9	89	3/20	81	3/23	86	Supplement adverbs Program with games.
Caldor, John	3/10	76	3/15	75	3/20	75	Try Instructional Packages.
Friedman, Joan	3/10	96	3/12	98	3/17	100	Continue Programs; alternate with small groups; try a Contract or two.

(Dunn and Dunn, 1978, p. 178)

FIGURE 8-1. Record keeping form for programmed learning sequence.

Step 19

Begin the process again and design a new program to teach another topic in this way!

Sample Programmed Learning Sequence

Following is a sample of a reading PLS developed by a teacher and used successfully at different levels with children whose learning styles matched the approach intrinsic to programmed learning.

Intermediate: Idioms*

FRAME 1

If you wish to hear this Programmed Learning Sequence read to you, start the accompanying tape right after this card. Each time a question is read, turn the machine <u>off</u> (STOP BUTTON), write your answer, and then turn it back on to learn whether you were correct.

FRAME 2
Instructions

Each card in this program is called a frame. On one side of each frame, information is presented and a question is asked about it. Mark your answer on the frame itself with the pencil attached to this program.

    Then look at the back of each frame to see if your answer was correct. If it was, move to the next frame. If it was incorrect, study the frame to find out why your answer was wrong. It is important that you understand your error before going ahead.

    Turn to the next frame.

---

*This Programmed Learning Sequence on Idioms was designed by Eileen O'Keefe, teacher, American Martyrs School, Bayside, New York.

FRAME 3

Hello! In this Programmed Learning Sequence, you will be learning about idioms. Idioms are colorful and useful expressions in our language.

By the time you finish this program, you will be able to recognize idioms and match idioms with their real meanings. You also will learn about the origins, or backgrounds, of some common idioms.

Let's get the ball rolling!

FRAME 4

Before you begin working on this program, you need to know what is meant by the word, <u>idiom</u>. An idiom is a group of words which, when used together, has a very different meaning from each individual word in the group.

A group of words which, when used together, has a very different meaning from the individual words in the group is an _____i———m_____.

Fill in the missing letters.

Turn over.

BACK OF FRAME 4

<u>ANSWER:</u>

　　• i <u>d</u> i <u>o</u> m

Idioms do not mean exactly what their words suggest. For example,

————————————————————▶

Turn to Frame 5.

FRAME 5

Sometimes idioms can make a very funny picture in our mind. For instance, the expression "on pins and needles" is an idiom. Can you imagine really being on pins and needles? What does this expression really mean?

The expression "on pins and needles" is an example of an _____.

BACK OF FRAME 5

ANSWER:
- idiom

Are you on pins and needles while using this Program?

FRAME 6

Little Timmy was on pins and needles as he waited to open his birthday presents.

Write the idiom in the sentence above.

_____.

BACK OF FRAME 6

<u>ANSWER:</u>

- on pins and needles

FRAME 7

The expression "on pins and needles" does not mean that someone is actually sitting, standing, or lying on pins and needles. What it really means is that someone is nervous, anxious, or uneasy.

The idiom "on pins and needles" really means that a person is _____.

BACK OF FRAME 7

<u>ANSWERS:</u>

- nervous
  or
- anxious
  or
- uneasy

Any of the above is correct. If you wrote <u>all</u> these words, you are completely correct!

FRAME 8

The sentence:

"Little Timmy was on pins and needles as he waited to open his birthday presents," means Timmy was anxious to begin to open his birthday presents.

The idiom in the sentence above tell us that Timmy was _____ about his presents.

BACK OF FRAME 8

ANSWERS:
- nervous
   or
- anxious
   or
- uneasy

If you ever become nervous about something, you can say, "I am on pins and needles."

FRAME 9

There are thousands of idioms in our language like "pins and needles." You are probably familiar with many of them already.

Can you underline the idiom in the sentence below?

Mom will blow her top if she finds out you've eaten that cake!

BACK OF FRAME 9

ANSWER:
- blow her top

What does this idiom really mean?

FRAME 10
When someone "blows his (or her) top," that person is very, very angry. He or she may yell or scream. It does not mean, however, that the top of the person's head blows off!

A person who "blows his top" is very _____.

BACK OF FRAME 10

ANSWER:
- angry

Now that we have gotten the ball rolling, you should <u>not</u> be on pins and needles!

FRAME 11

Now let's try another sentence. Underline the idiom:

Yesterday it was raining cats and dogs.

BACK OF FRAME 11

<u>ANSWER:</u>

- <u>raining cats and dogs</u>

Can you imagine what would happen if it <u>really</u> rained cats and dogs?

FRAME 12

What does that idiom mean?

We all know that we won't see hundreds of animals pouring down from the sky! If it's "raining cats and dogs," it is raining extremely hard.

Fill in the missing words.

It is raining _____ if it's raining cats and dogs.

BACK OF FRAME 12

ANSWER:
- extremely hard

  or
- very hard

If it <u>really</u> were raining cats and dogs, those animals surely would be on pins and needles!

FRAME 13

Try this idiom!

After losing their third game, the team was ready to throw in the towel.
Underline the idiom in the sentence above.

BACK OF FRAME 13

ANSWER:
- <u>throw in the towel</u>

FRAME 14

In the sentence, "After losing their third game, the team was ready to throw in the towel," the idiom "throw in the towel" does not mean the players were actually going to throw a towel onto the playing field. Rather, it means the team was ready to give up.

The idiom "throw in the towel" means to _____.

BACK OF FRAME 14

<u>ANSWER:</u>
- give up

<u>Another example:</u>

When Liz was in a ten-minute race, she ran as quickly as she could. After nine minutes, she realized that she was far behind everyone else. She had no energy left, so she threw in the towel!

. . . .

Would <u>you</u>?

FRAME 15

Time flies when you're having fun.

Underline the idiom in the sentence above.

BACK OF FRAME 15

ANSWER:

- time flies

ANOTHER EXAMPLE:

It seemed as if Barbara had just arrived, but her watch showed that it was nearly dinner time. "My, how time flies," Barbara groaned.

. . . .

When does time fly for <u>you</u>?

FRAME 16

Of course, clocks do not have wings, and they do not fly. The idiom "time flies" means that time seems to pass very quickly sometimes.

"Time flies" is an _____ which means that

_____.

BACK OF FRAME 16

ANSWERS:

- idiom
- time seems to pass quickly sometimes

FRAME 17

Now that you have become more familiar with idioms and can explain their real meanings, it is time for a mini-quiz.

Below are two columns. The first column lists idioms, and the second lists meanings. Draw lines from the idioms to their correct meanings.

- on pins and needles
- blow your top
- raining cats and dogs
- throw in the towel
- time flies

- give up
- raining very hard
- very angry
- time seems to pass quickly
- nervous, uneasy, or anxious

BACK OF FRAME 17

<u>ANSWERS:</u>

- on pins and needles
- blow your top
- raining cats and dogs
- throw in the towel
- time flies

- give up
- raining very hard
- very angry
- time seems to pass quickly
- nervous, uneasy, or anxious

If you had all of these right, go on to the next frame. If not, review the necessary frame or frames to find the correct answers before continuing.

FRAME 18

Of the many idioms in the English language, some are not much older than you, while the origins of others may go back hundreds of years or more.

Did all the idioms we use today come into being at the same time? _____

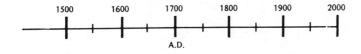

1500   1600   1700   1800   1900   2000

A.D.

BACK OF FRAME 18

ANSWER:

- no

Some idioms are not very old, yet others may be hundreds of years old or more.

FRAME 19

For instance, when you have to take all the blame for something, you are "left holding the bag." This idiom is believed to have started in the United States in the early 1800s.

Can you estimate how long ago the idiom "left holding the bag" began to be used in our country?

_____

BACK OF FRAME 19

ANSWER:

It began in the 1800s, so it is

- Almost 200 years ago
    -or-
- More than 185 years ago
    -or-
- Between 150 and 200 years ago

FRAME 20

One place we might find the idiom "lead by the nose" is in the Bible. It was first used by the prophet Isaiah almost 3,000 years ago. Some sayings last a very long time!

The idiom "lead by the nose" was probably first used almost_____ years ago.

BACK OF FRAME 20

<u>ANSWER:</u>

• 3,000

To lead someone by the nose is to tell them what to do without explaining why. If they do what you say, they may be left holding the bag for whatever happens!

FRAME 21

The idioms "have a bone to pick" and "blow your own horn" started in England in the 1500s. This means they have been around for more than 400 years!

Two idioms which started in England in the 1500s were _____

and _____.

BACK OF FRAME 21

ANSWERS:
- Have a bone to pick
- Blow your own horn

Could someone have a bone to pick with you because you always blow your own horn?

. . . .

What do you think?

FRAME 22

As you may have noticed, some of the idioms we read and use as part of our English language today do not have their origins in our country. In fact, many of them began in countries in Europe.

Many of the idioms we use in America

had their origins in _____ countries.

BACK OF FRAME 22

ANSWERS:
- different
    -or-
- other
    -or-
- European

If an idiom begins in one country, can the people of that country blow their own horn because of it?

. . . .

What do you think?

FRAME 23

The saying "have a bone to pick" with someone comes from England. At one time, people who disagreed thought of dogs fighting over a bone, and began to use the idiom when they had something to argue about.

The expression "have a bone to pick" probably started in

_____ many years ago.

BACK OF FRAME 23

ANSWER:

- England
- If your friend wanted to lead you by the nose, would you have a bone to pick with him?
- If your friend wanted you to do things that you didn't fully understand, would you argue with him?

Do these two sentences mean the same thing?

FRAME 24

When you pay too much money for something, you "pay through the nose." This idiom probably began in Ireland about 1,200 years ago. The Vikings who ruled at that time wanted the Irish people to pay them money and gifts. If an Irishman refused, his nose was slit with a sword. To avoid that unpleasant experience, they paid, but said it was "paying through the nose."

The idiom "paid through the nose" began about

1,200 years ago in _____ .

BACK OF FRAME 24

ANSWER:

- Ireland

To lead by the nose and pay through the nose mean very different things. One is to guide someone without explaining, and the other is to pay more than something is worth.

FRAME 25

Now let's see how well you can remember the origins of some idioms. Match the idiom in the left column with the country it came from in the right column by drawing lines to connect them. (Two of the idioms started in the same country.)

- Left holding the bag
- Have a bone to pick
- Paid through the nose
- Blow your own horn

- Ireland
- England
- The United States

BACK OF FRAME 25

ANSWERS:

- Left holding the bag
- Have a bone to pick
- Paid through the nose
- Blow your own horn

- Ireland
- England
- The United States

If you had all these correct, take the test which follows. If you had one or more incorrect, reread the necessary frames to find out why they were wrong, then take the test.

FRAME 26
TEST YOURSELF

1. A group of words which, when used together, have a very different meaning

   than the meanings of the individual words in the group is an _____.

2. A person who is on pins and needles is really _____,

   or _____.

3. Someone who blows his top is very _____.

4. The idiom which means that it's raining very hard is _____

   _____.

5. An example of an idiom which began in the United States in the 1800s is

   _____.

FRAME 27

6. Isaiah was the first person to use the idiom _____

   _____ almost 3,000 years ago.

7. The idiom which started in England when people saw dogs fighting over a

   bone is _____.

8. The idiom "throw in the towel" means to _____.

9. Besides "have a bone to pick," another idiom which started in England in

   the 1500s was _____ .

10. True or False: All the idioms in our language started in different countries

    at the same time. _____.

BACK OF FRAME 27

<u>ANSWERS:</u>

1. Idiom	6. Lead by the nose
2. Nervous, anxious, or uneasy	7. Have a bone to pick
3. Angry	8. Give up
4. It's raining cats and dogs	9. Blow your own horn
5. Left holding the bag	10. False

If you had all ten (10) correct, you are ready to use the task cards with idioms. If you had one or two incorrect, go back to the program and reread the frames that explain the ones that were wrong. If you can't understand why they were wrong, or if you had three or more incorrect, talk to your teacher about your answers.

FRAME 28

Idioms can be fun to use!

The ones mentioned in this program are just a few of hundreds. You will be more aware of them now and will probably be able to spot some idioms while you are reading or even in everyday conversation.

Be on the lookout for idioms. When you see or hear one, write it and share it with your teacher! In that way, you will get the ball rolling!

FRAME 29

Wipe off all your answers with a damp cloth.

If you were using the tape for this program, please rewind it so it will be ready for the next person.

Then, return the program and special pencil along with the tape and tape recorder to where they were before you took them.

If you know most of the idioms in this program, you may blow your own horn to any grownup you know tonight!

Summary

The Programmed Learning Sequences included in this chapter represent one way in which many youngsters can learn new material without necessarily being excellent readers. The use of a cassette to assist in the reading process eventually makes difficult vocabulary familiar and reduces the tension that many poor readers often feel. Good readers who require structure and sequencing also will appreciate this step-by-step approach to learning.

Why not photocopy the program on idioms for your students to learn? Have the illustrations colored, cut out the frames, and arrange them into proper sequence. Bind them together and make a tape that reads the text and answers in a pleasant, natural, but dramatic manner. You may add comments of your own if you care to do so.

Identify students whose learning styles would be responsive to a PLS and introduce them to this resource by explaining how to use it. Then step back and watch the reactions. When a program has been completed, the concepts or facts taught always should be reinforced through a tactual resource, such as Task Cards, a Pic-A-Hole, a Learning Circle, or a Flip-Chute. Then ask the student to take a posttest. Compare each youngster's score with his or her own baseline data on previous tests. We believe that you will be delighted with the results.

9

Teaching Children to Read through Contract Activity Packages

Contract Activity Packages (CAPs) are one of the three basic methods of personalizing reading instruction through individual learning styles, interests, ability and achievement levels. They are extremely effective for gifted and above-average students and can be modified to stimulate the interests of average youngsters by adding many multisensory resources and a great deal of structure. Hodges (1982) used them with underachievers. CAPs are superior to many typical approaches used in the classroom such as reading groups, teacher–student question and answer sessions, large group instruction, story time, one-to-one direct instruction, and peer tutoring.

Learning Styles Differences

Contract Activity Packages for reading permit learning through individual preferences, provided that the youngsters assigned to them are relatively motivated, persistent and responsible. Ironically, Contract Activity Packages can *increase* motivation, persistence and responsibility through interest, and they permit learning to occur through individual style preferences. They also encourage reading and academic success at the student's appropriate achievement level by permitting self-pacing and self-selected resources. Independent students can work by themselves, and those who prefer to learn with peers or adults (including the teacher) can experience improved self-image through choices, self-assessment of results, and the gratifying realization of self-growth. Indeed, all elements of learning style may be accommodated when students meet assigned objectives through Contract Activity Packages.

Varied Academic Levels and Independent Learning

Contract Activity Packages permit individualization based on varied academic levels in several ways:

- Resource alternatives may be provided at various levels of difficulty.
- Objectives may be assigned in order of difficulty and through selection of different numbers of objectives based on academic ability and achievement.
- Pretest and subsequent self-assessment and posttest questions may be limited to specific achievement levels.
- Circles of Knowledge, Team Learnings, Brainstorming, and other small group techniques may be designed to teach and to reinforce learning at different levels.

Because students may select the resources they use (from a list of approved ones), their motivation is improved and they are able to work in ways with which they feel most comfortable. Self-pacing permits them to learn as quickly as they can, but thoroughly enough to retain what they have studied. As they become accustomed to exercising freedom of choice and assuming responsibility, they become increasingly independent of their teacher and learn to use resources to their advantage.

Basic Principles of the Reading Contract Activity Package

A reading Contract Activity Package (see Figure 9-1) is an individual educational plan that facilitates basic reading skills and comprehension because it includes all of these elements: Objectives; Resource Alternatives; Activity Alternatives; Reporting Alternatives; small group techniques; and a pretest, a self-test and a posttest.

Objectives

Simply and clearly stated objectives that itemize exactly what the student is required to learn are central to the Contract Activity Package.

Resource Alternatives

Multisensory resources are used by the student to learn the information that the objectives indicate must be mastered. Students are given a list of available resources that they may use to learn the information required by their objectives. The resources should be multisensory: visual materials such as books, films, filmstrips, study prints or transparencies; auditory materials such as tapes, records, cassettes or movies; tactual materials such as task cards, learning circles and games; and interesting kinesthetic learning experiences.

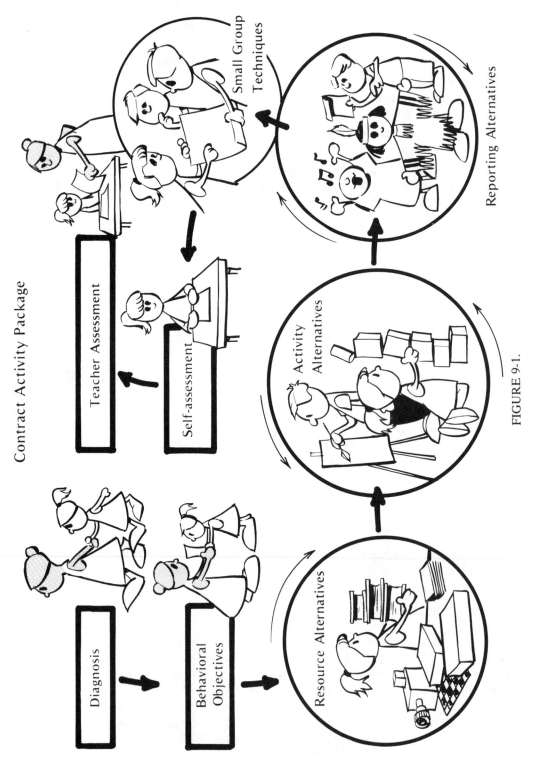

Contract Activity Package

Diagnosis

Behavioral Objectives

Resource Alternatives

Activity Alternatives

Reporting Alternatives

Small Group Techniques

Teacher Assessment

Self-assessment

FIGURE 9-1.

Activity Alternatives

Activity Alternatives are applications of the newly learned knowledge. Students use their new information in a creative way by developing a project, writing a poem, drawing, pantomiming or developing other experiences designed to reinforce what has been learned through the resources.

Each student's strongest modality preference may be utilized when selecting an Activity Alternative to complete for each objective. In fact, each objective should be followed by three to five Activity Alternatives, each of which is designed to appeal to a different perceptual strength, e.g.,

1. Audio—taped responses or presentation: Auditory.
2. Written reports, compositions, or charts: Visual Words.
3. Drawings, diagrams or illustrations: Visual Pictures.
4. Interviews, building, floor games, projects, trips, role-playing: Kinesthetic.
5. Task cards, textured games, electroboards, flip chutes, learning circles: Tactual.

Reporting Alternatives

This is a series of alternative ways in which creative activities developed by one student may be shared with one to five classmates.

Small Group Techniques and Games

Individualization does not imply that children must work or learn in isolation. Rather, it suggests that each student's learning style be identified and that each learner be permitted to learn in ways that complement his or her style. Because many students prefer to work in small groups or in a pair, while others evidence this preference only when their requirements become difficult, at least three small-group techniques (of the teacher's choice) are added to each Contract Activity Package so that difficult sections of the CAP may be attacked (and conquered) by a few students working together. These small-group techniques may include, but are not limited to, Team Learning, Group Analysis, Role-playing, Brainstorming, Simulations, Circle of Knowledge and Case Study. Crossword puzzles, games and other visual–tactual activities aid in reinforcing what has been learned and may be added to a CAP based on the teacher's discretion. These should be included in the Resource Alternative section.

A Pretest, a Self-Test and a Posttest

Each Contract Activity Package has a single test attached to it. This test may be used to assess the student's knowledge of the information required by the

CAP's behavioral objectives before the CAP is assigned, so that students who have already mastered those concepts and skills need not be burdened with the same subject matter again.

The assessment device may also be used by the student to identify how much of the information required by the behavioral objectives he or she has already mastered and how much remains for the student to learn after he or she completes the CAP. Self-assessment builds ownership of the contract and its objectives.

Finally, you may use the same assessment device to test the student after the behavioral objectives have been mastered, the resources have been used, the Activity Alternatives have been completed and shared with selected classmates, the three small-group techniques have been done and the self-test has been taken. This approach establishes a pattern of revealing what is expected, removes the mystery and builds motivation. It is an excellent way to assess knowledge and use of vocabulary, comprehension, specific reading skills, spelling, grammar and syntax and nuances of meaning.

Step-by-Step Guide to Designing a Contract Activity Package for Reading

Step 1

Begin by identifying a topic, concept or skill that you want to teach. There are two kinds of CAPs. The first, a curriculum CAP, covers a topic that you would like to teach all or most of the students in your class. The second, an individual CAP, deals with a topic in which only one (or a few) students might be interested.

Step 2

Write the name of the topic, concept or skill that you have decided to teach as a title at the top of a blank sheet of paper. Examples:

Ready to Read

Learning to Use the Encyclopedia

Alphabetical Order

Step 3

List the things about this topic that you believe are so important that every student in your class should learn them. Many of the secondary list of important items will be required of some, and some of the more difficult items will be required of a few advanced students. The way in which you assign the number of required objectives will help you to individualize the Contract Activity Package.

Step 4

Translate the important items into behavioral objectives. When students are given a list of items that should be learned, these items are called objectives, and they become the students' short-term instructional goals. Since acquired information can be demonstrated in many ways, it is important that youngsters be given an idea of how they will be expected to demonstrate what they have learned. Recognizing individual differences, we acknowledge that people are capable of evidencing knowledge through different skills and talents. We therefore give students: (1) a general indication of how they can verify mastery of their instructional objectives, and (2) specific alternatives to (a) increase their motivation and (b) capitalize on their strengths.

Step 5

Design at least three or four Activity Alternatives for each behavioral objective (or for a group of related objectives) so that students may choose how they will demonstrate that they learned what their objectives require of them.

In effect, the Activity Alternatives permit students to select the conditions under which they will perform or demonstrate their mastery. Each Activity Alternative should appeal to different perceptual strengths, and some should be global while others are analytic.

Step 6

Create a Reporting Alternative for each of the Activity Alternatives you have designed. The Activity Alternative gives students a choice of how they will use the information they have learned so that it is reinforced. Once an activity has been completed, most students enjoy sharing their product with others. In addition, sharing provides additional reinforcement.

Step 7

List all the resources you can locate that students may use to gain the information required by their behavioral objectives.

Try to find multisensory resources. Categorize the materials under separate lists, for example, books, transparencies, tapes, records, magazines, games, and—if you have them—programs, instructional packages, task cards or learning circles. Use these broad divisions as titles; underline the title and below it list the names of the available resources. Students may use additional materials if they wish, but they should either show them to you or refer to them in their work. Because students may select which resources they will use, these materials are called Resource Alternatives.

Step 8

Add at least three small-group techniques to the developing Contract Activity Package.

Identify the most difficult objectives in your CAP. Develop a Team Learning experience to introduce those objectives that require in-depth knowledge, insight or extensive explanation. Design a Circle of Knowledge to reinforce what you taught through Team Learning. Use any of the remaining strategies—such as Brainstorming, Group Analysis or Case Study—to help peer-oriented youngsters gain information. Circles of Knowledge are simple to create; try a few. Team Learnings require more time, but they are well worth the effort for they will enhance learning for many of your students and simultaneously free you to work directly with the ones who are authority-oriented and need your supervision and guidance.

Step 9

Develop a test that is directly related to each of the behavioral objectives in your CAP. An assessment instrument or exam that is directly related to stated objectives is called a *criterion-referenced test.* Questions for such tests are formed by either restating the objective or by phrasing it in a different way.

For example, if the behavioral objective was "List at least three (3) reasons why the Pilgrims left England," then the question on the examination should be "List at least three (3) reasons why the Pilgrims left England."

Step 10

Design an illustrated cover for the Contract Activity Package. It should be colorful and attractive (see Figure 9-2) and include the CAP title in nicely printed or typed letters.

Step 11

Develop an information top sheet. On the page following the illustrated cover, provide information that you believe is important. Some items that may be included are:

● The name of the Contract Activity Package
● The student's name

Name: _____

Objectives completed: _____

Date received: _____

Date completed: _____

By the time you have finished this Contract Activity Package, you will become an expert on alphabetical order through the completion of each objective listed on the following pages.

This Contract Activity Package on The Alphabet Circus was designed by Maureen Carnonas, Graduate Student, St. John's University, New York.

FIGURE 9-2.

- The student's class
- The objectives that have been assigned to or selected by that student
- The date the CAP should be completed
- The dates selected parts of the CAP should be completed (for students in need of structure)
- Space for a pretest grade ⎫
- Space for a self-test grade ⎬ All three may be the same.
- Space for a final test grade ⎭
- The names of the classmates who may have worked on this CAP as a team
- Directions to the students for working on or completing the CAP:

    1. Take the pretest. If you did not get ___%, note what you did not know.

    2. Look at the CAP objectives. Check the ones you knew for the pretest. Put a star next to the ones you still have to master.

    3. Find the Resource Alternatives that can teach the information you do not know.

    4. Use the Team Learnings to learn the information. Reinforce it, so that you remember it, with the Circle of Knowledge.

    5. Write the answers to the information you did not know on the pretest.

    6. When you think you know all the information cited in the CAP objectives, complete one Activity Alternative for each objective you had to master.

    7. Then share your completed Activities with a classmate or two, as directed by the Reporting Alternative paired with the Activity you chose.

    8. Take the self-test. If you score ___% or better, take the posttest. If your mark is lower than ___%, study more.

Step 12

Reread each of the parts of the Contract Activity Package to be certain that they are clearly stated, well-organized, in correct order and grammatically written. Check spelling and punctuation.

Step 13

Add illustrations to the pages so that the CAP is attractive and motivating.

Step 14

Duplicate the number of copies that you will need.

Step 15

Design a record-keeping form so that you know which students are using and have used the Contract Activity Package and how much of it they have completed successfully.

Step 16

Try a CAP with students who can work well with any three small-group techniques. Be prepared to guide and assist the students through their first experience with a CAP. Establish a system whereby they can obtain assistance if needed. Placing an "I Need You" column on the chalkboard or on a chart and having youngsters sign up for help when they are stymied is usually effective.

Primary Level

When Contract Activity Packages are used with young children who are not yet reading well, each section should be (a) typed on a primary (large print) typewriter, (b) printed on large oaktag or poster board, (c) displayed prominently in a section of the room or in an instructional area such as a learning station and (d) read onto a cassette so that the youngsters can hear the CAP sections while they read the words (follow the tape and the text simultaneously).

For primary pupils it is important to add tactual games, such as an electroboard, a learning circle or task cards to the resource alternative list (see Chapter 7).

If this is your pupils' first experience with CAPs, assign only one or two objectives to slower youngsters. Give them a few opportunities to begin to feel secure with this method before deciding whether it is effective for each individual. If it stimulates certain children and provokes their thinking and knowledge skills, continue its use. If you find that some students do not respond well to it (even if they are permitted to work with one or two classmates), set aside the CAP system *for those youngsters* and introduce instructional packages to them.

The Contract Activity Package is most effective with gifted and above-average youngsters who are creative, peer-oriented, in need of mobility and interaction and not in need of much structure. You will note that it is an especially well-organized system, although it does permit flexible learning arrangements and provides options for students.

THE ALPHABET CIRCUS

The Alphabet Circus is a primary level Contract Activity Package designed to teach the letters of the alphabet and their correct sequence. Many youngsters will be able to learn how to locate words in a children's dictionary.

We suggest that you print each page, or each objective and its accompanying Activity and Reporting Alternatives, on large oaktag or construction board. Then record the material onto a cassette in a clear but interesting voice. Secure each tape to its matching oaktag section by placing it in a manila envelope and gluing the envelope to the bottom of the section. The envelope surface should clearly depict the CAP and the section to which it belongs, both in printed letters and in a colored illustration. In that way, children who wish to use the CAP—which should be mounted in sequential steps across a complete wall of the classroom— need only take the cassette from the envelope, insert it into a tape recorder that can be carried to the area in which the oaktag is mounted, insert the tape into the recorder and hear what must be done. Youngsters who are able to read the material on the oaktag need not use the recorder and cassette, except for passages that may be difficult for them. To facilitate independent usage among students whenever possible, write the CAP in the simplest words.

For children who do use a recorder, a listening set is helpful so that no one other than the user will hear the recording. For children who can read the CAP independently, it is wise to provide individual copies that may be used at their seats or at an instructional area in the room. Laminate the CAP so that it can be returned and used by another child when it has been completed by a previous user.

Youngsters who like to work either by themselves or with a friend or two will learn to read the words in a CAP gradually, without the tension that often accompanies group recitals, reading or being called on. CAPs are suggested for motivated students who prefer individual or small-group studies and who have either three perceptual strengths or two accompanied by strong motivation.

Objective 1

Name each letter of the alphabet in its correct order.
Do at least one (1) of the following:

	Activity Alternatives	Reporting Alternatives	
V/T/K*	1. Make an alphabet scrapbook in which each letter has at least three (3) pictures of objects that begin with the sound it makes.	1. Show and discuss your book with at least four (4) children. Have them check to see that the letters are in the correct order.	V/A
V/T/K	2. On a large sheet of paper, design the background of your own circus. Draw or look for pictures of animals that would be in your circus whose names begin with a letter of the alphabet. Paste the animals on your circus picture in ABC order.	2. Mount and display your circus picture on the bulletin board.	V/T
V/K	3. Use your body to form the letters of the alphabet.	3. Let two (2) friends try to guess the letter you form and tell what letter comes before and after that letter. Have a friend take photographs of you forming the alphabet.	V/K
A/K	4. Make believe you are making a record about the alphabet. Record your song on the tape recorder.	4. Sing and teach the song to four (4) classmates. Use the tape you have made to help you.	A/K

(A = Auditory; K = Kinesthetic; T = Tactual; V = Visual)

Objective 2

List words in ABC order according to the first letter.
Do at least two (2) of the following:

	Activity Alternatives	Reporting Alternatives	
V/T	1. Design a circus animal chart. Write the names of all the animals in the circus that begin with different letters. Arrange these names in ABC order.	1. Display the chart and explain what you have done to four (4) children.	A/V
V/T/K	2. Build a diorama of a circus parade. Label each object you make and arrange the objects in ABC order.	2. Display the diorama and then answer any questions that might arise.	A/V
A/T/K	3. Pretend you are the circus ringmaster. Design a puppet show for the circus. As the ringmaster, introduce each act in ABC order.	3. Present the puppet show to a small group of children (5 to 8).	A/K
V/T/K	4. Design a game in which you must choose at least six (6) words that begin with different letters and arrange them in ABC order.	4. Let a group of children play your game.	V/K

Objective 3

Arrange words in ABC order according to the second letter.
Do at least two (2) of the following:

	Activity Alternatives	Reporting Alternatives	
V/T	1. Find six (6) words in a magazine or newspaper that begin with the same first letter but have a different second letter. Arrange these words in ABC order on a piece of paper.	1. Show your work to two (2) friends and talk about what you did. Have them choose another six (6) words and arrange them in ABC order by the second (2nd) letter.	A/V/T
A/V/T/K	2. Construct five (5) clown puppets and give each a name that begins with the same first letter but a different second letter. Tape a story that will introduce them in correct ABC order and tell about their jobs at the circus.	2. Have a small group of children listen to your story and then help you dramatize it in the little theater area.	A/K

	Activity Alternatives	Reporting Alternatives	
V/T	3. Prepare a list on an overhead transparency of all the goodies you can eat at the circus. Arrange these words in ABC order. Be sure to look at the second letter if two words begin with the same letter.	3. Show your transparency to a group of children and explain what you have done. If they can think of any other circus goodies, add them to your list in correct ABC order.	V
V/T	4. With your eyes closed, select a letter from the box of sandpaper alphabet letters. Write a sentence of three or more words that begin with this letter but have a different second letter. Arrange the words in your sentence in ABC order.	4. Explain what you have done to two (2) children. Have them choose their own sandpaper letter, write their sentence, and then arrange the words in ABC order.	A/V/T

Objective 4

Locate words in a children's dictionary.
Do at least one (1) of the following:

	Activity Alternatives	Reporting Alternatives	
V/T/K	1. List six (6) words that are associated with the circus. Use the children's dictionary to locate the definitions of these words. Make a mobile to illustrate the words and definitions.	1. Show your mobile to several of your classmates and then mount it in your classroom.	V
V/T	2. Design a card game for students to match words and their definitions.	2. Have four (4) children play your game with you.	V/K
V/T	3. Choose five (5) words from the Vocabulary Word Box and arrange them in ABC order. Find the definitions of each of these words in the dictionary.	3. Present the definitions to a small group of children through pantomime. Have the children in the group try to guess what word you are acting out.	V/K
V/T	4. Make a list of some of the objects found at the circus. Use this list of words to help you design a crossword puzzle. Use the words and their definitions.	4. Make copies of the crossword puzzle and let at least five (5) other students try to complete it. Check and return their answers to them.	T/V

Resource Alternatives

BOOKS

Brown, Marcia. *Peter Piper's Alphabet*. Chicago: Scribner, 1959.

Crews, Donald. *We Read: A to Z*. New York: Harper and Row, 1967.

Duvoisin, Roger. *A for the Ark*. New York: Shepard, 1960.

Gag, Wanda. *ABC Bunny*. New York: Coward-McCann, 1964.

Garten, Jan. *The Alphabet Tale*. New York: Random House, 1964.

Greenaway, Kate. *A Apple Pie*. New York: Primary Press, 1965.

Hefter, Richard and Moskof, Martin. *The Great Big Alphabet Picture Book with Lots of Words*. New York: Grosset and Dunlap, 1972.

Sendak, Maurice. *Alligators All Around*. New York: Harper and Row, 1962.

Seuss, Dr. *Dr. Seuss's ABC*. New York: Random House, 1963.

Tudor, Tasha. *A is for Annabelle*. New York: Harper and Row, 1960.

Zacks, Irene. *Space Alphabet*. New York: Primary Press, 1973.

RECORDS

The Muppet Alphabet Album (Sesame Street)

Learning Basic Skills Through Music, Volume 1—Marching Around the Alphabet (Song #5)

The Simon Says Alphabet Album

Acting Out the ABCs (Walt Disney Records)

CASSETTES AND READ-ALONG BOOKLETS

The Troll Talking Dictionary

Miliken's Dictionary Skills Package

FILMSTRIPS

Curious George Learns About the Alphabet (Singer Films)

Putting the Alphabet in Order (Eyegate Films)

What Comes after A? (Coronet Films)

Alphabet Recognition (Eyegate Films)

TEACHER-MADE RESOURCES

Alphabet Learning Circle

ABC Order Task Cards

Juggler Jan's Word Toss Game

Tapes: A recording of the poem "The Circus Parade" to be used as part of the Team Learning Assignment

Worksheets

Vocabulary Word Box

GAMES

Keys to ABC Order (Trend and Co., St. Paul, MN)

Alphabet Sequence Cards (Trend and Co., St. Paul, MN)

Who Comes First? (Rhythms Productions, Los Angeles, CA)

MISCELLANEOUS

Tactile Letters—Manuscript Capitals and Lower Case

Magnetic Alphabet Board and Letters

Class Flannelboard and Letters

Sesame Street Poster on Forming the Alphabet with Your Body

WORKSHEETS

If you wish you may add a series of appropriate worksheets that reinforce knowledge obtained from each objective, e.g., "Correct Order By Lisa the Lioness," "The Clown's Riddle," "Circus Telegram," "Children at the Circus," "Dot to Dot Puzzle," "Clown's Clothes," "Three-Ring Words," "Juggler Jan," "Circus Dictionary."

Primary Level Independent Reading Contract

The Learning Person or *Contract Clown* is another type of reading contract suggested for primary students by faculty members of the Westorchard School in Chappaqua, New York (see Figure 9-3). Youngsters call this reading contract by either name—the Learning Person or the Contract Clown—because of its shape when completed, colored and stapled or pasted together on a bulletin board; it also may be suspended from overhead by thin wire or yarn. The finished product relates to all sections of a regular Contract Activity Package, but the headings are worded simply for younger children. When finished, a student signs his or her name and enjoys seeing the work displayed.

Each section—*What I Want to Learn, What I Can Use to Learn, What I Learned, How I Feel About What I Made,* (poem, drawing, music, game) and *How I Shared What I Learned*—is enlarged to fill an 8½ × 11 inch sheet, then put together when completed. These CAPs make excellent murals and corridor displays—a testimonial to total interest in reading contracts.

An easy way to begin involves discussing each section (What I Want to Learn [A], What I Can Use to Learn [B], etc.) with individuals, pairs and small groups of four or five students, depending upon their sociological learning preferences.

The children should hear and see you write alternative suggestions onto a sample Learning Person or Contract Clown. Gradually increasing degrees of independence should be permitted as students' reading achievement, interest and performance improves.

Descriptions and Samples of Small-Group Techniques

Circle of Knowledge

The Circle of Knowledge technique is highly motivating and is an ideal technique for reinforcing skills in any subject area. It provides a framework for review in which everyone learns more or solidifies what he or she has already mastered.

This instructional approach permits students to:

- Review previously learned information in an interesting way
- Focus thinking on one major concept at a time
- Contribute to a group effort as part of a team
- Serve as catalysts for additional responses

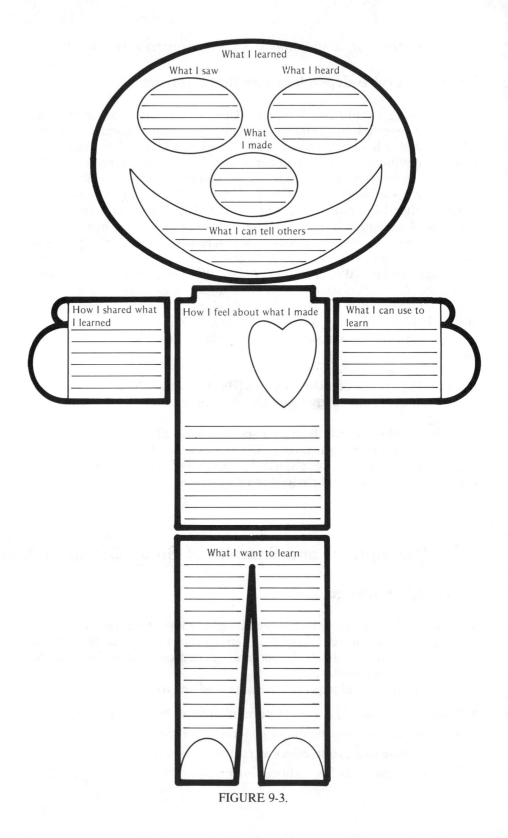

FIGURE 9-3.

- Develop ingenuity in helping team members to contribute
- Be exposed to and learn information without becoming bored

PROCEDURES

Several small circles of four to six chairs (no desks) are positioned evenly about the room. One student in each group volunteers or is drafted, appointed, or elected as the recorder; members also may take turns. Only the recorder writes, although everyone participates and concentrates on thinking of many possible answers.

A single question or problem is posed, and whether written and reproduced or printed on a chalkboard, it must have many possible answers. Examples include naming all fifty states, identifying the possible causes of war, citing the products of a country, or listing synonyms for the word "leader."

Each Circle of Knowledge responds to the same question simultaneously (but quietly). A member in each group is designated as the first to begin, and the answers are then provided by one member at a time, clockwise or counterclockwise. No member may skip his turn, and no one may provide an answer until the person directly before him has delivered his; therefore, the answers stop while a member is thinking or groping for a possible response. No teammate may give an answer to another, but anyone in the group may act out or pantomime hints to help the person remember an item, an answer, or a possible response. Only the recorder may write, and he jots down (in a phrase or two only) the suggestions (answers, responses, thoughts) of each participant as the circle of knowledge continues.

At the end of a predetermined period of time, the teacher calls a halt to the knowledge-sharing, and all recorders must stop writing the groups' answers. The number of responses produced by each group is noted, but credit is not given for quantity.

The teacher divides the chalkboard or overhead transparency into columns and numbers them so that each represents one of the groups. In turn, a representative from each circle offers one of the answers suggested by that group. When an answer is provided, the teacher writes it in that group's column, and all the recorders in the room look at the list of answers developed by their group. If that answer is on the Circle's list, the recorder crosses it off, thus gradually decreasing the length of the list until only the answers that have not yet been reported to the entire group and written on the board remain. This procedure continues until no circle has any remaining answers on its list.

The answers given by each Circle of Knowledge can be awarded points that then are recorded on the board to produce competition among the teams. The teacher might decide that each correct response will earn one point (or five or ten points), and that the Circle achieving the most points will be the winner. Any time an answer is challenged by a rival circle, the teacher must decide whether it is right or wrong. If the answer is right and the challenger incorrect, the challenger's Circle loses one point. If the answer is incorrect and the challenger was right, the Circle that sponsored the answer loses that potential point, and the challenger's Circle gains it. Answers are given from Team 1 through Team 6 and then reversed, pendulum style, with Team 6 supplying two answers each time and Team 1 offering two answers from the second round on.

The important thing to remember about Circles of Knowledge is that they may be used only to review something that already has been introduced and taught. Because the information required has been made available to the students previously, the time span permitted is usually short (2 to 5 minutes). Discipline improves if teams are told they may use answers they overhear from other teams.

Examples of Circle of Knowledge Problems

Primary   (Use a tape recorder to record each child's thoughts.)

- List all the words you can that begin with "b."
- Name as many words containing a short "a" sound as you can in three minutes.
- List all the boys' names that you can think of that begin with the letter "R."
- List all the foods you can think of that make up a good breakfast.
- Name as many compound words as you can in two minutes.

Intermediate

- List as many adverbs as you can.
- Write as many interogative sentences as you can in three minutes.
- Give as many synonyms as you can for the adjective "small."
- Cite all the spelling words you learned this year that have ten (10) or more letters in them.
- List as many rules as you can for writing a correct business letter.

Team Learning

Team Learning is an excellent technique for introducing new material. All the advantages of peer interaction and support described earlier are apparent in this approach. Enthusiasm, motivation, good spirits, positive results, division of labor, responsibility, persistence, self-image, and group recognition of individual efforts usually result. It also may be used to reinforce previously learned, difficult objectives.

PROCEDURES

Begin by writing original material or by copying sections of commercial publications to form short paragraphs containing new information to be learned. Young students who are beginning readers may be able to absorb three to six sentences collectively; older students should be able to read short poems, diagrams, and articles. By developing Team-Learning exercises of varied difficulty, you will not only be able to respond to different learning styles, but you will also be able to establish groups to work on new reading materials according to the ability level and rate of learning in each small team.

At the end of the printed reading (or diagrammatic) material, list a series of questions that should be answered by the group. Some of the questions should be related directly to the printed reading passages; others should be answered through inference and analysis by the group. A third type of question requires that students use the new information creatively. By finding answers in the assigned material through rereading, underlining, or discussion, the individuals in the group will learn how to seek and to obtain specific information. The more difficult inference questions will promote reasoning and group decision-making. The creative application will help students retain what is being learned.

When the printed materials are ready, assign students into groups of four to six (six should be the maximum for most small-group techniques). As students demonstrate responsibility, you might permit some degree of self-selection of teams. Groups should be allowed to sit on the floor or at clustered tables according to their preferences. Other variations include a round circle of chairs, hassocks, or a couch and chairs in a conversational grouping. The learning style elements of design, mobility, time, intake, temperature, and light should be considered as part of the team-learning assignment.

When comfortable, the group should elect, assign, or accept a volunteer to serve as Recorder. It is the Recorder (and only the Recorder) who writes the group's responses to the questions. Short, succinct answers are important to keep the discussion and learning process moving. Some of the other students may elect to write the answers, too, but only because they believe they'll remember the material through note-taking. Very young children or those not able to read or write well should use tape recorders until those skills are developed.

Any member may help other participants on the same team, but all effort must be concentrated within the group. One way to promote quiet and order if teams are in competition on a specific Team-Learning exercise is to tell the class that other teams are free to use answers that are overheard from adjacent groups working on the same exercise.

After one or two Team-Learning experiences, groups of students will develop team relationships and begin to question and analyze the material

(Recorded on a tape.)

Team Members:

1. _____   4. _____

2. _____   5. _____

3. _____   6. _____

Recorder: _____

(You may use the tape recorder to record your names and answers.)

Use the yellow-boxed, cassette tape, "Mr. Ss, The Snake," to help you read the following story.

Mr. Ss, The Snake

Hi, I am Mr. Ss. See how curvy I am. I have a body like a snake. I am easy to make; just follow my arrows 1, 2, 3.   My brother, lower case s, looks just like me, only smaller. Try to make us with your finger—1, 2, 3.

1. Which animal does Mr. S look like?

_____

2. Can you make Mr. S? Draw Mr. S in between the two lines below.

_____

_____

3. What is different about lower case s?

_____

4. Why is Mr. S fun to write or draw?

_____

_____

5. Make two (2) snake puppets to look like capital S and lower case s. You may use clay, or cloth, or wet spaghetti, or anything else you like!

FIGURE 9-4. Sample Format for Team Learning.

with enthusiasm and animated, but productive, conversation. You will need to walk around and assist with the process the first time or two, but you will discover newfound freedom to work with individuals or other groups very soon after the students gain initial experience with this teaching strategy.

Time limits may be imposed or left open, depending on the learning style and need for structure of the members of each group. An alternative to strict time limits is to assign some team-learning prescriptions to a group as homework or as a free-time activity.

For the purposes of comparison, participation, and reinforcement, the Recorders of teams working on the same assignment should be asked to share with the entire group the responses that were developed and approved by their membership. This is done by numbering each group and then asking team 1 for a response to a question, asking team 2 for a second answer, and so on, in rotation.

Write each Recorder's responses on the chalkboard or overhead projector and instruct students to cross an answer off their lists if it duplicates theirs; they thus will be left with only answers that have not yet been called out. Other team members should respond on the second or third round. The Recorders should pass their lists to the students who will be answering next. Eventually you and the class will proceed through all the questions, permitting most of the team members to participate. In this way, errors and misinformation are not likely to be retained. Moreover, all questions will be answered, and everyone will have had a chance to participate actively.

As with the Circles of Knowledge, you and your class may elect to use a team competition approach with points based on the correct number of answers given by each team. Competition among teams is usually friendly and stimulating; often different teams win. Furthermore, the competition does not pit one individual against another where loss of self-image is a serious risk.

Team Learning presents new material in a fashion that responds to such important learning style elements as structure, design, time, mobility, intake, learning with peers, motivation, persistence, responsibility, and visual and auditory perceptual strengths. (Kinesthetic and tactual resources could be added to team learning exercises for those who require them.) A sample team learning is shown in Figure 9-4.

Brainstorming

Brainstorming is an exciting group participation technique designed to develop multiple answers to a single question, alternate solutions to problems, and creative responses. It is an associative process that encourages students to call out—one of the few times this is permitted in our schools. Thus, it responds to personal motivation and does not suppress natural spontaneity.

In addition to increasing motivation, the technique of brainstorming offers many practical advantages. Brainstorming is:

- *Stimulating.* It offers a unique, freewheeling, exciting, and rapid-fire method that builds enthusiasm in nearly all participants.
- *Positive.* Quiet and shy students usually become active participants because they are not put down; their contributions are masked by the group process. Conversely, those who usually dominate endless discussions are structured into offering succinct suggestions.
- *Focused.* Diversions and distractions are eliminated. Stories and speeches irrelevant to the questions or otherwise not pertinent are eliminated.
- *Spontaneous and creative.* Students serve as a sounding board that generates new ideas. Creativity is released during the momentum of the process.
- *Efficient and productive.* Dozens of suggestions, facts, ideas, or creative solutions are generated in a matter of minutes. Additional steps or plans of an activity can be brainstormed, as well as more specific answers for general responses (subset brainstorming).
- *Involving and image-building.* Self-image is enhanced for students who see their ideas listed. Group pride and cohesiveness increase, too, as the members begin to feel a part of the unit that created the lists.
- *Ongoing and problem-solving.* The results are recorded and may be modified and used in new situations.

PROCEDURES

The Brainstorming leader also acts as Recorder. His or her functions include writing all responses, asking for clarification or repetition, synthesizing large phrases into short key ideas, and keeping the group focused on each single topic. The leader should not comment, editorialize, or contribute; his or her effort should be concentrated on producing an effective and productive session.

SETTING

Five to ten students should form a fairly tight semi-circle of chairs facing the leader. (Larger groups can be effective at times.) Behind the leader is a wall containing three to five large sheets of lecture pad paper or newsprint double-folded to prevent strike-through marks on the wall (see Figure 9-5). These sheets, approximately twenty to twenty-four inches wide and thirty to thirty-six inches high, should be attached to the wall with masking tape and placed a few inches apart at a comfortable height for recording. The leader should use a broad-tipped felt marker for instant visibility by the entire group. A timekeeper should be appointed for the two- or three-minute Brainstorming segments, but he or she may participate. It is useful to have additional sheets available and an overhead projector to permit groups to analyze, plan, or participate in subset brainstorming for specific aspects of general answers.

RULES FOR PARTICIPANTS

1. Concentrate on the topic—storm your brain.
2. Fill the silence—call out what pops into your head.
3. Wait for an opening—don't step on someone's lines.
4. Record the thoughts in short form.
5. Record *everything*, no matter how tangential.
6. Repeat your contribution until it is recorded.
7. Be positive: no put downs, negative body language, or editorial comments.
8. Stay in focus—no digressions.
9. Use short time spans—one to three minutes.
10. Analyze later—add, subtract, plan, implement.
11. Brainstorm from general to specific subsets.

Primary: List all the new words you learned to read this year.

Intermediate: Call out all the synonyms you can think of for "leader."

Intermediate: Instead of using a cliché such as "Quiet as a _____" (mouse is usually given), let's brainstorm: "As quiet as a _____ _____ing."
    You will soon have delighted groups calling out as quiet as a "snowflake falling," an "eyelid closing," a "mosquito landing," or a "mother worrying." You might do this for all the usual clichés found in compositions, and praise those who use creative substitutions.
—or—
Provide synonyms for an entire sentence, one word at a time:

	(adjective)	(noun)	(verb)			(noun)
The	large	boy	ran	to	the	hill.

    Take one minute (60 seconds) for each word. Then consider the limitless number of combinations to find the funniest sentence, most precise description, most creative arrangement, and so forth.

FIGURE 9-5. Sample format for Brainstorming

FIGURE 9-6. For optimum results, a Brainstorming session consists of a tight semi-circle of five to ten participants. This illustration was designed by Dr. Edward J. Manetta, Chairman, Department of Fine Arts, St. John's University, New York.

A Final Word on Small-Group Techniques

These three small-group techniques and others you use or devise are essential for building independence and for responding to those youngsters whose learning style clearly indicates a need to work with peers.

- *Circle of Knowledge* reviews and reinforces previously learned material.
- *Team Learning* introduces new material and uses factual and inference questions and creative assignments.
- *Brainstorming* releases creative energy and aids in planning and solving problems.

There are variations and other small-group techniques such as case studies, simulations, role-playing, group analysis, task forces, and research committees. Select or develop those that will respond to varied learning styles, and your instructional role will take less effort and eventually will be far more rewarding for you and for your individual students as they learn to read more and more difficult material.

When used in a CAP, small group techniques are included in the Resource Alternative section. They teach and reinforce what has to be learned and help to develop higher level thinking skills.

Summary

We encourage you to experiment with having motivated, high and gifted achievers learn through CAPs. Be certain that you explain how the CAP system works, and that students:

a. Examine the objectives carefully so they know exactly what must be learned.

b. Locate the resources listed on the Resource Alternatives page and use those that are preferred. However, if any are marked "required," be certain those are used too.

c. After they know all the answers to the first objective, choose one Activity Alternative to do. That will help them reinforce the information; they then will remember it better and longer.

d. Share their completed activity with a friend or two, or the teacher, as indicated in the Reporting Alternative that matches the activity selected.

e. Use the Team Learning to teach themselves something that either is difficult or unclear. They may work alone or with a friend or two, as preferred. They need to remember to work very quietly so that no one else hears what they are doing.

f. Use the Circles of Knowledge to reinforce what they have learned. You will be surprised at how much they remember after trying that small group technique. If they prefer, they may do the Circle of Knowledge alone with a timer and see how many answers they can create in the few minutes allotted for each task.

g. Try all the small group techniques in each CAP. In that way they will remember almost everything important. They also will be *very* proud of themselves!

Be honest with yourself and the students. This is your opportunity to see how much can be learned by individuals. When they are finished, they will need to take a test—so encourage them *to do their best!*

10

Teaching Children to Read through Multisensory Instructional Packages (MIPs)

Poor readers, students who lag behind others in developing visual and auditory acuity, and youngsters who cannot learn through the traditional methods of reading instruction, can benefit most from Multisensory Instructional Packages. Indeed, these resources, when constructed properly, utilize a student's perceptual strengths, promote the success-motivation-success cycle, and lead ultimately to reading achievement and enjoyment with conventional books.

The Multisensory Instructional Package (MIP) is an important teaching approach because it responds to the entire set of learning style characteristics that typify the student who is having problems learning to read, or learning anything for that matter.

In our view, there are very few *learning disabled* children. Aside from actual physical or genetic damage, the LD term as generally used in this nation, is a misnomer. Children learn if taught through their perceptual strengths and under conditions which respond to their learning styles. We believe, therefore, that *Learning Different* should be substituted for the LD label. We all have learning differences—not learning disabilities. It is the rare adult who has not struggled with a specific subject, a particular teacher, or an application of some knowledge during the learning process. All humans have learning strengths and weaknesses—which comprise their *Learning Differences*.

Therefore, if students do not learn in the way that we teach them, we must teach them in the way that they learn. The Multisensory Instructional Package is an approach that appeals to many youngsters with varied learning differences. It is a strategy that helps teachers remove the negative LD label—meaning Learning Disabled, and demonstrates how responding to learning differences promotes reading success.

Learning Style Characteristics Responsive to Multisensory Instructional Packages

The typical profile of students who experience difficulty when learning to read often includes low or negative scores on motivation, persistence, responsibility, self-structure, and auditory and visual perceptual abilities; occasionally they also lack tactual or kinesthetic strengths. Multisensory Instructional Packages are designed to respond directly to such negative characteristics and to help children achieve in spite of them.

Motivation, Persistence and Responsibility

Motivation springs from success and accomplishment, improved self-image, high self-esteem, external or internal recognition, interest, immediate feedback, non-existent or limited failure, higher order tasks, and personal growth. Persistence and responsibility are enhanced for the same reasons.

Multisensory Instructional Packages for reading are especially motivating to students who are slow starters when learning to read.

Success and Accomplishment

Youngsters who cannot decode or read fluently often require repetition and varied approaches through many senses—particularly through *tactual and kinesthetic materials and games*. This type of youngster usually can begin to learn *only* through his or her sense of touching, manipulating and doing. Moreover, the package, which contains taped and written scripts, permits multiple-repetition at any point within the sequence or for the entire set of materials until its objectives are mastered. The student for whom the package is appropriate grows through his strengths, often only tactual and/or kinesthetic, toward utilization of visual and auditory skills. Youngsters receive immediate feedback on their work, and by repeating activities that guarantee eventual success, their self-image is enhanced, and self-esteem is raised. Indeed, we've watched previously failing students return to these packages again and again until objectives were mastered completely. This elimination, or at least limitation, of failure also increases motivation.

As students complete a package, they receive approval and recognition from the teacher, internalize their own success, and develop new insights into their personal growth and potential. This type of motivation and sense of self-worth is not limited to elementary school youngsters. After successfully using an MIP, one eleventh grade student in an advanced humanities class reported, "I bet I can learn Chaucer and Shakespeare this way! I'm not afraid to go to class any more." His classmates, all of whom elected that course with a teacher who believed in this approach, agreed with his observation.

Students can be given higher-order tasks and responsibilities in conjunction with their newly found success and growth. They are asked to repair, restore, return, catalog, and show others how to use the packages. They can design and author new materials or even entire packages.

With respect to the interests of students, packages can be designed around themes or current heroes to their age groups, e.g., E.T., Rocky, Star Trek, Snoopy, Superman, a favorite video game, sports team, television series, movie, etc. The objectives are learned using one of these unifying themes of interest to the student.

Persistence increases through the successful completion of short-term, specific objectives provided in the Multisensory Instructional Package. Directions written and taped by the teacher guide this type of slowly achieving student through each task. *Structure* is provided through the sequencing of tactual and/or kinesthetic activities and learning experiences designed for the package. Success, increased motivation, persistence, and teacher-provided structure promote *responsibility* and improvement in all aspects of reading.

Accommodating Other Elements of Learning Style

The Multisensory Instructional Package can accommodate a variety of other learning style characteristics.

Time of Day. Obviously, packages can be utilized during the student's best time zone for learning by assigning objectives during the individual's peak productivity period. Most slowly achieving students learn best in the afternoon, evening or late morning. Packages can be used at any time and even may be taken home for night studies.

Light. The amount of light in the instructional environment can be matched to the student's needs through the use of darker areas, windows, lamps and/or shades. The proper use of reading light at home should be suggested, based on each student's strong preference.

Temperature. Extra or lesser clothing and varied placement, both in a classroom and at home, can be adapted to the degree of temperature present when the student uses a package at the correctly matched time of day or evening.

Intake. Nutritious food can be eaten while working on a Multisensory Instructional Package if indicated. Usually, however, the activities in a package occupy student attention and require tactual and kinesthetic involvement that precludes eating or drinking, except only while listening to the tapes.

Sound. When youngsters who need quiet use packages, they can work in a corner of the room away from major activities, wear earmuffs, earplugs or a head set, and/or turn their backs to the classroom interaction to decrease the amount of distraction to which they are subjected. For the few who *prefer* sound, headphones or a listening set permit music which their classmates do not hear.

Mobility. Packages permit youngsters to stop, take a few minutes off and then return to their studies. The very nature of this resource, which includes a series of multisensory activities, encourages movement for those who require activity *while* processing and allows youngsters who prefer passivity to work quietly.

Design. Packages may be taken to a formal area, such as a desk, table, Interest Center or Learning Station, or they may be used in an informal design—on the floor, on carpeting, on a couch, or on a bed.

Sociological Elements. Generally, packages are used by individuals working on specific objectives which they are required to master. They may, however, be used in pairs, in a small group, with a teacher, or in a variety of sociological patterns—as students' learning styles dictate.

How Instructional Packages Facilitate Reading Achievement

Instructional packages are multisensory, self-contained teaching units that appeal to students who learn slowly or whose learning style characteristics respond to this method. All packages have certain basic elements in common.

Each Package Focuses on a Single Concept. Whether the package deals with vowels, spelling, adverbs, comprehension, blends, possessive form, or following directions, students know precisely what the focus is. After the teacher trains youngsters in their use and guides them to and through packages appropriate to each student's academic and learning style needs, they often begin to select additional packages based on interest and growth. The cover and title always reveal what the package contains.

At Least Four Senses Are Used to Learn the Contents. A typewritten script that is repeated by the taped voice of the teacher gives clear directions to students to construct, manipulate, piece together, write, draw, complete, play games and, in several ways, use their sense of touch and their entire bodies in kinesthetic activities related to the objectives of the package.

Feedback and Evaluation Are Built In. Tests are included in the package, and students may respond by writing, taping, or showing results. Correct answers and responses may be checked as the items to be learned are completed. The directions allow for immediate feedback and self-evaluation.

Mistakes can be corrected through repetition of the taped and printed directions and by comparing the students' answers with ones prepared for the games and activities

Learning Is Private and Aimed at Individual Learning Styles.   Only the teacher and student know how well the youngster is doing. Self-image and success are enhanced as progress increases without peer competition for the slower students. The multisensory approach, colorful materials and packaging, working alone, motivating choices, selection of when, where and how, and the ability to move about and to eat if necessary make the instructional package an effective teaching aid for many students. In some cases, pair, team and peer interaction may be appropriate for youngsters who learn well with others.

A Step-by-Step Guide to Designing an Instructional Package

Step 1.   Identify the topic. For example, you may want your students to understand concepts or acquire skills related to parts of speech, comprehension exercises, sounds of certain letter combinations, finding the main idea, and so forth.

Step 2.   List the things you want the student to learn about the topic.

Step 3.   Plan to tape-record simple learning objectives for your students. Use such words as *explain, describe, list* and *identify*. For example, if you were constructing a package on nouns, the taped objective might be: "By the time you finish this package, you will be able to explain what a noun is and to recognize one in a sentence." (For specific instructions, see the section of this chapter on "How to Tape Directions for Instructional Packages.")

Step 4.   Pretend you are teaching your class the most important aspects of the selected topic. Write out exactly what you would say. Plan to tape-record this explanation.

Step 5.   Develop a visual, a tactual, and a kinesthetic activity that emphasizes these aspects in different ways. Write the directions for each of the activities exactly as they will be taped.

Step 6.   Make up a short test that will reveal whether the student has learned the skills and concepts after using the package. This may be recorded as well as written.

Step 7.   Use a colorful cardboard box with a design that reveals the topic and contents. Cover the entire box, including the typewritten topic and contents, with clear plastic or laminate them to ensure longevity.

Examples of Appropriate Instructional Package Topics for Reading

Selected reading skills, parts of speech, grammar, spelling, comprehension exercises or stories are all appropriate content. Consider:

Recognizing and Using Idioms	The Alphabet
What Does an Adverb Do?	How to Develop Complete Sentences
Knowing Nouns	When to Use the Possessive Form
When to Use Capital Letters	How to Follow Directions
How to Solve Problems	The _____ Word Family
How to Write an Original Ending	Quotation Marks: Where Do They Go?
Compound Words	Using the Dictionary
Sound off: A E I O U	Consonant Blends
Context Clues: What to Look For	Reading Readiness
Punctuation	Drawing Conclusions
Using Vocabulary	How to Find the Main Idea
Antonyms	Synonyms

How to Tape Directions for Instructional Packages

The cassette tape is, perhaps, the most important part of a multisensory package. To be effective, the tape must provide simple, concise directions and explanations so that students can use the package without your assistance. The following suggestions can help you develop a good tape:

1. State the objectives clearly and simply.

2. Speak slowly and vary your speech pattern, tone, and inflection to add listening interest. Be dramatic, but not overly so.

3. Avoid picking up background noises or taping where electrical appliances can cause interference.

4. Use explicit directions for each action that the child must do. For example, request that the package's cover be placed onto the table, that items be taken out carefully, that each envelope be returned to the box, and so on.

5. Pause after giving directions so that the listener has time to consider them and carry them out. Or, to allow longer periods of time, you could say, "Turn off the tape recorder while you are putting these materials away. But remember to turn the recorder back on when you are ready to continue."

6. Don't ask questions that require only "yes" or "no" responses. Avoid saying, "Are you ready to begin the next activity?" or "Did you know the answer to that riddle?" Instead say, "I hope you are ready for the next activity! Please take out the blue box with the cotton cloud on

it." Or, "I hope you knew that the answer to that riddle was 'a clock.' A clock has 'hands' but never washes them!"

7. Be certain that the tape is completely self-instructional. Put yourself into the student's place and see if you can work alone without assistance or additional resources and without having to leave the area.

8. Repeat important directions or difficult passages in a slightly different way to reinforce in an interesting manner.

9. Use good grammar and appropriate vocabulary.

10. Be certain that the tape and the materials are self-corrective. If you ask questions, pause sufficiently and then provide answers.

11. Use supplementary sounds (music, bells, animals, other people's voices).

12. Use a good tape recorder and fresh batteries; place the microphone in a comfortable position for you; place a "Taping" sign on your door to avoid bells and other intrusions; take the telephone off the hook; leave enough footage at the beginning of the tape so that your introduction is recorded in its entirety; watch that the tape does not run out while you are still speaking; check the volume; and test as you are recording to be certain the pickup is clear.

13. For primary level children, color-code the tape recorder's buttons.

If you have never taped material for students to hear and use, it is wise to try portions of the text over and over again until you are satisfied with the results. Play one or two objectives with directions for other teachers; ask them to be critical. Then experiment by using the tape with a few students to see their reactions. When criticisms and suggestions disappear, you are ready to complete the tape for the specific package.

Sample Multisensory Instructional Packages

Nongraded Multisensory Instructional Package: FOLKTALES*

Chapter 8 included Programmed Learning Sequences suggested for use with highly visual students in need of structure. Despite their learning style characteristics, many youngsters will enjoy a PLS for the first few times exposed to that type of instructional resource, but after several

---

*This Multisensory Instructional Package on Folktales was designed by Jeannette Bauer and Mary Dawber, graduate students, St. John's University, New York.

experiences with the extremely analytic and structured format, may become hyperactive and unable to maintain concentration. For that kind of child, a Multisensory Instructional Package (MIP) is a far more effective teaching tool. MIPs consistently appeal to students who do not listen intently, find it difficult to concentrate while someone is speaking for any length of time, do not really pay attention when reading or looking at either materials or people, and who find it difficult to remain involved in learning for anything other than the briefest of time intervals. Such children tend to be only tactual/kinesthetic learners; they often have no perceptual strengths. They also tend to require a great deal of mobility, an informal design, frequent breaks, intake, and either peer interaction or an authoritative figure present.

The teacher's voice provides a sufficiently authoritative base for most youngsters to follow directions on a sequential basis. What the MIP does that a real teacher rarely can is to teach globally through at least four different, short, multisensory, hands-on activities that *directly involve* the learner. In addition, MIPs permit youngsters to learn without much tension and in private—thus protecting self-image and status. The materials can be used repeatedly until the skills or concepts are mastered, and the child feels a tremendous sense of accomplishment when the tasks ultimately are mastered.

This MIP on Folktales can be used successfully with students in grades 2 through 8—depending upon their vocabulary and comprehension levels.

LEARNING ABOUT FOLKTALES

Tape:

Hello! I'm very glad you chose this package on analyzing Folktales. I do hope you enjoy working with it. By the time you finish this package, you will be able to identify certain characteristics about folktales.

Most folktales use at least two (2) of the following:

1. a typical opening line
2. a heroic figure
3. animal characters that have human traits—which is called *personification*
4. the technique of cleverness to outwit another character
5. an ending with a moral, or
6. the use of exaggerated qualities for their characters.

Now, open your reading text to page 403, and let's read one folktale together.

A long time ago, on the west side of Oahu, there was a cornfield that a grasshopper had grown. A coyote lived at the south side, and she was an old coyote. One day she went outside, and she saw the cornfield and the grasshopper who sat and watched it. There were lots of corn, melon, and all kinds of vegetables. As the old lady coyote came close to the grasshopper, she heard the grasshopper singing.

"Oh, that is such a beautiful song. I could learn it and sing it to my grandchildren when they are ready for bed. I think I will go ask him to teach me the song," she said to herself and then went down to the cornfield. When she came upon the cornfield, she saw the grasshopper sitting in the shade. "Whose vegetables and fruits are these?" she asked.

"They are mine," the grasshopper answered.

"What were you singing about?" she asked.

"I was praying for the vegetables to grow quickly," he told her.

"I heard you singing. That is why I came," she said. "You sing your song for me, and I will learn it. I would like to sing it to my grandchildren," the coyote told him.

The grasshopper said, "You sit down here and listen so you will learn." Then the grasshopper sang. After he finished, he asked, "Did you learn it?"

"Yes," she said, "I will go now and sing it to my grandchildren." She started running as soon as she left the cornfield. When she was halfway home, a flock of pigeons in the cornfield flew in front of her. She fell backward. When she got up, she tried to remember the song, but had forgotten it. "I think I will go back and ask the grasshopper to sing again. I am sure he stays there all the time. He'll probably sing it for me again." She turned around and went back. When she arrived, he was still sitting in the same place as when she had left him.

"Why have you come back?" he asked her.

"A flock of no-good pigeons scared me on my way, and I forgot the song. So I came back to ask you to sing for me again." After he sang for her, she said, "Now I will go sing for my grandchildren." She ran down the hill, but a rodent scurried in front of her. The old coyote got frightened and forgot the song again. She started off by singing, "Tu-Wee, Tu-Wee," but she forgot the rest of the song.

The grasshopper saw the old coyote coming in the distance. He said to himself, "This time I am getting tired. I won't sing to her." He curled up in a ball and just sat there.

When the coyote got close, she said, "You help me again. That rodent ran in front of me, and I forgot my song again." She waited for him to sing for her, but he didn't sing anything. "Aren't you going to sing for me again?" The grasshopper sat there without saying a word. "If you won't sing for me after I have asked you four times, I am going to eat you!" the coyote threatened him. She asked once, then twice, then the third time and the fourth. Then she threatened him again by saying, "I am going to eat you up if you won't sing for me." The grasshopper didn't move an inch. He just sat there all curled up. Then the coyote put the grasshopper in her mouth. Just before she ate him, he turned into a rock. When she took a bite, to her surprise, the rock caused her front teeth to break. That is why coyotes have teeth that are short in front and long in the back.

If you would like to read the other tales in this book, rewind this tape, replace it into its plastic holder, and turn off the tape recorder. When you have read as much as you care to, look into the Learning About Folktales box and find the tape that says Activity 1. Insert that tape into the recorder, and we will be ready to work a bit more on identifying the characteristics of folktales. If you are going to read the book now, get comfortable and enjoy the reading. Remember to find the second tape when you have finished the stories that interest you!

Activity 1 (Tape #2)
Hello, again! Now let's have some fun in identifying the characteristics of folktales. Look inside the Learning About Folktales box and take out the folder labeled Task Cards. Take out the cards that are inside the folder. Place them in front of you. These task cards are a game that will help you to remember the characteristics of folktales. There should be 12 different cards in front of you. Spread them out. What you really have are 12 halves of task cards. The parts must fit together to form 6 examples of the folktale's characteristics. The examples were taken directly from the reading. You will need to match the characteristic to the example to form the whole task card. (See Figure 7-9, page 158.)

Turn off the tape while you are working. Here's a hint for the task cards. Once properly joined together, each will form a picture of a characteristic found in the folktales. Good luck! Remember, turn the tape back on when you are finished.

● ● ● ●

I hope you liked working with the Task Cards. I'm sure you put them all together correctly. Notice that only correct examples can be matched. Hold up the cards. The cards are shape-coded, and they will fit together when they are right for each other. Just to be on the safe side, you should have pictures of a castle, a coyote, a frog, a hero, a grasshopper, and a goat on the backs of the cards when matched correctly. What *are* the characteristics of Folktales? They include:

- a typical opening line
- a heroic figure—a hero or a heroine
- animals that behave like people

● people who think cleverly

● a moral, or

● people with extreme qualities

Activity 2

Now you are ready for the next activity. Put the task cards back into their folder and set them aside. Next, find the folder labeled Learning Circles. Take out the wheel and place it onto the table with the different colored writing facing you. Now take the 8 clothespins and place them in front of you so that the words, *riddle, moral, exaggerated, typical opening line, folktales, cleverness, personification,* and *heroic figure* can be seen. The object of the game is to match the folktale characteristic on it. While you turn the wheel, read each definition. When you have found the characteristic's definition, clip the clothespin to that section; then go on to the next one. There are eight (8) definitions in all. Now turn off the tape recorder and do your best to match each word or set of words with the correct definition. Sit back and relax while you work. Please remember to turn the tape back on when you are through. Good luck!

●   ●   ●   ●

Here we go again. How did you do? To check your work in defining the characteristics of a folktale, simply turn the Learning Circle over. If the symbols on the back of each clothespin match the symbol to which it is clipped, your answer is correct. Take some time to check. (Pause.)

●   ●   ●   ●

How many did you get right? This wasn't difficult at all! I'm certain that you are doing well. I hope you are ready for the next game! First put the Learning Circle back into the folder, and clip the clothespins to the outside of the folder. Place the folder onto the table or desk near you.

Activity 3

Now look into the large box again and find the box labeled Scrambled Word Game. There is a game board that goes with it. That is in the folder marked Scrambled Word Game Board which is also inside the box. Now find the 68 alphabet letters in the same box. When correctly placed together, they will form the words for the characteristics of most folktales. Look at the game board. See how it is divided into sections for each answer. The first and last letter of each word are written in front of you. I will give you additional clues as you go on. While you are working to solve each word, be certain to turn off the tape. After you have solved each word scramble, turn the tape on to receive your next clue. Get ready, get set, go! Here is your first clue:

1. This word means the lesson taught by a story. (Pause.) Try to remember what the word is! (Pause.)
2. This word means to give human qualities to an object or an animal. (Pause.) That is a long word. It has 15 letters in it! (Pause.)
3. This word means to overstate an idea beyond the truth. (Pause.)
4. This word means to come up with an ingenious action to overcome an opponent. (Pause.)
5. This word means a puzzling question. (Pause.)
6. This word is a brief story told throughout history. (Pause.)
7. These words mean a person identified for courage, strength, and valor. (Pause.)

•   •   •   •

Since you turned the tape back on, you must be finished. Go back to the box labeled Scrambled Word Game. Look at the inside of the boxtop. You will see a secret compartment. Take the card labeled Answer Key, and compare your answers to the key. When you are ready, stop the tape, but turn it back on when you have completed checking. Good luck! Remember to turn the tape back on when you are finished.

•   •   •   •

How did you do? Did you have the correct answers, but some spelling errors? Those were difficult words, so it is not bad if you did. Now that you have completed the Scrambled Word Game, return all the alphabet letters to the box and be certain to place the Answer Key back into its secret compartment. Now that you have completed the three activities, you are ready to take a short quiz to see if you have mastered the characteristics of folktales.

Activity 4

Go back into the Learning About Folktales box. Look inside and take out the folder labeled Folktales Characteristics Quiz. Open it. You should see a sheet with 10 questions on it. You also should see a pencil. Take the pencil and read each question on the sheet with me. At the end of each question you will see a "T" and an "F." The "T" stands for True, and the "F" stands for False. After you read and listen to each question, decide if the question is True or False. Then circle either the "T" or the "F" depending upon which answer is correct. Are you ready? Follow me by referring to the quiz sheet. After you have finished, you may turn the tape off to review your answers but remember to turn the tape back on when you have finished checking your answers. (Pause.)

1. The lesson that is learned at the end of the story is called a moral.   T F
2. A heroic figure is a disliked character.   T F
3. A riddle is a puzzling question.   T F
4. Folktales have only been around for two (2) years.   T F
5. "Once upon a time" is a typical opening line for a folktale.   T F
6. Ingenious actions or cleverness may be present in a folktale.   T F
7. To describe a character truthfully is known as exaggeration.   T F
8. Personification is when an object or animal has human qualities.   T F
9. An animal talking is an example of personification.   T F
10. "And they lived happily ever after" is a typical opening line for a folktale.   T F

Please bring your paper to my desk after you have completed listening to this tape. Would you please be kind enough to place each folder and game back into the large box? Then rewind the tape and place it back into its pocket in the box. When you have done all that, put the cover back onto the box and put the box back into its place in the Learning Center.

I hope you have enjoyed this package, because I enjoyed making it for you. Remember to put your quiz sheet into the bin for Completed Work on my desk and to return the package. I will read and score your quiz as soon as I can. We then will talk about what you have learned from this package.

Thank you and goodbye for now!

Summary

Teachers often do not have the time to teach and reteach each student who needs individualized attention. Instructional packages can do both and offer a variety of other benefits, too. They develop listening skills, encourage independent work, and teach students to follow directions. They provide a new teaching method when all else has failed. They make youngsters aware of their own academic growth and thus build positive self-image. They are private; no one except the learner and the teacher knows who is learning what and how. They eliminate direct interaction between teacher and child when a poor or negative relationship exists. And, of course, they are fun! Instructional packages are a practical and effective strategy for aiding slowly achieving youngsters to read—and to read well.

Appendix A
Learning Style Inventory

**Preparing Young Children
to Understand Their
Learning Styles**

Before you administer the LSI, explain learning style to the students you plan to analyze. For very young children (K-4) the Learning Styles Network distributes a booklet, *Elephant Style* (Perrin, 1978), which explains the concept in storybook form. You also can obtain a Primary Version of the LSI (Perrin, 1981, 1982a, 1982b) to identify the styles of girls and boys in the first or second grade from Learning Styles Network, St. John's University, Grand Central Parkway, Jamaica, N.Y. 11439 for $30.00.

Tell the youngsters that whether their eyes are brown, black, blue, green or hazel is not important; what matters is that they can see. Neither is it important whether they learn while sitting on a wooden or steel chair, on the floor or on carpeting; what matters is that they learn.

Be certain they understand that there are no "right" or "wrong" answers—only the ones that are correct for each person. Compare and contrast their styles and get them relaxed. Then read the Inventory's questions to them as they either look at the Primary Version's illustrations or read the LSI along with you. Avoid tension; becoming aware of how each of them learns should be an interesting, pleasant experience.

The Primary Version is hand-scorable. If you obtain one Specimen Set, you have the author's permission to duplicate as many copies as you need.

When each youngster's individual Profile is in hand, distribute and discuss them with the children. Again, compare their styles and have them explain how it feels when they have to study, learn, or concentrate in an environment that is antithetical to what they prefer. Be certain they realize there are no "good" or "bad" styles.

Figures A-1 through A-3 are charts titled "My Learning Style Profile." Duplicate the charts and encourage each student to write his or her name on the ditto and to color—on the appropriate half of each illustration—the elements that are "GO!" in green and those that are "NO!" in red. (After they've discussed [verbal/auditory] and examined [visual] the elements that are strong for them, we want them to reinforce the concept tactually by coloring.) Then ask them to explain to their parents what they've learned about their own styles and to ask which elements affect their mothers' and fathers' styles.

The Learning Style Inventory (LSI)

The *LSI* is a comprehensive approach to the identification of an individual's learning style. The instrument analyzes the conditions under which students in grades 3-12 prefer to learn;

DIAGNOSING LEARNING STYLE

FIGURE A-1. My Learning Style Profile, Chart 1.

this diagnosis is accomplished through an assessment of 18 environmental, emotional, sociological, and physical characteristics. The LSI uses dichotomous items and can be completed in approximately 30 to 40 minutes. It reports a Consistency Key to reveal the accuracy with which each respondent has answered its questions. The Ohio State University's National Center for Research in Vocational Education conducted a two-year survey of all the instruments that purportedly revealed individual styles and reported that the LSI evidenced "impressive reliability and face and construct validity" (Kirby, 1979). Since that time, the LSI also has yielded predictive validity (Della Valle, 1984; Hodges, 1985; Krimsky, 1982; Lynch, 1981; MacMurren, 1985; Murrain, 1983; Pizzo, 1981; Shea, 1983; Spires, 1983; Virostko, 1983;

White, 1980). It is the LSI's comprehensiveness and quality that led to Keefe's verification that it "is the most widely used assessment instrument in elementary and secondary schools" (1982, p. 52). Individualized group summary Learning Style Inventory printouts may be obtained from: Price Systems, Inc., Box 7818, Lawrence, KS 66046-0067, (913) 843-7892.

Teaching Students through Their Individual Learning Styles: The Research

The LSI was used to examine and compare the styles of underachievers (Dunn, Dunn and Price, 1977; Dunn, 1979); students in alternative education (Dunn and Dunn, 1974, 1975); the

HERE'S MY LEARN- ING STYLE...

SOCIO- LOGICAL

WORK WITH

SELF
PEERS
PAIR
TEAM
ADULT
VARIED

ENVIRONMENTAL

QUIET · NOISE
BRIGHT · DIM
COOL · WARM
FORMAL DESIGN INFORMAL DESIGN

MOTIVATION
SELF · ADULT · TEACHER
PERSIST · STOP
RESPONSIBLE · GUIDED
LONG-RANGE · IMMEDIATE STRUCTURE

EMOTIONAL

PERCEPTUAL
EYES · EARS
HANDS · BODY
EAT · ABSTAIN
EARLY A.M.
LATE A.M.
AFTERNOON
P.M.
SIT · MOVE

PHYSICAL

There is no one like me... I am unique... There is no one like you... You are unique... Alone and together, ...we will

LEARN FOR LIFE

FIGURE A-2. My Learning Style Profile, Chart 2. Designed by Myrna Dupler of Worthington Middle School, Ohio.

Your Learning Style Profile

Student's Name: _____

Stimuli | Elements

Environmental

| 1. Quiet | 3. Bright | 5. Cool | 7. Formal |
| 2. Noise | 4. Dim | 6. Warm | 8. Informal |

Emotional

9. Self	13. Persistent	15. I AM RESPONSIBLE	17. Needs M T W Th F
10. Adult	14. Not	16. Not very	18. Needs little
11. Teacher			Structure
12. Un-motivated			

Sociological

| 19. Self | 20. Peer | 21. Peers | 23. Adult |
| | 22. Several | | 24. Varied |

Physical

25. Perceptual / Auditory	29. Intake	31. a.m.	35. Mobility
26. Visual 27. Kinesthetic 28. Tactile	30. No	32. Late a.m.	36. No
		33. p.m.	
		34. Evening	

FIGURE A-3. My Learning Style Profile, Chart 3. Copyright December 1979 by Nancy Haimeri.

256

handicapped (Cole and Dunn, 1977; Dunn and Cole, 1979, 1980); the gifted (Dunn, Bruno, and Gardiner, 1984; Dunn and Dunn, 1979; Dunn and Price, 1980; Price, Dunn, Dunn and Griggs, 1981); good and poor readers (Dunn and Carbo, 1979; Dunn and Dunn, 1978; Dunn, Price and Sanders, 1981); good and poor mathematicians (Dunn and Dunn, 1978; Hodges, 1985); students with high and low self-concept (Dunn, Price, Dunn and Sanders, 1979); and individuals with strong hemispheric inclinations (Zenhausern, Dunn, Cavanaugh and Eberle, 1981; Dunn, Cavanaugh, Eberle and Zenhausern, 1982).

Once students' learning preferences were identified, alternative methods were used to measure the academic gains made (Dunn and Dunn, 1977a,b; Dunn and Dunn, 1978). After a number of years, other researchers began to experiment by matching and mismatching students' learning style preferences with complementary instructional approaches and resources. Whenever students were taught through their identified styles, statistically significant increases occurred in achievement (Cafferty, 1980; Carbo, 1980; Della Valle, 1984; Douglass, 1979; Domino, 1970; Farr, 1971; Freeley, 1984; Hodges, 1985; Krimsky, 1982; MacMurren, 1985; Martin, 1977; Murrain, 1983; Perrin, 1984; Pizzo, 1981; Shea, 1983; Trautman, 1979; Urbschat, 1977; Virostko, 1983; Weinberg, 1983; Wheeler, 1983; White, 1981). In addition to increases in achievement, students taught through their learning styles evidenced improved attitudes (Copenhaver, 1979; Martin, 1977; Pizzo, 1981; Shea, 1983) and reduced numbers of discipline problems (Carruthers and Young, 1980; Hodges, 1982, 1983; Lynch, 1981).

Eventually many practitioners began to implement learning styles' instructional programs based on our model. Their consistent successes are noteworthy (Ballinger and Ballinger, 1982; Cavanaugh, 1981; K. Dunn, 1981; Fisk, 1981; Gardiner, 1983; Hodges, 1982, 1983; Jenkins, 1982; Lemmon, 1982; Legal, 1983; Vigna and Martin, 1982). Ultimately, researchers at a variety of universities began to explore the learning style model that we had observed, synthesized and described in publications (Cupke, 1980; Cody, 1983; Dean, 1982; Kaley, 1970; Kulp, 1982; Murray, 1980; Ramirez, 1982; Spires, 1983; Steinauer, 1981; Tappenden, 1983; Wingo, 1981; Wolfe, 1983).

Option 1: Individual Summary

The individual summary (see Figure A-4 for an example) for the LSI includes: the student's name or number, sex, date LSI was administered, school, grade and class number; a consistency score, which indicates how accurate the responses are for that student; and the learning style profile for the student based on the way he or she responded to the series of questions for each subscale. The teacher is referred to the appropriate page in the LSI manual for suggestions in designing the learning environment for that particular student.

Option 2: Class Summary

The LSI sample class summary (see Table A-1 for an example) is a single page breakdown for all the students in the class. It includes each student's name or student number, preferred learning styles and consistency score. The teacher uses this summary to individualize instruction and form groups of students with similar, preferred learning styles. For instance, all the students with an X under subscale 1 indicate they need quiet and all the students with an X under subscale 8 indicate they study best when structure is provided. Detailed suggestions for arranging the learning environment to meet a student's learning style are in *Teaching Students through Their Individual Learning Styles* (Dunn and Dunn, 1978, Chapter 2). The class printout summarizes all the information for each student on each subscale.

Option 3: Subscale Summary

The LSI subscale summary (see Table A-2 for an example) indicates the number and percent

INDIVIDUAL PROFILE
LEARNING STYLE INVENTORY

Name: Edgar Bright   **Sex:** M   **Year In School:** 7   **Date of Birth:** 5/70   **I.D. No.:** 398

Group Identification: Deer Park School   **Special Code:**   **Date:** 10-26-1982   **Group No.:** 816

PREFERENCE SUMMARY

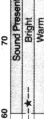

Raw Score	Standard Score	#	Preference	Low — High scale
0	0	1	Noise Level	Quiet — Sound Present
4	62	2	Light	Low — Bright
3	48	3	Temperature	Cool — Warm
2	52	4	Design	Informal — Formal
5	60	5	Motivation	
2	40	6	Persistent	
5	61	7	Responsible	
3	56	8	Structure	
5	64	9	Learning Alone / Peer Oriented	
3	75	10	Authority Figures Present	
3	65	11	Learn in Several Ways	
3	53	12	Auditory	
3	65	13	Visual	
6	61	14	Tactile	
6	60	15	Kinesthetic	
0	0	16	Requires Intake	
6	62	17	Evening - Morning	
3	59	18	Late Morning	
5	65	19	Afternoon	
4	59	20	Needs Mobility	
4	60	21	*Adult Motivated	
4	60	22	*Teacher Motivated	
		23		

CONSISTENCY: 100   *These scales are on LSI profile only.   **PROFILE NO.:**

FIGURE A-4. Individual Summary Example. Copyright 1982, Price Systems, Inc., P.O. Box 7818, Lawrence, KS 66044.

TABLE A-1. Learning Style Inventory

Learning Style Summary for Students Having Standard Score Equal to or Greater Than 60

Price Systems, Inc. Date: May 25, 1982

Group Identification: State Tech. Inst. Group No.: 434

Name	Consistency Score	1	2	3	4	5	6	7	8	9	10	11	12	13	14	15	16	17	18	19	20	21	22
Powell, Pam	0.85	X				X	X	X	X	X		X	X		X	X	X						
Freeland, J. Camille	0.85		X		X	X	X	X	X		X		X		X	X	X		X				
Mills, Thomas Scott	1.00	X	X		X	X	X	X	X			X	X		X	X	X						
Boldreghini, James J.	1.00	X	X			X	X	X	X			X	X		X	X	X						
Appleton, Toni J.	0.46	X				X	X	X	X		X	X	X	X	X		X	X				X	
Kerley, Stephanie P.	0.85	X	X			X	X	X	X			X	X	X		X	X	X					
Brown, Ed	0.92	X			X	X	X	X		X					X	X	X					X	
Holzworth, Charlene	0.85		X			X	X	X	X			X	X		X		X						
Monasterio, Patricia	0.92		X		X	X	X	X	X			X	X		X	X	X						
Riels, Carol Ann	1.00					X	X	X	X	X	X	X	X		X	X	X	X	X			X	
Cooper, Tony	1.00		X		X	X	X	X	X	X	X	X	X		X	X	X	X					
Van Housen, Julia L.	1.00	X			X	X	X	X	X	X	X	X	X		X	X	X						

259

TABLE A-2. Learning Style Inventory
Total Responses by Subscale for Standard Score Equal to or Greater than 60:
05-25-1982

Group Identification: Morningside Elementary   **Group No.: 434**

LSI Area	*Subscale*	*Responses*	*Percentage*
Noise Level	1	6	50.00
Light	2	6	50.00
Temperature	3	0	0.00
Design	4	6	50.00
Motivation	5	12	100.00
Persistent	6	11	91.67
Responsible	7	11	91.67
Structure	8	10	83.33
Learning Alone/Peer Oriented	9	1	16.67
Authority Figures Present	11	10	83.33
Learn in Several Ways	12	10	83.33
Auditory	13	2	16.67
Visual	14	10	83.33
Tactile	15	11	91.67
Kinesthetic	16	12	100.00
Requires Intake	17	1	8.33
Evening-Morning	18	2	16.67
Late Morning	19	0	0.00
Afternoon	20	0	0.00
Needs Mobility	21	3	25.00
Adult Motivated	22	0	0.00
Teacher Motivated	23	0	0.00

Total Number of Students: 12   Total Responses: 130

of the total group that identified each factor as important to their learning style. For instance, only two students—17 percent of the group—indicated that they learn best in the morning (subscale number 18). Using the LSI manual and supplementary references, the teacher can design the program and learning environment to complement each group of students' needs.

Interpreting the Learning Style Inventory Individual Printouts

The LSI reveals how individual students prefer to study, concentrate, and learn new or diffi-cult information or skills. It describes each person's learning style.

The following instructions and charts will assist you in interpreting an individual Student Profile; it will help you "read" the Profile, understand its implications, and then suggest strategies for helping that student learn more, more easily and to remember it better than ever before.

Reading an Individual Student Profile

Look at our Sample Individual Profile (see Figure A-5). Notice that 23 items are printed from top to bottom through the center of the oblong. Those are the elements of learning style that affect most youngsters. We are going to identify which of those elements affect the student whose printout you have.

Few people are affected by all the elements; most have between six and 14 that are important to them (Dunn, 1983a). When an element is *unimportant*, people are unaware of their reactions to it, because they have none. When an element *is* important to them, most people can describe their preferences and dislikes accurately.

Very Low Preferences and Their Implications

Look at the sample Individual Profile. Across the top of the oblong, moving from left to right, is a series of numbers that begins with 20 and ends with 80. Any element that falls between 20 and 30 is a Very Low Preference and has been important to that student for a long time. Very Low Preferences affect learning and are the *opposite* of the element's name. Thus, if the element is noise, and the score is anywhere between 20 and 30, the student needs the opposite of noise when he is trying to learn; he needs quiet. If he scores between 20 and 30 on light, he has a Very Low Preference for light—which means that he needs low or dim light when concentrating.

Low Preferences and Their Implications

Elements that fall between 30 and 40 are called "Low Preferences." Students do not learn easily with Low Preferences either; in fact, they do better when they avoid them. Thus, a score between 30 and 40 on noise suggests that a student usually learns better in quiet. Although a youngster may find it difficult to learn with sound in the environment if he or she scores between 30 and 40, that student would have an *extremely* difficult (if not impossible) time trying to read or learn if he or she scores in the 20–30 range.

Unimportant Elements and Their Implications

When an element falls between 40 and 60, it is classified as "Not Important." Sometimes we call those the "It Depends Elements" because they, themselves, really do not affect learners; what *is* important is the task being done. For example, if a youngster scores 45 on noise, whether the environment in which he or she is trying to study is quiet or noisy is of little importance. If a student is trying to do something in which he or she is interested, the youngster can do it—and do it well—regardless of the amount of sound present. If the student is bored with what he or she is doing, or does not want to do it, the noise will disturb and prevent the youngster from concentrating.

Preferences and Their Implications

Elements in the 60–70 range are Preferences. We all learn easily and remember better when we learn through our Preferences. Sometimes, though, if we are extremely motivated, we can overcome either our Preferences or Low Preferences; the best we can do when we must learn through our Very Low Preferences is to *function*—rather than learn easily and well—when we encounter new and difficult knowledge.

Very Strong Preferences and Their Implications

As you probably surmise, those elements between 70 and 80 comprise our Very Strong Preferences. Like the 20–30 group, they are very important and tend to be fairly stable—meaning that, if they change at all, they do so over a comparatively long period of time (Copenhaver, 1979, 1980; Virostko, 1983). Very Strong Preferences help us to learn, and our Very Low Preferences inhibit us from doing so unless conditions are matched.

Combining Elements to Identify Individual Style

Every element that falls between 20 and 40 and between 60 and 80 on an Individual Profile is part of that person's style. After testing students, count all the asterisks that you find in those two sections; do not count those in the 40–60 group. How many asterisks do you see when you combine all those in the 20–40 and in the 60–80 sections? Those are the number of elements that are important to that student. Another way of phrasing that is, "Which elements comprise the most important aspects of that student's learning style?"

If you find it difficult to see all the asterisks, look at the left-hand column immediately next to the oblong on the sample Individual Profile; it is titled, "Standard Score." Hold a piece of paper level across the Profile extending from the name of the element in the center of the oblong to the numeral in the Standard Score column, and you can read the response in number (rather than asterisk) form.

Although most students have between six and 14 elements that are important to them, some have as many as 17 or 18—or, on occasion, more. Who has a more difficult time learning—the one affected by six elements or the one to whom 16 are important? (The more elements that are over 60 and below 40 on the Profile, the more important it is to find the "right" instructional environment or conditions, and the more tension the student feels when the setting is "wrong.") The difference between two or three points on the LSI means very little; the numbers merely indicate students' approximate reactions to the various elements and whether they should have or avoid them when trying to concentrate.

Grouping Certain Elements

Some elements "go together;" that is, they need to be examined in relation to each other. Let's consider some of those that should be viewed

as a pair and then discuss what can be done to respond to them (Dunn, 1983b).

Motivation and Persistence. These two elements often interact. Students who score above 60 on both sometimes experience conflicting emotions. Those who score above 70 on motivation are always strongly task-oriented; they enjoy accomplishment. When such youngsters are asked to stop what they are doing and to begin another assignment, their high persistence is frustrated; their inclination is to complete what has been initiated before embarking on another task.

If children are high on both motivation and persistence, allow them plenty of time to finish one thing before the pressure of the next intrudes. If the child's teacher does not recognize his or her persistence quotient, share his or her LSI Individual Profile and explain why it is important that the work be sequenced, allowed to come to fruition and be completed before the youngster can embark on the next endeavor.

On the other hand, if he or she has high motivation and low persistence, or is low on both, that student must learn the discipline of completing important tasks before beginning another—or many will remain incomplete and only partially designed; the youngster will develop a reputation for dabbling. (If the student is low on responsibility, he couldn't care less!) In such cases, divide the task into several small parts; write the dates and times during which each portion should be done. The student should stay with each smaller unit until it is complete. He may not deviate from the time line; he may only add extra time for incompleted work, but that extra period must be inserted before the time allocated for the next phase. It will be painful in the beginning; it may remain painful for awhile; but if he is working with others, they are counting on him to carry his "load"—or he'll be causing them to adopt his style.

If the student is low on motivation, again, be certain to divide each task into smaller sections. If his Profile indicates that he is authority-oriented, have him show his developing material to you or another adult at periodic intervals. If he is collegial or peer-oriented, arrange to have a friend review what he is doing to provide feedback. Keep the deadlines that you have; thus establishing and encouraging work toward the completion of each small section.

Motivation and Responsibility. If youngsters are high on both motivation and responsibility, they face conflict whenever they do not agree with what they are supposed to do/achieve/learn. Their high motivation characteristics instinctively say "Go!" when they agree with a task, but when they disagree, internal fighting begins! Their desire to achieve urges, "Do it and get it over with!" (particularly if they are highly persistent!), but their intolerance for something which they do not believe in causes little red lights to flash, "I will not!"

- If they are high on motivation, high on responsibility and disagree with either the task, its value, or how it ought to be done, occasionally they will compromise, and at other times they will not.

- If their motivation scores are approximately 8–10 points higher than their responsibility scores, they will struggle with a decision about doing things that they feel they "ought" to do but with which they disagree, but invariably will end up doing what they believe in or want to do rather than what they "should."

- If their motivation scores are about 60 and their responsibility scores are below 40, they usually do exactly what they want to do—and have no qualms about it!

Motivation and Structure. Remember that structure is the need for explicit directions before beginning a task; such people feel better about knowing exactly what has to be accomplished, what the parameters are, when it is due, and so on, as opposed to those who merely want to know what the assignment is and then prefer doing it their way.

Many people are motivated to accomplish assignments, but cannot begin without sufficient directions. Such people will give all kinds of rationalizations; they (a) "work better under pressure," (b) have so much to do that certain things just have to wait for later, (c) don't like to do the task they haven't begun, (d) "need time to think it through," and so on. If youngsters belong to this group, establish a time line for them. Take every task that eventually must be accomplished and place it onto a continuum wherein they know what they will do on Monday at 9:00, what will be done next, what can be discarded, what can be assigned to someone else and what they may never really get to. They must maintain that schedule. Before the day assigned, specify all the parameters of the assignment: length, complexity, score to be achieved, format, and whatever. It also helps to divide the assignment into small sections and attack one section for a specific amount of time. If it is completed before the allocated time, reward with a "break" or by letting the student do something he is more motivated to do.

On the other hand, some people impose a great deal of structure on themselves. They explain that they feel a kind of tension when they know they have something that must get done. Such people feel better when they complete the task and can relax. If the student is the kind of person who tries to get things done "now" because "Who knows what can happen?"; if he feels better about having the task done than worrying about when it will get done, you need only continue as you have been. You know he will do it early; you should not impose extra tension.

Learning Alone, with Peers, with Authorities or in Several Ways. These elements should be examined in relation to each other. Students who achieve 60 or better on the continuum learning alone/peer-oriented, strongly need to learn with peers; those who score below 40, prefer to learn alone. The closer the score is to 0, the more learning alone is preferred. Scores in the 40–60 range suggest that whether the youngster works well alone or with peers depends on the task, the interest, and the peers.

For example, a score between 40 and 60 on learning alone suggests that sometimes the student likes to work/study alone and sometimes he doesn't. His interest in what he is doing is more important than his need to work alone or with others.

Over 60 on several ways reveals the kind of person who must have variety; he becomes irritated and dissatisfied if he has to do the same thing repeatedly in the same way. Avoid routines and assembly lines; give responsibilities that enable him to utilize creativity. Incidentally, several ways may refer to two other possibilities. He may learn/work in a variety of patterns; alone, with peers, with authorities, and so on. It also describes people who do not like to work with others, and do not have the independence skills to work alone; such people often like to learn or produce with media or computers; they like to work with "things" rather than people, and they do so very well indeed!

Auditory, Visual, Tactile, and Kinesthetic. If students score below 40 on any of the above modalities, they should use that means as the last way to learn/produce; it can serve as a reinforcement device, but do not permit new material to be introduced through their least effective modality. Rather, be certain that new and/or difficult material is always/usually in-troduced through their strongest modality.

Early Morning, Late Morning, Afternoon, and Evening. Examine these four elements in relation to each other. Early morning and evening are on a continuum; students who score above 60 prefer learning in the morning; students who score below 40 are evening people; that's when they become most alert. Scores of above 60 on late morning and afternoon indicate that those are good times for learning; when the scores go below 40 on those two, they signify that those time intervals should be avoided. Should students' scores on any of these four items fall into the 40–60 range, that time of day is not important to them. What is important is their interest in the task or how they are feeling. In other words, any element between 40–60 can be disregarded; their reaction to it depends on things other than the element itself—like interest or the weather.

Teacher-Motivated. This item is very important. A score of above 60 indicates that student wants teacher approval, attention, and support. When that occurs, examine the same student's score on Authority Figures Present. A score there of above 60 suggests that the student needs an authoritative teacher; a score of below 40 may be interpreted as meaning that the student prefers a collegial teacher.

Appendix B
The Reading Style Inventory

The Reading Style Inventory (RSI) (Carbo, 1979, 1981) is the first instrument to identify a student's natural "reading style." The RSI generates personalized, computerized RSI individual and group profiles which describe how to teach students to read, based on each youngster's natural reading style strengths. The RSI can be administered in approximately 15 to 30 minutes, to individuals or groups in grades 1–12. RSI profiles may be obtained by utilizing an RSI floppy diskette, or by sending RSI answer sheets to Learning Research Associates for processing.

For information about reading styles seminars, conferences, on-site consultants, and ordering RSI materials, write or call:

Learning Research Associates
P.O. Box 39
Roslyn Hts., NY 11577
1-800-331-3117
(516)248-8002 (NY, Hawaii, Alaska)

Students can take the Reading Style Inventory directly on the computer, or in RSI test booklets. RSI computer diskettes score students' answers and print their RSI profiles. An RSI scoring device is also available from Learning Research Associates. (Photograph courtesy of the Sacred Heart Seminary, Hempstead, New York)

265

Sample Items from The Reading Inventory

A) I like to choose what I read.	B) I like my teacher to tell me what to read.	C) Sometimes I like my teacher to tell me what to read. Other times I like to choose what I read.

A) I usually feel warmer than most people. I like to read where it's cool.	B) I usually feel colder than most people. I like to read where it's warm.	C) I feel about the same in cool or warm rooms. When I read, temperature isn't important to me.

A) When I read, I always like to eat or drink something.	B) When I read, I don't like to eat or drink something.	C) When I read, sometimes I like to eat or drink something and sometimes I don't.

A) When I read, I like to sit on a hard chair at a desk.	B) When I read, I like to sit on something soft, like pillows, a soft chair, or a rug.	C) When I read, I usually sit in different places. Sometimes I like a hard chair and sometimes I like a soft chair.

A) I like my reading work checked as soon as I finish it.	B) I like my reading work checked about one day after I finish it.	C) It's not important to me to have my reading work checked often.

A) When I write words, sometimes I mix up the letters.	B) When I write words, I almost never mix up the letters.

A) I almost never lose my place on the page when I'm reading.	B) I usually lose my place on the page when I'm reading.

A) When I look at words, I often mix up letters like "b" and "d".	B) When I look at words, I almost never mix up letters like "b" and "d".

A) If I stop to sound out new words, I often forget what I'm reading.	B) If I stop to sound out new words I don't forget what I'm reading.

A) Tracing over a word with my finger would not help me to remember it.	B) Tracing over a word with my finger would help me to remember it.

A) I like to read alone.	B) I don't like to read alone.

FIGURE B-1. Sample items from the Reading Style Inventory.

Reliability of the Reading Style Inventory®

A test-retest reliability study was conducted with the RSI in 1981 with 293 students in grades two, four, six and eight, who were identified as good, average and poor readers. The sample was drawn from both inner-city and suburban schools located in New York City and Nassau County, New York, respectively.

Test-retest reliability coefficients for the 13 RSI subscales ranged from .63 to .77. The RSI scales with reliabilities of .70 or higher for all grade levels were: sound (.72), design (.71), motivation (.70), structure (.72), auditory perception (.74), visual perception (.77), kinesthetic perception (.75) and mobility (.76) (see Table 1). Additional research with larger and more representative populations of students is planned for the near future.

Validity of the Reading Style Inventory®

Content Validity

The RSI has established initial content or "face" validity, which is concerned with how well an instrument measures what it claims to measure. All RSI items were based on careful observation and testing of the reading styles of hundreds of students from 1976 to 1980. In 1981, articles in national journals and newsletters invited educators to evaluate the representativeness and appropriateness of the items on the RSI, and the clarity of the language (Dunn & Reckinger, 1981; "Selecting the 'Right' Reading Approach," 1981). A total of 87 practitioners from 23 states responded; 93 percent reported that the RSI accurately measured the elements of reading style.

TABLE 1. Test–Retest Reliability Coefficients for Reading Style Inventory Scales

Scale	All Grades	Grade 2	Grade 4	Grade 6	Grade 8
Sound	.72	.70	.73	.75	.78
Light	.69	.63	.68	.76	.66
Temperature	.65	.61	.66	.68	.62
Design	.71	.74	.67	.71	.68
Motivation	.70	.63	.72	.72	.68
Persistence	.63	.62	.64	.65	.60
Responsibility	.64	.70	.70	.72	.64
Structure	.72	.72	.70	.72	.70
Sociological	.67	.69	.55	.64	.76
Perception					
Auditory	.74	.67	.75	.78	.76
Visual	.77	.76	.71	.81	.79
Tactual	.69	.70	.68	.64	.67
Kinesthetic	.75	.72	.74	.69	.77
Intake	.67	.62	.59	.76	.72
Time of day	.66	.69	.63	.63	.68
Mobility	.76	.70	.73	.75	.78

From the *Reading Style Inventory Research Supplement* by Marie Carbo, 1983, p. 16.

Concurrent Validity

A second type of validity, concurrent validity, is determined by submission of an instrument to experts in the field, and demonstration of high correlation to other measures of the same variable with high validity and reliability. Beginning research has evidenced correlations between the *Reading Style Inventory* and the *Learning Style Inventory* (Carbo, 1982; 1983a; b; Price, Dunn & Sanders, 1980; Zenhausern, Dunn, Cavanaugh & Eberle, 1981).

In 1982, the National Center for the Study of Learning/Teaching Styles conducted a nationwide survey to identify the learning style instruments (K–12) that had been utilized by practitioners, reported in at least one research study and evidenced "reliability and validity" ("Network Undertakes Instrument Classification System," 1982). Its "report to the field," was "based on the data collected after one full year of careful investigation" (p. 1, Freeley, 1983). The RSI was one of fourteen instruments that qualified for inclusion in the *Learning Styles Network's Instruments Assessment Analysis.*

Parents, students and teachers have indicated that the RSI printouts are accurate. For example, of 147 parents who participated in a research study conducted with the RSI, 96 percent found that the RSI printouts were accurate. (The Juanita Project, 1983) (see Table 3); and the students in Hamiltons' sixth grade noted that "the items on the RSI printouts were quite truthful, and they agreed with what was said" (p. 2, Hamilton, 1983).

The actual behavior of students has been compared to the preferences and strengths described on their RSI printouts. The following is a typical observation of Hamilton's:

... the nine students who had said (on their RSI) that they preferred snacks and worked best with snacks were the ones who consistently, day after day, week after week, and month after month, continued to bring in snacks for themselves. ... it seemed to calm them down quite a bit, and I got quite a bit of extra work out of them. (p. 3)

Dixon (1983), a high school reading specialist, also noted that the RSI printouts were corroborated by teacher observations. She wrote:

The results (of the RSI) were very revealing and were on target with the findings experienced in the Communication Skills Lab. The descriptions matched what was observed with the students over the past six months. (p. 4)

Both the *Reading Style Inventory* (Carbo, 1981) and the *Learning Style Inventory* (Dunn, Dunn & Price, 1979), have yielded similar data regarding the style differences of good and poor readers, and those of students across grade levels. When administered the RSI (Carbo 1982, 1983b), good readers and poor readers differed significantly on nine of the eleven elements identified with the LSI (Price, Dunn & Sanders, 1980). And, significant differences between right and left activators on the LSI subscales (Zenhausern, Dunn, Cavanaugh & Eberle, 1981) were identical to those reported by Carbo (1982, 1983b) with the RSI. Comparisons of the learning styles of students across grade levels, as measured by the LSI ("Which Learning Style Elements . . . ," 1980), closely matched those obtained with the RSI (Carbo, 1982; 1983a).

Predictive Validity

A third kind of validity, called predictive or criterion-related validity, is "characterized by prediction to an *outside* criterion and by checking a measuring instrument . . . against some outcome or measure" (p. 460, Kerlinger, 1973). Learning style research has demonstrated significant increases in reading achievement when students learn through their individual styles (see Chapter 1).

Initial research with the RSI indicates that the instrument has predictive validity. Educators who have identified individual reading styles, and implemented the RSI prescriptions have noted increased reading achievement, decreased discipline problems, improved student attitudes, increased reading for plea-

TABLE 2. Average Reading Gains* of Remedial Reading Students In Grades 1–6 After Implementation of the Reading Style Inventory Prescriptions During the 1982–1983 School Year

n=24 Grade Level	September 1982	May 1983	Average Gain
1	1.3	2.8	1.5 years
2	1.8	3.8	2.0 years
3	3.2	6.5	3.3 years
4	3.3	6.9	3.6 years
5	3.7	7.1	3.4 years
6	4.0	8.1	4.1 years

*Grade 1—Wide Range Achievement Test
Grades 2 through 6—Stanford Diagnostic Achievement Test

(*Source:* Hutchinson Public Schools, reading support program: end-of-year report, Roosevelt School, Hutchinson, Kansas, May 1983.)

sure, and positive changes in the teacher's role and ability to teach reading (Adams, 1983; Carbo, 1984 a, b, c; Hamilton, 1983; Hodges, 1984, 1985; LaShell, 1983, 1985; Lemmon, 1983; Sudzina, 1986 (see Table 2).

Construct Validity

An important question when considering the construct validity of an instrument is whether or not it discriminates among known groups.

As part of the test-retest reliability study described previously, a series of ANOVAS was performed on the data to determine if the RSI discriminated among the identified groups. Good, average and poor readers differed significantly on ten elements of reading style; significant differences among mean scores emerged on ten reading style elements across grade levels; and boys and girls differed significantly on three reading style elements.

The results of a statistical analysis of the RSI subscales among ability groups indicated

TABLE 3. Juanita Project Parent Questionnaire Summary After Implementing The Reading Styles Inventory Prescriptions

n=147

1. I have observed the following changes in my child during this program. My child:

	Juanita	Summer
reads more for pleasure	52%	71%
asks to be read to	7%	57%
enjoys a wider variety of reading materials	42%	50%
talks more about what he/she has read	54%	50%
is more interested in the library	35%	36%
enjoys reading more	54%	71%

2. I found the Reading Style Inventory:

	Juanita	Summer
generally accurate for my child	95%	100%
of value to me as a parent	70%	100%
helped me better understand my child	68%	100%

The Juanita Project took place during the 1982–1983 school year. Twenty-three teachers and 550 students (grades K–6, all reading levels) participated. One hundred twenty elementary students with reading problems attended the summer program.

(*Source:* Juanita Elementary School, Lake Washington School District, Kirkland, Washington.)

TABLE 4. Juanita Project Teacher Survey Results After Implementing the Reading Style Inventory Prescriptions

n=23

1. The time I have available for the planning of reading instruction achieves the following results with students:

	Pre	Post
Excellent	0%	10%
Good	30%	45%
Fair	70%	45%
Poor	0%	0%

2. In general, I believe that students learn differently.

	Pre	Post
Strongly Agree	70%	86%
Agree	30%	14%
Disagree	0%	0%
S. Disagree	0%	0%
No Opinion	0%	0%

3. Most children need and benefit from a highly structured reading program, such as a basal program.

	Pre	Post
Strongly Agree	9%	0%
Agree	35%	43%
Disagree	30%	48%
S. Disagree	9%	10%
No Opinion	4%	5%

4. I believe that most children will learn to read best with high-interest reading materials, such as those in an individualized program.

	Pre	Post
Strongly Agree	22%	25%
Agree	49%	60%
Disagree	17%	10%
S. Disagree	4%	0%
No Opinion	9%	5%

5. I am comfortable with the methods I use to manage my program.

	Pre	Post
Strongly Agree	14%	20%
Agree	39%	60%
Disagree	39%	20%
S. Disagree	4%	0%
No Opinion	0%	0%

6. I believe children learn to read best with many audio-visual materials and games.

	Pre	Post
Strongly Agree	35%	38%
Agree	0%	43%
Disagree	17%	5%
S. Disagree	4%	5%
No Opinion	12%	5%

7. My students use/apply the skills they learn during reading in other subject areas.

	Pre	Post
Often Occurs	41%	55%
Sometimes Occurs	54%	45%
Rarely Occurs	5%	0%

8. I use teaching techniques developed in my reading program in other subject areas.

	Pre	Post
Often	48%	60%
Sometimes	48%	35%
Rarely	4%	5%

(*Source:* Juanita Elementary School, Lake Washington School District, Kirkland, Washington.)

that poor readers were significantly less visual/auditory and more tactile/kinesthetic than good readers (Carbo, 1982; 1983b). Identical results were obtained by Koch (1983) when the RSI was administered to good and poor readers on the college level. There is ample research in the field that corroborates those findings. Reading performance has been found to be strongly related to perceptual abilities (Dykstra, 1966; Morency, 1968); good readers have demonstrated preferences for learning through their visual and auditory modalities, whereas poor readers have higher preferences for learning tactually and kinesthetically (Adams, 1978; Bakker, 1966; Mills, 1956; Murray, 1980; Price, Dunn & Sanders, 1980; Walters & Kosowski, 1963); and, poor readers tend to have difficulty shifting between and integrating auditory and visual stimuli (Beery, 1967; Birch & Belmont, 1965; Heckerl, 1971).

Although boys comprise the great majority of poor readers in schools in the United States, no significant differences have been found between the reading abilities of boys and girls in England; in Germany boys are superior to girls (Johnson & Greenbaum, 1980). The RSI subscales that discriminated significantly between boys and girls all dealt with the emotional stimulus; boys were significantly less persistent and responsible, and more peer-motivated than girls. Those results suggest that, as hypothesized by Johnson and Greenbaum, boys may develop reading difficulties, in part, due to cultural/emotional causes.

Statistical analyses of students' reading styles across grade levels indicated that when compared to intermediate and junior high students, primary youngsters were significantly more tactile/kinesthetic, teacher-motivated, and self-motivated. They also had lower visual and auditory strengths, and stronger preferences for intake, mobility, structure, reading in the morning and reading with adults or adults and peers. Similar findings were reported previously by Price, Dunn, and Sanders (1980).

Many research studies verify the strong preferences intermediate students have for choices of reading materials, high-interest reading materials and prolonged reading periods (Heathington, 1979; Moray, 1978; Stanchfield & Fraim, 1979). When the RSI was administered to 139 youngsters in grades four and five, the students' reading styles matched significantly more often with storybooks and individualized methods, rather than basal readers, regardless of previous reading experiences in school ("Kansas Discovers Reading Materials . . . ," 1983).

Appendix C
Publishers and Suppliers of Commercial Reading Materials

Sample Basal Reader Programs

Whole-Word Emphasis Basal Readers

1. Allyn and Bacon Pathfinder (K-8)
   Allyn and Bacon, Inc.
   7 Wells Avenue
   Newton, MA 02159
   Note: First grade preprimers are strongly linguistic matching an analytic/auditory reading style.

2. D. C. Heath Readers (K-6)
   125 Spring Street
   Lexington, MA 02173

3. Ginn and Company (K-8)
   P.O. Box 2649
   1250 Fairwood Avenue
   Columbus, OH 43216
   (See Figure 5-2)

4. Harcourt, Brace and Jovanovich (1-8)
   757 Third Avenue
   New York, NY 10017

5. Open Court (K–6)
   LaSalle, IL 61301
   Note: Lessons for Grades K and 1 contain many multisensory phonic exercises appropriate for analytic/auditory youngsters.

6. Reading Basics Plus (K-8)
   Harper & Row, Publishers, Inc.
   School Division
   10 East 53rd Street
   New York, NY 10022

7. Houghton Mifflin Reading Series (K-8)
   One Beacon Street
   Boston, MA 02107
   Note: Workbooks contain some difficult exercises requiring a strongly analytic/auditory reading style.
   (See Figure 5-7)

8. Macmillan Publishing Company (K-8)
   Front and Brown Streets
   Riverside, NJ 08370

9. Modern Curriculum Press (K-2)
   Real Or Make-Believe? series
   13900 Prospect Rd.
   Cleveland, OH 44136
   Difficult, high-interest preprimers

10. Scott Foresman Reading (K-8)
    1900 East Lake Avenue
    Glenville, IL 60025
    (See Figures 5-6 and 5-8)

Adapted from the "Selection Guide For Matching Reading Programs and Reading Styles" by Marie Carbo and Elizabeth Burton, and the list, "Publishers and Suppliers of Reading Materials," in the *Reading Style Inventory Manual*, pp. 45–53; 74–75.

Strong Phonic-Emphasis Basal Readers

1. Addison-Wesley (K-8)
   320 E. 46 Street
   New York, NY
   Word-for-word recordings of some stories at beginning levels are available.

2. Economy Keys to Reading (K-8)
   Economy Company
   5455 West 84th Street
   Indianapolis, IN 46268

3. Modern Curriculum Press Primary Readers (1-3)
   13900 Prospect Road
   Cleveland, OH 44136
   Word-for-word recordings of readers are available. (See Figure 5-9)

4. Distar® (N-3)
   Science Research Associates
   155 North Wacker Drive
   Chicago, IL 60606
   (See Figure 5-10)

Strong Linguistic-Emphasis Basal Reader Programs

1. Benziger Readers (K-3)
   Glencoe Publishing
   17337 Ventura Blvd.
   Encino, CA 91316

2. Lippincott Basal Reading (K-6)
   Harper & Row, Publishers, Inc.
   School Division
   10 E. 53rd Street
   New York, NY 10022

3. McGraw-Hill Programmed Reading (K-3)
   by Sullivan and Buchanan
   1221 Sixth Avenue
   New York, NY 10017
   Students write in self-checking programmed workbooks that present linguistic exercises in small, sequential steps. A cloze format is utilized. These materials respond to a strongly analytic/auditory youngster with a high need for structure and immediate feedback.
   (See Figure 5-12)

4. Merrill Linguistic (1-6)
   Charles E. Merrill Publishing Co.
   1300 Alum Creek Drive
   Columbus, OH 43216

5. SRA Basic Reading Series (K–2)
   Science Research Associates
   155 North Wacker Drive
   Chicago, IL 60606
   Word-for-word recordings of beginning level readers are available.
   (See Figure 5-11)

Sample Language-Experience Reader Programs

1. *Feathers in My Cap* (N, k)
   Acropolis Books, Ltd.
   Washington, DC 20009
   Teacher's resource book utilizing an unstructured approach that contains stories, teacher-made games and activities to stimulate writing.

2. Language Experiences In Reading (LEIR Multimedia Kit) (1-4)
   Encyclopedia Britannica Education Corp.
   425 North Michigan Avenue
   Chicago, IL 60611
   Structured approach with a teacher's manual containing story writing ideas and skill lessons, as well as a daily lesson plan guide, story cards, filmstrips and tape recordings. (See Figure 5-13)

3. *Success in Reading*
   Goodyear Publishing Company, Inc.
   Santa Monica, CA 90401
   Teacher's manual describing a structured approach. Contains story writing ideas and skill lessons.

4. *The Language Experience Approach to Reading*
   by Denise D. Nessell and Margaret B. Jones
   Teachers College, Columbia University
   New York, NY
   Teacher's resource book for implementing a fairly structured language-experi-

ence program, including writing ideas, skill work and evaluation.

5. *The Language-Experience Approach to the Teaching of Reading*
by Russell G. Stauffer
Harper and Row, 1980.
Complete, detailed resource; sample lessons for implementing an LEA program.

Sample Individualized Programs

1. Dell Publishing Co. (K-6)
245 E. 47th Street
New York, NY 10017
Collections of paperback books.

2. Random House Reading Program (1-8)
Random House School Division
400 Hahn Road
Westminster, MD 21157
Hard-covered books with self-directing, self-correcting cards describing activities to be done before and after reading a book. Separate skill development kits are available. Early primary programs have accompanying tape recordings, games and puzzles.

3. Scholastic Book Services (K-12)
904 Sylvan Avenue
Englewood Cliffs, NJ 07632
Collections of paperback books. Some books have accompanying tape recordings, duplicating masters and a teacher's guide.
Selections of paperback books are available that correlate with most major basal reader series.

4. Weekly Reader Paperback Kits (K-12)
Weekly Reader Multimedia Materials
1250 Fairwood Avenue
Box 16629
Columbus, OH 43216
Kits of paperbook books; some have accompanying tapes, duplicating masters, posters and teacher's guide.

Sample Supplementary Reading Materials

Games

1. ABC School Supply, Inc.
6500 Peachtree Industrial Blvd.
Box 4750
Norcross, GA 30071

2. Curriculum Associates, Inc.
5 Esquire Road
North Billerica, MA 91862

3. Developmental Learning Materials
Box 4000
One DLM Park
Allen, TX 75002
(See Figure 5-14)

4. Lamtex, Inc.
1182 Salway S. W.
Canton, OH 44720
Easy-to-make learning circles, task cards, electroboards, activity cards (see Chapter 7, pp. 147, 154, 172, 173).

5. Scott Resources, Inc.
Box 2121
1300 Blue Spruce Drive, Suite B
Fort Collins, CO 80522

Activity Cards

1. Frank Schaeffer (1-8)
23770 Hawthorne Blvd.
Torrance, CA 90505

2. Good Apple (1-8)
Box 299
Carthage, IL 62321

3. World Record Publications, Ltd. (1-8)
Box 41
Williston Park, NY 11596

Reading Kits

1. Audio Reading Progress Laboratory (K-8)
Educational Progress
Box 45663
Tulsa, OK 74145

Graded booklets with stories that are followed by comprehension, vocabulary and decoding exercises. Accompanying tutorial tapes provide step-by-step instruction to guide the student through the reading activities; self-checking.

2. Glass Analysis For Decoding Only (1-12)
Easier-to-Learn, Inc.
Box 329
Garden City, NY 11530
Four kits that contain word cards and books for teaching decoding through recognition of letter clusters in words, ranging from simple to difficult levels. Students usually work individually or in small groups with a teacher.

3. SRA Reading Laboratory (1-12)
Science Research Associates
155 North Wacker Drive
Chicago, IL 60606
Graded packets of cards containing stories followed by comprehension, vocabulary and word attack exercises; self-checking.

Skill Development Books and Duplicating Masters

1. Barnell Loft (1-12)
958 Church Street
Baldwin, NY 11510
Books containing specific, concentrated and sequential practice in a variety of skill areas.

2. Continental Press (K-12)
Elizabethtown, PA 17022
Large selection of duplicating masters that practice a wide range of reading skills.

3. McGraw-Hill Reading For Concepts (2-6)
1221 Avenue of the Americas
New York, NY 10020
A series of books containing brief stories and articles followed by comprehension questions.

4. Milliken (K-12)
1100 Research Blvd.

St. Louis, MO 63132
Large selection of duplicating masters that practice reading skills.

5. Oceana Educational Communications, Inc. (1-12)
Dobbs Ferry, NY 10522
Reading programs comprised of books with a variety of formats providing sequential practice in many reading skill areas.

6. Reader's Digest (1-9)
Educational Division
Pleasantville, NY 10570
A series of books containing brief stories and articles, followed by comprehension questions; tape recordings of some materials available.

7. World Record Publications (1-8)
Box 41
Williston Park, NY 11596
Duplicating master books with brief stories and reading comprehension exercises based on unusual, true events (see Figures 5-1 and 5-3).

Audio-Visual Materials

1. Bell and Howell
7100 McCormick Road
Chicago, IL 60645
Language Master System (K-12)
Card reader with visual perception and beginning reading skills programs.

2. Borg-Warner Critical Reading (4-8)
Borg-Warner Educational Systems
600 University Drive
Arlington Heights, IL 60004
Reading software for Systems 80 computer.

3. Time-Share Corporation
Department 39
Box 683
Hanover, NH 03755
Dolphin Curricula Reading (3-8)
Computer software based on Houghton Mifflin paper-and-pencil reading materials.

4. Educational Insights
   150 W. Carob
   Compton, CA 90220
   Computer-like electronic device, called "Charlie," with accompanying reading software and programmable cards.

5. EDL Controlled Reader (K-12)
   Educational Developmental Laboratories
   McGraw-Hill
   Avenue of the Americas
   New York, NY 10020
   Controlled reader with visual perception and beginning reading skills programs.

6. ESP Incorporated (1-12)
   1201 E. Johnson
   P.O. Drawer 5037
   Jonesboro, AR 72401
   Skillsheets and filmstrips with accompanying tape recordings.

7. Films, Inc. Movie Strips (K-8)
   Movie Strip Division
   50 Rindge Avenue Extension
   Cambridge, MA 02140
   Tape recorded filmstrips of famous children's movies with accompanying worksheets.

8. Media Materials, Inc. (K-12)
   2936 Remington Avenue
   Baltimore, MD 21211
   Booklets, filmstrips, duplicating masters, computer software, and tape recordings to develop reading skills.

9. Milliken Computer Courseware Comprehension Power (4-12)
   1100 Research Blvd.
   St. Louis, MO 63132
   Computer software to teach reading comprehension.
   (See Figure 5-16)

10. Slosson Educational Publications, Inc. (2-6)
    Box 280-T
    East Aurora, NY 14052
    Computer-like machine called "Rainbow," with reading comprehension software, including programmable "Write Your Own" cards.

11. Texas Instruments Speaking Learning Aids (1-8)
    Texas Instruments
    Box 53
    Lubbock, TX 79408
    A variety of electronic teaching machines with recordings that interact with the student.

12. Troll Read-A-Longs (K-8)
    Troll Associates
    320 Route 17
    Mahwah, NJ 07430
    Books with word-for-word recordings appropriate for average and good readers. Generally, too much material is recorded and the pace is too fast for poor readers (see Chapter 6 for recording techniques for poor readers).

References

Chapter 1

Ballinger, R. and Ballinger, V. Steps in managing the diagnostic-prescriptive process in the foreign language classroom. *Student Learning Styles and Brain Behavior*. Virginia: National Association of Secondary School Principals, 1982, 33–37.

Barbe, W. and Swassing, R. *Teaching students through their modality strengths*. Ohio: Zaner-Bloser, 1979.

Biggers, J. L. Body rhythms, the school day and academic achievement. *Journal of Experimental Education*, Fall, 1980, *49*, 1, 45–47.

Brooks, A. The inner clock: a new timepiece for learning. *Teacher*, April, 1980, 48–50.

Cafferty, E. An analysis of student performance based upon the degree of match between the educational cognitive style of the teacher and the educational cognitive style of the student. Doctoral Dissertation, University of Nebraska, 1980.

Carbo, M. Teaching reading with talking books. *The Reading Teacher*. 1978, *3*, 267–273.

Carbo, M. Reading styles change from second to eighth grade. *Education Leadership*, February, 1983(a), 40, 1, 56–59.

Carbo, M. Research in reading and learning style: Implications for exceptional children. *Exceptional Children*, April, 1983(b), 49, 6, 486–494.

Carbo, M. An analysis of the relationship between the modality preferences of kindergartners and selected reading treatments as they affect the learning of a basic sight-word vocabulary. Doctoral Dissertation, St. John's University, 1980.

Carruthers, S. A. and Young, L. A. Preference of condition concerning time in learning environments of rural versus city eighth grade students. Unpublished manuscript in G. Price (ed.) Research on Learning Style. Paper presented at First Annual Conference on Teaching Students Through Their Individual Learning Styles, New York, July, 1980.

Cavanaugh, D. Student learning styles: a diagnostic/prescriptive approach to instruction. *Kappan*, 1981, *63*, 3, 202–203.

Cole, R. W. and Dunn, R. A new lease on life for education of the handicapped: Ohio copes with 94–142. *Kappan*. Indiana: Phi Delta Kappa, September, 1977, *59*, 1, 3–6, 10, 22.

Copenhaver, R. W. The consistency of learning styles as students move from English to mathematics. Doctoral Dissertation, Indiana University, 1979.

Copenhaver, R. W. The consistency of learning styles. *The Teacher Educator*, Winter, 1979–1980, *15*, 3, 2–6.

Cupke, L. F. The effects of similarity of instructor preferred teaching style and student preferred learning style on student achievement in selected courses in a metropolitan community college. Doctoral Dissertation, University of Missouri—Kansas City, 1980.

Cody, C. Learning styles, including hemispheric dominance: a comparative study of average, gifted, and highly gifted students in grades five through 12. Doctoral Dissertation, Temple University, 1983.

Dean, W. L. A comparison of the learning styles of educable mentally retarded students and learning disabled students. Doctoral Dissertation, The University of Mississippi, 1981.

DeBello, T. A critical analysis of the effects on achievement and attitudes, of administrative assignments to social studies instruction based on individual eighth grade students' learning style preferences for learning alone, with peers, or with teachers. Doctoral Dissertation, St. John's University, 1985.

Della Valle, J. An experimental investigation of the relationship(s) between preference for mobility and the word recognition scores of seventh grade students to provide supervisory and administrative guidelines for the organization of effective instructional environments. Doctoral Dissertation, St. John's University, 1984.

Domino, G. Interactive effects of achievement orientation and teaching style on academic achievement. *ACT Research Report*, 1970, *39*, 1–9.

Domino, G. Interactive effects on achievement orientation and teaching style on academic achievement. *Journal of Educational Psychology*. 1971, *62*, 427–431.

Douglass, C. Making biology easier to understand. *The American Biology Teacher*, May, 1979, *41*, 4, 277–279.

Dunn, K. Madison prep: alternative to teenage disaster. *Educational Leadership*. Virginia: Association for Supervision and Curriculum Development, 1981, *38*, 5, 386–387.

Dunn, K. Small-group techniques for the middle school. *Early Years*. Darien, Connecticut: Allen Raymond, Inc. *15*, 5 (January, 1985): 41–43.

Dunn, R. Editorial. *Learning Styles Network Newsletter*. New York: National Association of Secondary School Principals and St. John's University, Summer, 1982 a, *3*, 2, 2.

Dunn, R. Would you like to know *your* learning style—and how you can learn more and remember better than ever?

Early Years, Darien, Connecticut, Allen Raymond, Inc. 13, *2*, October, 1982 b, 27–29, 70.

Dunn, R. You've got style: now's the time to find out what it is. *Early Years*. Connecticut: Allen Raymond, Inc. January, 1983 a, *13*, 5, 25–31, 58–59.

Dunn, R. Now that you know your learning style—how can you make the most of it? *Early Years*, Darien, Connecticut: Allen Raymond, Inc., February, 1983 b, *13*, 6, 49–54.

Dunn, R. Now that you understand your learning style—what are you willing to do to teach your students through *their* individual styles? *Early Years*, Connecticut, March, 1983 c, *13*, 7, 41–43, 62.

Dunn, R. Learning style and its relationship to exceptionality at both ends of the spectrum. *Exceptional Children*. Reston, Virginia: The Council for Exceptional Children *49*, 6 (April, 1983): 496–506.

Dunn, R. Teacher-made materials. In *Instructional Leadership Handbook*. Reston, Virginia: National Association of Secondary School Principals 5, 3 (Autumn, 1984).

Dunn, R. How should students do their homework? Research vs. opinion. *Early Years*. Darien, Connecticut: Allen Raymond, Inc. *15*, 41 (December, 1984): 43–45.

Dunn, R. Learning style: State of the science. In *Theory Into Practice XXIII*, 1 (Winter, 1984): 10–19.

Dunn, R., Bruno, A. and Gardiner, B. Put a cap on your gifted program. *Gifted Child Quarterly*, *28*, 2 (Spring, 1984): 70–72.

Dunn, R. and Carbo, M. The reading gamble: how to increase the odds for every youngster. *Learning*, Palo Alto, California, August/September, 1979, *8*, 1, 34–43.

Dunn, R. and Carbo, M. Modalities: an open letter to Walter Barbe, Michael Milone and Raymond Swassing. *Educational Leadership*. Virginia: Association for Supervision and Curriculum Development, February, 1981, *38*, 5, 381–382.

Dunn, R., Cavanaugh, D. P., Eberle, B. M., and Zenhausern, R. Hemispheric preference: the newest element of learning style. *The American Biology Teacher*. Virginia: National Association of Biology Teachers, May, 1982, *44*, 5, 291–294.

Dunn, R. and Cole, R. W. Inviting malpractice through mainstreaming. *Educational Leadership*. Washington, D.C., Association for Supervision and Curriculum Development, February, 1979, *36*, 5, 302–307.

Dunn, R. and Dunn, K. Practical approaches to individualizing instruction: contracts and other effective instructional strategies. New York: Parker Publishing Company, Division of Prentice-Hall, Inc., 1972.

Dunn, R. and Dunn, K. Learning style as a criterion for placement in alternative programs. *Kappan*, Indiana, December, 1974, 275–279.

Dunn, R. and Dunn, K. Educator's self-teaching guide to individualizing instructional programs. New York: Parker Publishing Company, Division of Prentice-Hall, Inc., 1975.

Dunn, R. and Dunn, K. How to raise independent and professionally successful daughters. Englewood Cliffs, New Jersey: Prentice-Hall, Inc., 1977 a.

Dunn, R. and Dunn, K. Be a better teacher: how to diagnose learning styles. *Instructor*, New York, September, 1977 b, 2, *LXXXVII*, 122–144.

Dunn, R. and Dunn, K. Teaching students through their individual learning styles. Englewood Cliffs, New Jersey: Prentice-Hall, Inc., 1978 a.

Dunn, R. and Dunn, K. Ten ways to make the classroom a better place to learn. *Instructor 4*, XCIV (November/December, 1984): 84–88, 139.

Dunn, R., Dunn K., and Freeley, M. E. Practical applications of the research: Responding to students' learning styles—step one. *Illinois Research and Development Journal*. Illinois State University; The Illinois Association for Supervision and Curriculum Development *21*, 1 (Fall, 1984): 1–21.

Dunn, R., Dunn, K., and Freeley, M. E. Tips to improve your inservice training: Know your learning style. *Early Years*. Darien, Connecticut: Allen Raymond, Inc. *15*, 8 (April, 1985): 30–31.

Dunn, R., Dunn, K., and Price, G. Diagnosing learning styles: a prescription for avoiding malpractice suits against school systems. *Kappan*, Indiana, January, 1977, 418–420.

Dunn, R. and Griggs, S. A. Selected case studies of the learning style preferences of gifted students. *Gifted Child Quarterly 28*, 3 (Summer, 1984): 115–119.

Dunn, R., Dunn, K., and Price, G. *Learning style inventory (LSI)*, 1974, 1979, 1981, 1985). Available from Price Systems, Box 7818, Lawrence, KS 66044.

Dunn, R., Dunn, K., and Price, G. *Learning style inventory research manual* (1974, 1979, 1981, 1985). Available from Price Systems, Box 7818, Lawrence, KS 66044. $9.

Dunn, R. and Price, G. The learning style characteristics of gifted students. *Gifted Child Quarterly*, 1980, *24*, 33–36.

Dunn, R., Price, G. E., Dunn, K., and Saunders, W. Relationship of learning style to self-concept. *The Clearing House*. Washington, D.C.: Heldref Publications, November, 1979, 53, 3, 155–158.

Dunn, R., Price, G., and Sanders, W. Reading achievement and learning styles. *The Clearing House*. Washington, D.C.: Heldref Publications, January, 1981, *54*, 5, 223–226.

Dunn, R. and Shockley, A. That a child may reach: expanded education in Freeport. New York: Freeport Public Schools, Pursuant to a U.S. Office of Health, Education and Welfare grant under the supervision of the New York State Education Department (1971).

Dunn, R., Zenhausern, R., Barretto, R., Bacilious, Z., Gemake, J., Griggs, S. A., Sanders, W., Schwartz, V., Sinatra, R., Spiridakis, J., and Swanchak, J. How brainy are you about the brain? *Early Years*. Darien, Connecticut: Allen Raymond, Inc. *15*, 1 (August/September, 1984): 46–48.

Farr, B. J. Individual differences in learning: predicting one's more effective learning modality. Doctoral Dissertation, Catholic University, 1971.

Fiske, E. B. Teachers adjust schooling to fit students' individuality. *The New York Times*, Tuesday, December 29, 1981, p. c1, c4.

Flesch, R. Why Johnny can't read, and what you can do about it. New York: Harcourt Brothers, 1955.

Freeley, M. E. An experimental investigation of the relationships among teachers' individual time preferences, inservice workshop schedules, and instructional techniques and the subsequent implementation of learning style strategies in participants' classrooms. Doctoral Dissertation, St. John's University, 1984.

Freeley, M. E. Learning styles and computers: Do they mesh? *Early Years.* Darien, Connecticut: Allen Raymond, Inc. *14*, 8 (April, 1984): 63–64.

Hart, L. A. Human brain and human learning. Longman, 1983.

Hodges, H. Madison prep: alternative through learning styles. Student Learning Styles and Brain Behavior. Virginia: National Association of Secondary School Principals, 1982, 28–32.

Hodges, H. Learning styles: R_x for mathaphobia. *Arithmetic Teacher*, 1983, *30*, 7, 17–20.

Hodges, H. An analysis of the relationships among preferences for a formal/informal design, one element of learning style, academic achievement, and attitudes of seventh and eighth grade students in remedial mathematics classes in a New York City Alternative Junior High School, Doctoral Dissertation, St. John's University, 1985.

Hunt, D. E. Learning style and student needs: an introduction to conceptual level. *Student Learning Styles: Diagnosing and Prescribing Programs*. Virginia: National Association of Secondary School Principals, 1979, 27–38.

Jenkins, J. M. Teaching to individual learning styles. *The Administrator*. 1982, 9, 1, 10–12.

Johnson, C. D. Identifying potential school dropouts, Ph.D., United States International University, 1984.

Kaley, S. B. Field dependence/independence and learning styles in sixth graders. Doctoral Dissertation, Hofstra University, 1977.

Keefe, J. W. School applications of the learning style concept. *Student Learning Styles: Diagnosing and Prescribing Programs*. Virginia: National Association of Secondary School Principals, 1979, 127.

Keefe, J. W. Assessing student learning styles: an overview. *Student Learning Styles and Brain Behavior*. Virginia: National Association of Secondary School Principals, 1982, 43–53.

Kirby, P. Cognitive style, learning style, and transfer skill acquisition. Columbus, Ohio: The Ohio State University's National Center for Research in Vocational Education, 1979.

Kintsch, W. Concerning the marriage of research and practice in beginning reading instruction. In Resnick, L. B., and Weaver, P. A. *Theory and Practice of Early Reading*, New Jersey: Lawrence Erlbaum Associates, Publishers, 1979, 1.

Krimsky, J. S. A comparative study of the effects of matching and mismatching fourth grade students with their learning style preferences for the environmental element of light and their subsequent reading speed and accuracy scores. Doctoral Dissertation, St. John's University, 1982.

Kroon, D. K. An experimental investigation of the effects on academic achievement and the resultant administrative implications of instruction, congruent and incongruent with secondary, industrial arts students' identified learning style perceptual preferences. Doctoral Dissertation, St. John's University, 1985.

Kulp, J. J. A description of the processes used in developing and implementing a teacher training program based on the Dunn's concept of learning style. Doctoral Dissertation, Temple University, 1981.

Learning style inventory (LSI) (Dunn, Dunn and Price, 1979) for students in grades 3–12, obtainable through Price Systems, Box 7818, Lawrence, Kansas 66044. Specimen Set: $12.00.

Learning style inventory research manual (Dunn, Dunn, and Price, 1974, 1979, 1981, 1985). Available from Price Systems, Box 7818, Lawrence, KS. $9.

Learning style inventory: primary version (LSI:P) (Perrin, 1981) for students in grades 1 and 2, obtainable through the Center for the Study of Learning and Teaching Styles. New York: St. John's University. Cost of LSI:P and Manual $30.00.

Learning style questionnaire (LSQ) (Dunn

and Dunn, 1975, 1977) for students in grades 3–12. In Dunn, R. and Dunn, K. *How to Raise Independent and Professionally Successful Daughters*, Prentice-Hall, Inc., (1977).

Legal, O. Analysis of the preferred learning styles of former adolescent psychiatric patients. Doctoral Dissertation, Kansas State University, 1983.

Lemmon, P. Step by step leadership into learning styles. *Early Years*, 1982, *12*, 5, 36, 14.

Lerner, B. Vouchers for literacy: second chance legislation. *Phi Delta Kappan*. December, 1981, 252, 255.

Levy, J. What do brain scientists know about education? *Learning Styles Network Newsletter*. New York: National Association of Secondary School Principals and St. John's University, Autumn, 1982 a, *3*, 3, 4, 8.

Levy, J. Children think with whole brains. *Student Learning Styles and Brain Behavior*. Virginia: National Association of Secondary School Principals, 1982 b, 173–184.

Lynch, P. An analysis of the relationships among academic achievement, attendance and the individual learning style time preferences of eleventh and twelfth grade students identified as initial or chronic truants in a suburban New York school district. Doctoral Dissertation, St. John's University, 1981.

MacMurren, H. A comparative study of the effects of matching and mismatching sixth-grade students with their learning style preferences for the physical element of intake and their subsequent reading speed and accuracy scores. Doctoral Dissertation, St. John's University, 1985.

Maeroff, G. L. Rule tying promotion to reading skill stirs worry. *New York Times*. April 3, 1982, 27, 28.

Martin, M. K. Effects of the interaction between students' learning styles and high school instructional environments. Doctoral Dissertation, University of Oregon, 1977.

Murray, A. C. The comparison of learning styles between low and high reading achievement subjects in the seventh and eighth grades in a public middle school. Doctoral Dissertation, United States International University, 1980.

Murrain, P. G. Administrative determinations concerning facilities utilization and instructional grouping: an analysis of the relationship(s) between selected thermal environments and preferences for temperature, an element of learning style, as they affect word recognition scores of secondary school students. Doctoral Dissertation, St. John's University, 1983.

Ohio learning "disabled" do not necessarily feel that they are. *Learning Styles Network Newsletter*. New York: National Association of Secondary School Principals and St. John's University, Autumn, 1982, *3*, 3, 6.

Panero, J. and Zelnick, M. Human dimension and interior space: a sourcebook of design reference standards. New York: Whitney Library of Design, 1980.

Perrin, J. Elephant style. Obtainable through the Center for the Study of Learning and Teaching Styles. New York: St. John's University, 1978. Cost: $8.00.

Perrin, J. Who's learning how? *Early Years*. Connecticut: Allen Raymond, Inc., January, 1982 a, *12*, 5, 37–38, 61.

Perrin, J. The identification of learning styles among young children. *Student Learning Styles and Brain Behavior*. Virginia: National Association of Secondary School Principals, 1982 b, 119–126.

Perrin, J. An experimental investigation of the relationships among the learning style sociological preferences of gifted and nongifted primary children, selected instructional strategies, attitudes, and achievement in problem solving and rote memorization. Doctoral Dissertation, St. John's University, 1984.

Pizzo, J. An investigation of the relationships between selected acoustic environments and sound, an element of learning style, as they affect reading achievement of male and female sixth grade students. Doctoral Dissertation, St. John's University, 1981.

Price, G. Research using the learning style inventory. Paper presented at Second Annual Conference on Teaching Students

Through Their Individual Learning Styles, New York, July, 1980.

Price, G. Research on learning style. Paper presented at Third Annual National Conference on Teaching Students Through Their Individual Learning Styles, New York, July, 1981.

Price, G., Dunn, K., Dunn, R., and Griggs, S. Studies in students' learning styles. *Roeper Review.* Michigan: Roeper City and Country School, November, 1981, *4*, 2, 38–40.

Progress report on learning styles: A formative evaluation model and the results from several assessments, Worthington, Ohio: Worthington City Schools (1980): 52.

Ramirez, A. I. Modality and field dependence/independence: learning style components and their relationship to mathematics achievement in the elementary school. Doctoral Dissertation, The Florida State University, 1982.

Reading style inventory (RSI) (Carbo, 1981) for students in grades 1–12.

Restak, R. *The brain: the last frontier.* New York: Doubleday and Co., 1979.

Shea, T. An investigation of the relationship among preferences for the learning style element of design, selected instructional environments, and reading test achievement of ninth grade students to improve administrative determinations concerning effective educational facilities. Doctoral Dissertation, St. John's University, 1983.

Spires, R. D. The effect of teacher in-service about learning styles on mathematics and reading achievement. Doctoral Dissertation, Bowling Green State University, 1983.

Steinauer, M. H. Interpersonal relationships as reflected in learning style preferences: a study of eleventh grade students and their English teachers in a vocational school. Doctoral Dissertation, Southern Illinois University, 1981.

Tanenbaum, R. An investigation of the relationship(s) between selected instructional techniques and identified field dependent/independent cognitive styles as evidenced among high school students enrolled in studies of nutrition. Doctoral Dissertation, St. John's University, 1982.

Tappenden, V. J. Analysis of the learning styles of vocational education and non-vocational education students in eleventh and twelfth grades from rural, urban and suburban locations in Ohio. Doctoral Dissertation, Kent State University, 1983.

Thies, A. A brain-behavior analysis of learning style. *Student Learning Styles: Diagnosing and Prescribing Programs.* Virginia: National Association of Secondary School Principals, 1979, 55–61.

Trautman, P. An investigation of the relationship between selected instructional techniques and identified cognitive style. Doctoral Dissertation, St. John's University, 1979.

Urbschat, K. A study of preferred learning modes and their relationship to the amount of recall of cvc trigrams. Doctoral Dissertation, Wayne State University, 1977.

Vigna, R. and Martin, M. Learning styles at Bishop Carroll high school. *Student Learning Styles and Brain Behavior.* Virginia: National Association of Secondary School Principals, 1982, 38–42.

Virostko, J. An analysis of the relationships among academic achievement in mathematics and reading, assigned instructional schedules, and learning style time preferences of third, fourth, fifth and sixth grade students. Doctoral Dissertation, St. John's University, 1983.

Weinberg, F. An experimental investigation of the interaction between modality preference and mode of presentation in the instruction of arithmetic concepts to third grade underachievers. Doctoral Dissertation, St. John's University, 1983.

Wheeler, R. An alternative to failure: teaching reading according to students' perceptual strengths. *Kappa Delta Pi Record.* Indiana: Kappa Delta Pi, December, 1980, *17*, 2, 59–63.

Wheeler, R. An investigation of the degree of academic achievement evidenced when second grade, learning disabled students' perceptual preferences are matched and mismatched with complementary sensory approaches to beginning reading instruction. Doctoral Dissertation, St. John's University, 1983.

Which learning style elements are stable and

which tend to change? *Learning Styles Network Newsletter.* New York: National Association of Secondary School Principals and St. John's University, Autumn, 1980, *1*, 3, 1.

Wingo, L. H. Relationships among locus of motivation, sensory modality, and grouping preferences of learning style to basic skills test performance in reading and mathematics. Doctoral Dissertation, Memphis State University, 1980.

White, R. M. An investigation of the relationship between selected instructional methods and selected elements of emotional learning style upon student achievement in seventh grade social studies. Doctoral Dissertation, St. John's University, 1981.

White, R. M., Dunn, R., and Zenhausern, R. An investigation of responsible versus less responsible students. *Illinois School Research and Development.* Fall, 1982, *19*, 1, 18–25.

Wolfe, G. L. Learning styles and the teaching of reading. Doctoral Dissertation, Akron University, 1983.

Zenhausern, R. Hemispheric dominance. *Learning Styles Network Newsletter.* New York: National Association of Secondary School Principals and St. John's University, Spring, 1980, *1*, 2, 3.

Zenhausern, R., Dunn, R., Cavanaugh, D., and Eberle, B. Do left and right "brained" students learn differently? *Roeper Review.* Michigan: Roeper City and Country School, September, 1981, *4*, 1, 36–39.

Zenhausern, R. Education and the left hemisphere. *Student Learning Styles and Brain Behavior.* Virginia: National Association of Secondary School Principals, 1982, 192–196.

Chapter 2

Adams, D. Implementing the Reading Styles Inventory: The Juanita project. Paper presented at Teaching Reading Through Individual Reading Styles, inservice course for the Spokane Public Schools, August 1983.

Carbo, M. Teaching reading with talking books. Newark, Delaware: International Reading Association, December 1978, *32*, 267–273.

Carbo, M. How to play with a book. Darien, Conn.: Allen Raymond, Inc., February 1979, *9*, 6, 68; 72–74.

Carbo, M. Reading style: Diagnosis, evaluation, prescription. *Academic Therapy,* September 1980, *16*, 1, 45–52.

Carbo, M. *Reading Style Inventory Manual.* New York: Learning Research Associates, 1981.

Carbo, M. Reading style: Key to preventing reading failure. *Student Learning Styles and Brain Behavior.* Virginia: National Association of Secondary School Principals, 1982. Chapter 13.

Carbo, M. Reading styles change from second to eighth grade. *Educational Leadership.* Alexandria, Virginia: Association for Supervision and Curriculum Development, February 1983(a), *40*, 5, 56–59.

Carbo, M. Research in reading and learning style: Implications for exceptional children. *Exceptional Children.* Reston, Virginia: Council for Exceptional Children, April 1983(b), *49*, 6, 486–494.

Carbo, M. *Reading Style Inventory Research Supplement.* New York: Learning Research Associates, 1983(c).

Carbo, M. You can identify reading styles ... and then design a super reading program. *Early Years K-8,* Allen Raymond, Inc., April 1984(a), *14*, 8, 80–83.

Carbo, M. Research in learning style and reading: Implications for instruction. *Theory Into Practice.* Columbus, Ohio: Ohio State University, Winter 1984(b), 72–76.

Carbo, M. Five schools try reading styles programs ... and see how their kids have grown! *Early Years K-8.* Allen Raymond, Inc., 1984(c) *15*, 1, 52–60.

Carbo, M. Reading Styles: How principals can make a difference. *Principal.* National Association of Elementary School Principals, 1984(d), *64*, 1, 20–26.

Chall, J. The great debate: Ten years later, with a modest proposal for reading stages. *Theory and Practice of Early Reading.* New Jersey: Lawrence Erlbaum Associates, 1979, 29–55.

Dixon, G. A specialist's reading of the Carbo Reading Style Inventory. Report for the 1982–1983 Model Schools Learning Style Project (sponsored by the National Association of Secondary School Principals). Columbia, Maryland: Howard County Schools, 1983.

Hamilton, S. Reading styles: an experiment with sixth grade, poor readers. A report for the Norton, Ohio Public Schools, May 1983.

Hammill, D. and Larsen, S. The effectiveness of psycholinguistic training. *Exceptional Children.* Reston, Virginia: Council for Exceptional Children, 1974, *41*, 5–14.

Hodges, H. Using the RSI with junior high poor readers. Presentation delivered at the Fortieth National Conference of the Association for Supervision and Curriculum Development, Chicago, March 1984, and at the National Reading Styles Conference, New York City, July 1985.

Hutchinson public schools, reading support program: end-of-year report. Hutchinson, Kansas: Roosevelt School, May 1983.

LaShell, L. Teaching handicapped children to read through their individual reading styles. Report presented at Seattle-Pacific University course, Teaching Reading Through Individual Learning Styles, Seattle, Washington, April 1983.

LaShell, L. An analysis of the effects of reading methods on reading achievement and locus of control when individual reading style is matched for learning disabled students. Doctoral Dissertation, Fielding University, 1985.

Lemmon, P. Reading styles: Increasing the reading achievement of remedial reading students. Presentation delivered at Sixth Annual Conference on Teaching Students Through Their Individual Learning Styles, New York, July 1983.

Reading Style Inventory® (Carbo, 1981) for students in grades 1–12. Available through: Learning Research Associates, Box 39, Roslyn Hts., NY, 11577. Specimen set $14.00 (includes postage).

Sudzina, M. An investigation of the relationship between the reading styles of second graders and their achievement in three different basal reader programs. Doctoral Dissertation, Temple University, 1986.

The Juanita prcject. Kirkland, Washington: Lake Washington School District, June 1983.

There's more to reading than some folks say. A position statement issued by the Board of Directors of the International Reading Association, in a letter from the President, Roger Farr, November 3, 1979; reprinted in *The Reading Teacher*, May 1980, *33*, 8, 190.

Chapter 3

Adams, J. Visual and tactual integration and cerebral dysfunction in children with learning disabilities. *Journal of Learning Disabilities*, 1978, *11*, 197–204.

Bakker, D. J. Sensory dominance in normal and backward readers. *Perceptual and Motor Skills*, 1966, *23*, 1055–1058.

Bursuk, L. Sensory mode and lesson presentation as a factor in the reading comprehension improvement of adolescent retarded readers (Doctoral Dissertation, City University of New York, 1969). *Dissertation Abstracts International*, 1969, 30/06A, 2370. (University Microfilms No. 69-21180).

Carbo, M. Teaching reading with talking books. *The Reading Teacher*. Newark, Delaware: International Reading Association, December 1978, *32*, 267–273.

Carbo, M. Reading style: Diagnosis, evaluation, prescription. *Academic Therapy*, September 1980(a), *16*, 45–52.

Carbo, M. An analysis of the relationships between the modality preferences of kindergartners and selected reading treatments as they affect the learning of a basic sight-word vocabulary (Doctoral Dissertation, St. John's University, New York, 1980). *Dissertation Abstracts International*, 1980(b), 41/04A, 1389. (University Microfilms No. 80-21790).

Carbo, M. *Reading Style Inventory Manual.* New York: Learning Research Associates, 1981.

Carbo, M. Teaching reading the way children learn to read. *Early Years*. Darien, Conn.: Allen Raymond, Inc., February 1982(a), *12*, 6, 43–47.

Carbo, M. Reading style: Key to preventing reading failure. *Student Learning Styles and Brain Behavior*. Virginia: National Association of Secondary School Principals, 1982(b), Chapter 13.

Carbo, M. Reading styles change from second to eighth grade. *Educational Leadership*. Alexandria, Virginia: Association for Supervision and Curriculum Development, February 1983(a), *40*, 5, 56–59.

Carbo, M. Research in reading and learning style: implications for exceptional children. *Exceptional Children*. Reston, Va.: Council for Exceptional Children, April 1983(b), *49*, 6, 486–494.

Carbo, M. Reading style: Help a fairy tale come true. *Early Years*. Darien, Conn.: Allen Raymond, Inc., November 1983(c), *14*, 3, 10, 12, 15, 16.

Carbo, M. Five schools try reading styles programs . . . and see how their kids have grown! *Early Years K–8*. Darien, Conn.: Allen Raymond, Inc., 1984(a), *15*, 1, 52–60.

Carbo, M. Reading styles: How principals can make a difference. *Principal*. Reston, Va.: National Association of Elementary Principals, 1984(b), *64*, 1, 20–26.

Chall, J. The great debate: Ten years later, with a modest proposal for reading stages. In *Theory and Practice of Early Reading* Vol. 1, Resnick and Weaver (Eds.), New Jersey: Erlbaum Publishers, 1979, pp. 29–55.

Daniel, P. N. and Tacker, R. S. Preferred modality of stimulus input and memory for cvc trigrams. *Journal of Educational Research*, 1974, 67, 255–258.

Donovan, M. A. The relationship between modality preferences and programs used in initial reading instruction (Doctoral Dissertation, University of Hawaii, 1977). *Dissertation Abstracts International*, 1978, 39/01A, 85. (University Microfilms No. 78-10248).

Douglas, C. Making biology easier to understand. *The American Biology Teacher*, May 1979, *41*, 4, 277–279.

Dunn, R. Individualizing instruction—teaming teachers and media specialists to meet individual student needs. *Audio-visual Instruction*, May 1971, *15*, 5, 78–80.

Dunn, R. and Carbo, M. The reading gamble: How to improve the odds for every youngster. *Learning*. California: Education Today Company, August/September 1979, *8*, 1, 34, 36, 40, 43.

Dunn, R. and Carbo, M. Modalities: An open letter to Walter Barbe, Michael Milone, and Raymond Swassing. *Educational Leadership*. Alexandria, Virginia: Association for Supervision and Curriculum Development, February 1981, *38*, 5, 381–382.

Dunn, R., Carbo, M., and Burton, E. Breakthrough: How to improve early reading instruction. *Phi Delta Kappan*. May 1981, *62*, 9, 675.

Dunn, R. and Dunn K. *Teaching students through their individual learning styles*. Reston, Va.: Reston Publishing Co., Inc., 1978.

Fernald, G. Remedial techniques in basic school subjects. New York: McGraw-Hill, 1943.

Ingersoll, G. M. and DiVesta, F. J. Effects of modality preferences on learning and recall of bisensory stimuli. *Perception and Psychophysics*, 1974, *15*, 73–78.

Lilly, S. M. and Kelleher, J. Modality strengths and aptitude-treatment interaction. *Journal of Special Education*, 1973, *7*, 5–13.

Oexle, J. E. and Zenhausern, R. Differential hemispheric activation in good and poor readers. *International Journal of Neuroscience*, 1981, *15*, 31–36.

Orton, S. T. *Reading, Writing, and Speech Problems in Children*. New York: W. W. Norton & Co., Inc., 1937.

Price, G., Dunn, R., and Sanders, W. Reading achievement and learning styles. *The Clearinghouse*. Washington, D. C.: Heldref Publications, January 1981, *54*, 5, 223–226.

Purnick, J. Little decrease is found in school dropout rate. *New York Times*, March 15, 1983, B1; B4.

Reading Style Inventory® (RSI) (Carbo, 1981), for students in grades 1-12. Available through: Learning Research Associates,

Box 39, Roslyn Hts., NY, 11577. Specimen set $14.00 (includes postage).

Restak, R. The other difference between boys and girls. *Student Learning Styles: Diagnosing and Prescribing Programs*. New York: National Association of Secondary School Principals, 1979, 75–80.

Trautman, P. An investigation of the relationship between selected instructional techniques and identified cognitive style. Doctoral Dissertation, St. John's University, 1979.

Urbschat, K. A study of preferred learning modes and their relationship to the amount of recall of cvc trigrams. Doctoral Dissertation, Wayne State University, 1977.

Walters, R. H. and Kosowski, I. Symbolic learning and reading retardation. *Journal of Consulting Psychology*, 1963, 27, 75–82.

Wepman, J. M. and Morency, A. S. Perceptual development and learning: An experimental study on modality reading instruction. Section II. First report. U.S. Department of Health, Education and Welfare, 1975. (ERIC Document Reproduction Service No. ED 125 164).

Wheeler, R. An investigation of the degree of academic achievement evidenced when second grade, learning disabled students' preferences are matched and mismatched with complementary sensory approaches to beginning reading instruction. Doctoral Dissertation, St. John's University, 1983.

Chapter 4

Adams, D. Implementing the Reading Styles Inventory: The Juanita project. Paper presented at Teaching Reading through Individual Reading Styles, in-service course for the Spokane Public Schools, August 1983.

Ashton-Warner, S. *Teacher*. New York: Simon and Schuster, 1963.

Bloomfield, L. Linguistics and reading. *Elementary English Review*, 1942, *19*, 125–130; 183–186.

Burton, E. An analysis of the interaction of field independence/field dependence and

word type as they affect word recognition among kindergartners. Doctoral Dissertation, St. John's University, New York, 1980.

Carbo, M. Teaching reading with talking books. *The Reading Teacher*. Newark, Delaware: International Reading Association, December 1978, *32*, 267–273.

Carbo, M. Matching reading method and learning style. *Learning Styles Network Newsletter*. New York: National Association of Secondary School Principals and St. John's University, Winter 1980(a), *1*, 1, 5.

Carbo, M. Reading style: Diagnosis, evaluation, prescription. *Academic Therapy*, September 1980(b), *16*, 1, 45–52./

Carbo, M. *Reading Style Inventory Manual*. New York: Learning Research Associates, 1981.

Carbo, M. Teaching reading the way children learn to read. *Early Years*. Darien, Conn.: Allen Raymond, Inc., February 1982(a), *12*, 6, 43–47.

Carbo, M. Reading style: Key to preventing reading failure. *Student Learning Styles and Brain Behavior*. Virginia: National Association of Secondary School Principals, 1982(b), Chapter 13.

Carbo, M. Reading style: Help a fairy tale come true. *Early Years*. Darien, Conn.: Allen Raymond, Inc., November 1983, *14*, 3, 10–15.

Carbo, M. You can identify reading styles . . . and then design a super reading program. *Early Years*. Allen Raymond, Inc., April 1984 (a), *14*, 8, 80–83.

Carbo, M. Why most reading tests aren't fair. *Early Years K/8*. Darien, Conn.: Allen Raymond, Inc., May 1984(b) *14*, 9, 73–75.

Carbo, M. Advanced book recording: Turning it around for poor readers. *Early Years K/8*. Darien, Conn.: Allen Raymond, Inc., 1985, *15*, 5, 46–48.

Dunn, R. and Dunn, K. *Teaching Students Through Their Individual Learning Styles*. Englewood Cliffs, New Jersey: Prentice-Hall, Inc., 1978.

Fernald, G. *Remedial Techniques in Basic School Subjects*. New York: McGraw-Hill, 1943.

Fries, C. C. *Linguistics and Reading*. New York: Holt, Rinehart, and Winston, 1962.

Gillingham, A. and Stillman, B. *Remedial teaching for children with specific disability in reading, spelling and penmanship*. Cambridge, Mass.: Educator's Publishing Service, 1968.

Glass, G. *Teaching decoding as separate from reading*. Garden City, New York: Adelphi University Press, 1973.

Glass, G. and Burton E. How do they decode? Verbalizations and observed behaviors of successful decoders. *Education*, 1973, *94*, 58–63.

Goodman, K. S. and Goodman, Y. M. Learning to read is natural. *Theory and Practice of Early Reading, Volume 1*. New Jersey: Lawrence Erlbaum Associates, 1979, 137–154.

Harris, A. J. *Effective Teaching of Reading*. New York: David McKay Co., Inc., 1962.

Heckelman, R. G. The neurological impress method of remedial reading instruction. *Academic Therapy*, 1969, *4*, 277–282.

Jansson D. R. and Schillereff T. A. Reinforcing remedial readers through art activities. *The Reading Teacher*, February 1981, *33*, 548–551.

Moore, J. T. A systems approach to individualizing reading. *The Reading Teacher*, May 1979, *32*, 951–955.

Oexle, J. E. and Zenhausern, R. Differential hemispheric activation in good and poor readers. *International Journal of Neuroscience*, 1981, *15*, 31–36.

Orton S. T. *Reading, Writing, and Speech Problems in Children*. New York: W. W. Norton & Co., Inc., 1937.

Policies for the development of written individualized programs, Editorial, *Exceptional Children*, 1977, *8*, 544–555.

Raabe, J. A. *Hop On Hop Off*. Cleveland: Modern Curriculum Press, 1974.

Reading Style Inventory® (Carbo, 1981) for students in grades 1–12. Available through: Learning Research Associates, Box 39, Roslyn Hts., NY, 11577. Specimen set $14.00 (includes postage).

Rasmussen and Goldberg, *A Pig Can Jig*.

Chicago, Ill.: Science Research Associates, 1964.

Stauffer, R.G. *The language experience approach to the teaching of reading*. New York: Harper and Row, 1980.

Sinatra, R. and Stahl-Gemake, J. *Using the Right Brain in the Language Arts*. Springfield, Ill.: Charles C. Thomas, 1983.

Chapter 5

Aaron, E. E. et al. Studybook for *Ride The Sunrise*. Glenview, Illinois: Scott, Foresman and Company, 1981.

Aaron, E. E. et al. *Taking Off*. Glenview, Illinois: Scott, Foresman and Company, 1981.

Carbo, M. *Practical Ideas For Using Activity Cards*. New York: World Record Publications, 1976.

Carbo, M. Teaching reading the way children learn to read. *Early Years*. Darien, Conn.: Allen Raymond, Inc., February 1982, *12*, 6, 43–47.

Carbo, M. Reading styles change from second to eighth grade. *Educational Leadership*. Alexandria, Virginia: Association for Supervision and Curriculum Development, February 1983(a), *40*, 5, 56–59.

Carbo, M. Research in reading and learning style: Implications for exceptional children. *Exceptional Children*. Reston, Virginia: Council for Exceptional Children, April 1983(b), *49*, 6, 486–494.

Carbo, M. Reading style: Help a fairy tale come true. *Early Years*. Darien, Conn.: Allen Raymond, Inc., November 1983(c), *14*, 3, 10–16.

Carbo, M. Why most reading tests aren't fair. *Early Years K/8*. Darien, Conn.: Allen Raymond, Inc., May 1984(a) *14*, 9, 73–75.

Carbo, M. How to start your own super reading styles program. *Early Years K/8*. Darien, Conn.: Allen Raymond, Inc., 1984(b), *15*, 2, 46–48.

Carbo, M. and Burton, E. Selection guide for matching reading materials and reading styles. *Reading Style Inventory Manual.* New York: Learning Research Associates, 1981, 45–53.

Carbo, M. and Carbo, N. *Building Vocabulary.* New York: World Record Publications, 1980(a).

Carbo, M. and Carbo, N. *Reading Comprehension.* New York: World Record Publications, 1980(b).

Clymer, T. et al. Studybook for *Ride The Sunrise.* Lexington, Mass.: Ginn and Company, 1982.

Carus, M. et al. *On a Blue Hill.* LaSalle, Ill.: Open Court Publishing Company, 1982.

Comprehension Power. St. Louis, Mo.: Milliken Publishing Company.

Durkin, D. Some questions about questionable instructional materials. *The Reading Teacher,* October 1974, *28,* 13–18.

Engelmann S. and Bruner, E. C. *Distar® Reading I.* Chicago, Ill.: Science Research Associates, 1969.

Glass, G. *Glass-Analysis For Decoding Only.* New York: Easier-to-Learn, Inc.

Goodlad, J. *Behind the Classroom Door.* Worthington, Ohio: Charles Jones Publishing, 1970.

Kansas discovers reading materials mismatch students' styles. *Learning Styles Network Newsletter.* Autumn, 1983, *4,* 3, 6.

Language Experiences in Reading (LEIR). Chicago, Ill.: Encyclopedia Britannica Educational Corporation.

Maxwell, M. and Zenhausern, R. Teaching reading disabled readers by eliminating the necessity for a grapheme to phoneme conversion. Paper presented at the Eastern Psychological Association Convention.

Moray, G. What does research say about the reading interests of children in the intermediate grades? *The Reading Teacher.* Newark, Delaware: International Reading Association, April 1978, *31,* 7, 763–768.

Oexle, J. E. and Zenhausern, R. Differential hemispheric activation in good and poor readers. *International Journal of Neuroscience,* 1981, *15,* 31–36.

Rasmussen, D. and Goldberg, L. *A Pig Can Jig.* Chicago, Illinois: Science Research Associates, 1964.

Rosecky, M. Are teachers selective when using basal guidebooks? *The Reading Teacher,* January 1978, *31,* 381–385.

Stanchfield, J. M. and Fraim, S. R. A follow-up study on the reading interests of boys. *Journal of Reading,* May 1979, 748–752.

Stauffer, R.G. *The language experience approach to the teaching of reading.* New York: Harper and Row, 1980.

Sullivan. *Programmed Reading.* New York: McGraw-Hill Book Company, 1963.

Chapter 6

Barchas, S. E. *I Was Walking Down the Road.* New York, N. Y.: Scholastic, 1975.

Carbo, M. *Practical Ideas For Using Activity Cards.* New York: World Record Publications, 1976.

Carbo, M. A word imprinting technique for children with severe memory disorders. *Teaching Exceptional Children,* Fall 1978(a), *11,* 1, 3–5.

Carbo, M. Teaching reading with talking books. *The Reading Teacher,* December 1978(b), *32,* 267–273.

Carbo, M. How to play with a book. *Early Years.* Darien, Conn.: Allen Raymond, Inc. February 1979, *9,* 6, 68; 72–74.

Carbo, M. Making books talk to children. *The Reading Teacher,* November 1981, *35,* 2, 186–189.

Carbo, M. Teaching reading the way children learn to read. *Early Years.* Darien, Conn.: Allen Raymond, Inc., February 1982, *12,* 6, 43–47.

Carbo, M. Recorded books=remarkable reading gains. *Early Years K/8.* Darien, Conn.: Allen Raymond, Inc., 1984, *15,* 3, 44–47.

Carbo, M. Advanced book recording: Turning it around for poor readers. *Early Years K/8.* Darien, Conn.: Allen Raymond, Inc., 1985, *15,* 5, 46–48.

Ceprano, M. A. A review of selected research on methods of teaching sight words. *The Reading Teacher,* December 1981, *35,* 3, 314–322.

Chomsky, C. After decoding, what? *Language Arts,* 1976, *53,* 288–296.

Dobrin, A. *Gerbils*. New York: Scholastic Book Services, 1971.

Flack, M. *The Story About Ping*. New York: Scholastic Book Services, 1961.

Gag, W. *Millions of Cats*. London, Eng.: Faber & Faber, Ltd., 1929.

Goodman, K. Reading: The key is in the children's language. *The Reading Teacher*, March 1972, *25*, 505–506.

Hart, L. Programs, patterns and downshifting in learning to read. *The Reading Teacher*, October 1983, *37*, 1, 5–11.

Hodges, H. Using the RSI with junior high poor readers. Report presented at the Sixth Annual Conference on Teaching Students Through Their Individual Learning Styles, New York, July 1983.

Kimura, D. Left differences in the perception of melodies. *Quarterly Journal of Experimental Psychology*, 1964, 16, 355.

King, F. L. and Kimura, D. Left-ear superiority in dichotic perception of vocal nonverbal sounds, *Com. Journal of Psychology*, 1972, *26*, 111.

Krauss, R. *The Happy Egg*. New York: Scholastic Book Services, 1967.

Lauritzen, C. Oral literature and the teaching of reading. *The Reading Teacher*. April 1980, *33*, 7, 787–790.

Reisberg, L. E. Individual differences in learning disabled students' use of contextual cuing. *Learning Disability Quarterly*, Spring 1982, *5*, 2, 91–99.

Stanchfield, J. M. Do girls learn to read better than boys in the primary grades? In *New Directions in Reading*. New York: Bantam Books, Inc., 1967, 60–61.

Vernon, M. D. *The Psychology of Perception*. Baltimore, Maryland: Penguin Books, 1962.

Warner, S. A. *Teacher*. New York: Simon and Schuster, 1964.

Notes

Davis, J. Personal letter to Marie Carbo, February 25, 1983.

LaShell, L. Personal letter to Marie Carbo, March 12, 1983.

Chapter 7

Barchas, S. E. I Was Walking Down the Road. New York: Scholastic Books, 1975.

Bishop, C. H. and Wiese, K. *The Five Chinese Brothers*. New York: Scholastic Books, 1967.

Bruno, A. and Jessie, K. Hands-on activities for children's writing. Prentice-Hall, 1983.

Carbo, Marie. How to play with a book. *Early Years K/8*. Darien, Connecticut: Allen Raymond, Inc., February 1979, 9, 6, 68–73.

Carbo, Marie. Teaching reading the way children learn to read. *Early Years*. Darien, Conn.: Allen Raymond, Inc., February 1982, 12, 6, 43–47.

Dunn, R. and Bruno, A. Learning through the tactual/kinesthetic senses. *Momentum*, Washington, D. C.: National Catholic Association, December, 1982, 10, *4*, 40–42.

Dunn, R. and Dunn K. Teaching students through their individual learning styles: A practical approach. Reston, Va.: Reston Publishing Company, Inc., 1978(a).

Dunn, R. and Dunn, K. How to create hands-on materials. *Instructor*. Dansville, New York: Instructor Publications, March, 1978(b), 7, *LXXXX*, 134–141.

Gardiner, B. Designing tactile/kinesthetic materials. Teaching students through their individual learning styles: A practical approach. New York: Leadership training conference, July, 1983, 115–119.

Moore, Eva. *Dick Whittington and his Cat*. New Jersey: Scholastic Books, 1974.

Stevenson, Robert L. *Dr. Jekyl and Mr. Hyde*. New Jersey: Scholastic Books, 1963.

Woods, B. *My Box and String*. New York: Scholastic Books, 1963.

Chapter 8

Dunn, R. and Dunn, K. Teaching students through their individual learning styles. Reston, Va.: Reston Publishing Company, Inc., 1978.

Poirier, G. A. Students' partners in team learning. Berkeley, Ca.: Center of Team Learning, 1970.

Scribner, H. B. Make your schools work. NY: Simon and Schuster, 1975.

Appendix A

UNIVERSITY RESEARCH CONDUCTED WITH THE LEARNING STYLE INVENTORY

Cody, C. Learning styles, including hemispheric dominance: A comparative study of average, gifted, and highly gifted students in grades five through twelve. Doctoral dissertation, Temple University, 1983.

Copenhaver, R. The consistency of student learning styles as students move from English to mathematics. Doctoral dissertation, Indiana University, 1979.

Cupke, L. F. The effects of similarity of instructor preferred teaching style and student preferred learning style on student achievement in selected courses in a metropolitan community college. Doctoral dissertation, University of Missouri-Kansas City, 1980.

Dean, W. L. A comparison of the learning styles of educable mentally retarded students and learning disabled students. Doctoral dissertation, The University of Mississippi, 1982.

Della Valle, J. An experimental investigation of the relationship(s) between preference for mobility and the word recognition scores of seventh grade students to provide supervisory and administrative guidelines for the organization of effective instructional environments. Doctoral dissertation, St. John's University. Recipient: Phi Delta Kappa National Award for Outstanding Doctoral Research, 1985; National Association of Secondary School Principals' Middle School Research Finalist Citation, 1984; and Association for Supervision and Curriculum Development National Finalist Award for Research in Supervision, 1985.

DeBello, T. A critical analysis of the effects on achievement and attitudes of administrative assignments to social studies instruction based on individual eighth grade students' learning style preferences for learning alone, with peers, or with teachers. Doctoral dissertation, St. John's University, 1985.

Freeley, M. E. An experimental investigation of the relationships among teachers' individual time preferences, inservice workshop schedules, and instructional techniques and the subsequent implementation of learning style strategies in participants' classrooms. Doctoral dissertation, St. John's University, 1984.

Hodges, H. An analysis of the relationships among preferences for a formal/informal design, one element of learning style, academic achievement, and attitudes of seventh and eighth grade students in remedial mathematics classes in a New York City alternative junior high school. Doctoral dissertation, St. John's University, 1985.

Johnson, C. D. Identifying potential school dropouts. Doctoral dissertation, United States International University, 1984.

Kaley, S. B. Field dependence/independence and learning styles in sixth graders. Doctoral dissertation, Hofstra University, 1977.

Kreitner, K. R. Modality strengths and learning styles of musically talented high school students. Master's dissertation, Ohio State University, 1981.

Krimsky, J. A comparative analysis of the effects of matching and mismatching fourth grade students with their learning style preferences for the environmental element of light and their subsequent reading speed and accuracy scores. Doctoral dissertation, St. John's University. Recipient: Association for Supervision and Curriculum Development First Alternate National Recognition for Best Doctoral Research, 1982.

Kroon, D. K. An experimental investigation of the effects on academic achievement and the resultant administrative implications of instruction, congruent and incongruent with secondary, industrial arts students' identified learning style perceptual preferences. Doctoral dissertation, St. John's University, 1985.

Kulp, J. J. A description of the processes used in developing and implementing a teacher training program based on the Dunns' concept of learning style. Doctoral dissertation, Temple University, 1982.

Learning style inventory (Dunn, Dunn, and Price, 1974, 1979, 1981, 1985). For grades 3–12. Available from Price Systems, Box 3067, Lawrence, KS 66044.

Legal, O. Analysis of the preferred learning styles of former adolescent psychiatric patients. Doctoral Dissertation, Kansas State University, 1983.

Lynch, P. K. An analysis of the relationships among academic achievement, attendance, and the individual learning style time preferences of eleven–twelfth grade students identified as initial or chronic truants in a suburban New York school district. Doctoral dissertation, St. John's University, 1981. Recipient: Association for Supervision and Curriculum Development National Finalist Award (Supervision) 1981.

MacMurren, H. A comparative study of the effects of matching and mismatching sixth grade students with their learning style preferences for the physical element of intake and their subsequent reading speed and accuracy scores and attitudes. Doctoral dissertation, St. John's University, 1985.

Murrain, P. G. Administrative determinations concerning facilities utilization and instructional grouping: An analysis of the relationship(s) between selected thermal environments and preferences for temperature, an element of learning style, as they affect word recognition scores of secondary students. Doctoral dissertation, St. John's University, 1983.

Murray, C. A. The comparison of learning styles between low and high reading achievement subjects in the seventh and eighth grades in a public middle school. Doctoral dissertation, United States International University, 1980.

Pizzo, J. An investigation of the relationships between selected acoustic environments and sound, an element of learning style, as they affect sixth grade students' reading achievement and attitudes. Doctoral dissertation, St. John's University. Recipient: Association for Supervision and Curriculum Development First Alternate National Recognition for Best Doctoral Research, 1981.

Ramirez, A. I. Modality and field dependence/

independence: Learning style components and their relationship to mathematics achievement in the elementary school. Doctoral dissertation, Florida State University, 1982.

Roberts, O. A. Investigation of the relationship between learning style and temperament of senior high school students in the Bahamas and Jamaica. Graduate research, Andrews University, 1984.

Ricca, J. Curricular implications of learning style differences between gifted and nongifted students. Doctoral dissertation, State University of New York at Buffalo, 1983.

Shea, T. C. An investigation of the relationship among preferences for the learning style element of design, selected instructional environments, and reading achievement of ninth grade students to improve administrative determinations concerning effective educational facilities. Doctoral dissertation, St. John's University. Recipient: National Association of Secondary School Principals' Middle School Research Finalist Citation, 1984.

Spires, R. D. The effect of teacher inservice about learning styles on students' mathematics and reading achievement. Doctoral dissertation, Bowling Green State University, 1983.

Steinauer, M. H. Interpersonal relationships as reflected in learning style preferences: A study of eleventh grade students and their English teachers in a vocational school. Doctoral dissertation, Southern Illinois University, 1981.

Tappenden, V. J. Analysis of the learning styles of vocational education and nonvocational education students in eleventh and twelfth grades from rural, urban, and suburban locations in Ohio. Doctoral dissertation, Kent State University, 1983.

Vigna, R. A. An investigation of learning styles of gifted and nongifted high school students. Doctoral dissertation, University of Houston, 1983.

Wheeler, R. An investigation of the degree of academic achievement evidenced when second grade, learning disabled students' perceptual preferences are matched and mismatched with complementary sensory approaches to beginning reading instruction. Doctoral dissertation, St. John's University, 1983.

White, R. An investigation of the relationship between selected instructional methods and selected elements of emotional learning style upon student achievement in seventh grade social studies. Doctoral dissertation, St. John's University. Recipient: Delta Kappa Gamma International Award for Best Research Prospectus, 1980.

Wingo, L. H. Relationships among locus of motivation, sensory modality and grouping preferences of learning style to basic skills test performance in reading and mathematics. Doctoral dissertation, Memphis State University, 1980.

Wolfe, G. Learning styles and the teaching of reading. Doctoral dissertation, Akron University, 1983.

Virostko, J. An analysis of the relationships among academic achievement in mathematics and reading, assigned instructional schedules, and the learning style time preferences of third, fourth, fifth, and sixth grade students. Doctoral dissertation, St. John's University. Recipient: Kappa Delta Pi International Award for Best Doctoral Research, 1983.

Appendix B

Adams, D. Implementing the Reading Styles Inventory: The Juanita project. Paper presented at Teaching Reading Through Individual Reading Styles, inservice course for the Spokane Public Schools, August 1983.

Adams, D. Visual and tactual integration and cerebral dysfunction in children with learning disabilities. *Journal of Learning Disabilities*, 1978, *11*, 197–204.

A directory of learning/teaching style practitioners. Compiled for the Learning/Teaching Style Subcommittee of the Curriculum Study Committee of the Association for Supervision and Curriculum Development, March 1983.

Bakker, D. J. Sensory dominance in normal and backward readers. *Perceptual and Motor Skills*, 1966, *23*, 1055–1058.

Beery, J. W. Matching of auditory and visual stimuli by average and retarded readers. *Child Development*, 1967, 38, 827–833.

Birch, H. G. and Belmont, L. Auditory-visual integration, intelligence and reading ability in school children. *Perceptual and Motor Skills*, 1965, *20*, 295–305.

Carbo, M. *Reading Style Inventory Manual.* New York: Learning Research Associates, 1981.

Carbo, M. Reading style: Key to preventing reading failure. *Student Learning Styles and Brain Behavior.* Virginia: National Association of Secondary School Principals, 1982. Chapter 13.

Carbo, M. Reading styles change from second to eighth grade. *Educational Leadership.* Alexandria, Virginia: Association for Supervision and Curriculum Development, February 1983(a), *40*, 5, 56–59.

Carbo, M. Research in reading and learning style: Implications for exceptional children. *Exceptional Children.* Reston, Virginia: Council for Exceptional Children, April 1983(b), *49*, 6, 486–494.

Carbo, M. *Reading Style Inventory Research Supplement.* New York: Learning Research Associates, 1983(c).

Carbo, M. Research in learning style and reading: Implications for instruction. *Theory Into Practice.* Columbus, Ohio: Ohio State University, Winter 1984 (a), 72–76.

Carbo, M. Five schools try reading styles programs . . . and see how their kids have grown! *Early Years.* Allen Raymond Publishers, September 1984(b), *15*, 1, 52–60.

Carbo, M. Reading styles: How principals can make a difference. *Principal.* National Association of Elementary Principals, September 1984(c), *64*, 1, 20–26.

Daniel, P. N. and Tacker, R. S. Preferred modality of stimulus input and memory for cvc trigrams. *Journal of Educational Research*, 1974, *67*, 255–258.

Dixon, G. A specialist's reading of the Carbo reading style inventory. Report for the 1982–1983 Model Schools Learning Style Project. Columbia, Maryland: Howard County Schools, 1983.

Dunn, R. and Carbo, M. Modalities: An open letter to Walter Barbe, Michael Milone and Raymond Swassing. *Educational Leadership.* Virginia: Association for Supervision and Curriculum Development, February, 1981, *38*, 5, 381–382.

Dunn, R. and Reckinger, N. Learning styles. *Educational Leadership.* Virginia: Association for Supervision and Curriculum Development, October 1981, *39*, 1, 75–76.

Freeley, M. E. *Learning Style Network's Instrumentation Assessment Analysis, an Interim Report.* New York: National Association of Secondary School Principals and St. John's University, 1983.

Gale, A. and Lynn, R. A developmental study of attention. *British Journal of Educational Psychology,* 1972, *42*, 290–266.

Hamilton, S. Reading styles: an experiment with sixth grade, poor readers. A report for the Norton, Ohio Public Schools, May 1983.

Heathington, B. S. What to do about reading motivation in the middle school. *Journal of Reading.* Newark, Delaware: International Reading Association, April 1978, *31*, 7, 763–768.

Heckerl, J. R. Integration and ordering of bisensory stimuli in dyslexic children (Doctoral dissertation, University of Michigan, 1971). *Dissertation Abstracts International,* 1972, *32/08-A.* (University Microfilms No. 72-4897).

Hodges, H. Using the RSI with junior high poor readers. Presentation delivered at the Fortieth National Conference of the Association for Supervision and Curriculum Development, Chicago, March 1984; and at the National Reading Styles Conference, New York City, July 1985.

Hutchinson public schools, reading support program: end-of-year report. Hutchinson, Kansas: Roosevelt School, May 1983.

Johnson, C. S. and Greenbaum, G. R. Are boys disabled readers due to sex-role stereotyping? *Educational Leadership.* Alexandria, Virginia: Association for Supervision and Curriculum Development, March 1980, *37*, 6, 492–496.

Kansas discovers reading materials mismatch students' styles. *Learning Styles Network Newsletter.* New York: National Association of Secondary School Principals and St. John's University, Autumn, 1983, *4*, 3, 6.

Kerlinger, F. N. *Foundations of Behavioral Research.* New York: Holt, Rinehart and Winston, Inc., 1973.

Koch, C. A. A comparison of responses of poor, average and good readers with the reading style inventory. Masters thesis, Emporia State University, 1983.

LaShell, L. Teaching handicapped children to read through their individual reading styles. Report presented at Seattle-Pacific University course, Teaching Reading Through Individual Learning Styles, Seattle, Washington, April 1983.

LaShell, L. An analysis of the effects of reading methods on reading achievement and locus of control when individual reading style is matched for learning disabled students. Doctoral dissertation, Fielding University, 1985.

Lemmon, P. Reading style: increasing the reading achievement of remedial reading students. Presentation delivered at Sixth Annual Conference on Teaching Students Through Their Individual Learning Styles, New York, July 1983.

Mills, R. E. An evaluation of techniques for teaching word recognition. *Elementary School Journal,* 1956, *56*, 221–225.

Morency, A. Auditory modality-research and practice. In H. K. Smith (Ed.) *Perception and Reading.* Newark, Delaware: International Reading Association, 1968.

Moray, G. What does research say about the reading interests of children in the intermediate grades? *The Reading Teacher.* Newark, Delaware: International Reading Association, April 1978, *31*, 7, 763–768.

Murray, A. C. The comparison of learning styles between low and high reading achievement subjects in the seventh and eighth grades in a public middle school. Doctoral dissertation, United States International University, 1980.

Network undertakes instrument classification system. *Learning Styles Network Newsletter.* New York: National Association of Secondary School Principals and St. John's University, Winter 1982, *3*, 1, 1.

Price, G., Dunn, R., and Sanders, W. Reading achievement and learning styles. *The Clearing House.* Washington, D.C. Heldref Publications, January 1980, 54, 5, 223–226.

Reading Style Inventory® (Carbo, 1979, 1981, 1982) for students in grades 3–12. Available through: Learning Research Associates, Box 39, Roslyn Hts., N.Y., 11577. Specimen set $14.00 (includes postage).

Selecting the "right" reading approach, Step 1: learning style analysis. *Learning Style Network Newsletter.* New York: National Association of Secondary School Principals and St. John's University, Winter 1981, *2*, 1, 8.

Stanchfield J. M. and Fraim, S. R. A follow-up study on the reading interests of boys. *Journal of Reading,* May 1979, 748–752.

Sudzina, M. An investigation of the relationship between the reading styles of second graders and their achievement in three different basal reader programs. Doctoral dissertation, Temple University, 1986.

The Juanita project. Kirkland, Wa.: Lake Washington School District, June 1983.

Walters, R. H. and Kosowski, I. Symbolic learning and reading retardation. *Journal of Consulting Psychology,* 1963, *27*, 75–82.

Wepman, J. M. and Morency, A. S. Perceptual development and learning: An experimental study on modality reading instruction. Section II. Final report. U.S. Department of Health, Education and Welfare, 1975. (ERIC Document Reproduction Service No. ED 125 164).

Which learning style elements are stable and which tend to change? *Learning Styles Network Newsletter.* New York: National Association of Secondary School Principals and St. John's University, Autumn, 1980, *1*, 3, 1.

Zenhausern, R., Dunn, R., Cavanaugh, D. P., and Eberle, B. M. Do left and right "brained" students learn differently? *Roeper Review,* September 1981, *4*, 1, 36–39.

Bibliography

Ball, A. L. The secrets of learning styles—your child's and your own. *Redbook*, November, 1982: 73–6.

Brennan, P. K. Teaching to the whole brain. *Student Learning Styles and Brain Behavior*, Reston, Virginia: National Association of Secondary School Principals, 212–213.

Bruno, A. Designing learning activities for the tactual learner. *Student Learning Styles and Brain Behavior*, Reston, Virginia: National Association of Secondary School Principals, 25–27.

Bruno, A. and Jessie, K. Hands-on activities for children's writing: *Innovative learning style resources*, Englewood Cliffs, New Jersey, 1983.

Burton, E. B. An analysis of the interactions of field independence/dependence and word type as they affect word recognition among kindergartners. Unpublished Doctoral dissertation, St. John's University, 1980.

Cafferty, E. An analysis of student performance based upon the degree of match between the educational cognitive style of the teachers and the educational cognitive style of the students. Unpublished Doctoral dissertation, University of Nebraska, 1980.

Carbo, M. *Practical Ideas For Using Activity Cards.* New York: World Record Publications, 1976.

Carbo, M. A word imprinting technique for children with severe memory disorders. *Teaching Exceptional Children.* Reston, Virginia: Council for Exceptional Children, Fall 1978(a), 11, 1, 3–5.

Carbo, M. Teaching reading with talking books. *The Reading Teacher.* Newark, Delaware: International Reading Association, December 1978(b), 32, 267–273. Reprinted in: *Education Digest.* Ann Arbor, Michigan: Prakken Publications, Inc., April 1979, 44, 8, 60–63. *Meeting the Needs of the Handicapped.* C. H. Thomas and J. L. Thomas (Eds.) Phoenix, Arizona: Oryx Press, 1980, 96–103.

Carbo, M. Wooing the Unwooable Parent. *Instructor.* Dansville, New York: Harcourt, Brace, Jovanovich, November 1978(c), 88, 4, 84; 86; 89.

Carbo M. How to play with a book. *Early Years.* Darien, Conn.: Allen Raymond, Inc. February 1979(a), 9, 6, 68, 72–74.

Carbo, M. Matching reading method and learning style. *Learning Styles Network Newsletter.* New York: National Association of Secondary School Principals and St. John's University, Winter 1980(a), 1, 1, 5.

Carbo, M. An analysis of the relationships between the modality preferences of kindergartners and selected reading treatments as they affect the learning of a basic sight-word vocabulary (Doctoral dissertation, St. John's University, New York, 1980). *Dissertation Abstracts International,* 1980(b), 41/04A, 1389. (University Microfilms No. 80-21790). Recipient: Association for Supervision and Curriculum Development Award for Best Doctoral Research, 1980.

An extensive *annotated* bibliography is available for $12.00 from the Learning Styles Network, St. John's University, Grand Central Parkway, Jamaica, New York 11439.

Carbo, M. Reading style: Diagnosis, evaluation, prescription. *Academic Therapy,* September 1980(c), 16, 1, 45–52. Abstracted in: Perceptions, Milburn, New Jersey: Perceptions, Inc., February 1981, 3, 6, 7.

Carbo, M. Learning style: Key to understanding the learning disabled. *Learning Styles Network Newsletter.* New York: National Association of Secondary School Principals and St. John's University, Autumn 1981(a), 2, 3, 5.

Carbo, M. *Reading Style Inventory Manual.* New York: Learning Research Associates, 1981(b).

Carbo, M. Making books talk to children. *The Reading Teacher.* Newark, Delaware: International Reading Association, November 1981(c), 35, 2, 186–189.

Carbo, M. Selling poor readers on reading. *Educational Dealer.* Dayton, Ohio: Peter Li, Inc., July 1981 (d), 6, 1, 97.

Carbo, M. Be a master reading teacher. *Early Years.* Darien, Conn.: Allen Raymond, Inc., February 1982(a), 12, 6, 39–42, 47.

Carbo, M. Teaching reading the way children learn to read. *Early Years.* Darien, Conn.: Allen Raymond, Inc., February 1982(b), 12, 6, 43–47.

Carbo, M. Reading style: Key to preventing reading failure. *Student Learning Styles and Brain Behavior.* Virginia: National Association of Secondary School Principals, 1982(c), 126–135.

Carbo, M. Reading styles change from second to eighth grade. *Educational Leadership.* Alexandria, Virginia: Association for Supervision and Curriculum Development, February 1983(a), 40, 5, 56–59.

Carbo, M. Research in reading and learning style: Implications for exceptional children. *Exceptional Children.* Reston, Virginia: Council for Exceptional Children, April 1983(b), 49, 6, 486–494.

Carbo, M. Reading style: Help a fairy tale come true. *Early Years.* Darien Conn.: Allyn Raymond, Inc., November 1983(c), 14, 3, 10–16.

Carbo, M. *Reading Style Inventory Research Supplement.* New York: Learning Research Associates, 1983 (d).

Carbo, M. You can identify reading styles . . . and then design a super reading program. *Early Years,* Allen Raymond, Inc., April 1984(a), 14, 8, 80–83.

Carbo, M. Why most reading tests aren't fair. *Early Years.* Darien, Conn.: Allen Raymond, Inc., May 1984 (b) 14, 9, 73–75.

Carbo, M. Five schools try reading styles programs . . . and see how their kids have grown! *Early Years.* Allyn Raymond, Inc., September 1984(c), 15, 1, 52–60.

Carbo, M. Reading Styles: How principals can make a difference. *Principal.* National Association of Elementary School Principals, September 1984(d), 64, 1, 20–26.

Carbo, M. How to start your own super reading styles program. *Early Years.* Darien, Conn.: Allen Raymond, Inc., October, 1984 (e), 15, 2, 53–56.

Carbo, M. Recorded books = remarkable reading gains. *Early Years.* Darien, Conn.: Allen Raymond, Inc., 1984 (f), 15, 3, 44–47.

Carbo, M. Research in learning style and reading: Implications for instruction. *Theory Into Practice.* Columbus, Ohio: Ohio State University, Winter 1984(g), 72–76.

Carbo, M. *Reading Styles Inservice Packet.* New York: Learning Research Associates, 1984 (h).

Carbo, M. Advanced book recording: Turning it around for poor readers. *Early Years.* Darien, Conn.: Allen Raymond, Inc., 1985, 15, 5, 46–48.

Carbo, M. and Burton, E. Learning style: Application to reading instruction for the gifted. *Gifted/Talented Education,* Branford, Conn.: Gifted/Talented Education, Inc., December 1978 (a), 3, 6, 4b.

Carbo, M. and Burton, E. Selection guide for matching reading programs and reading styles. *Reading Style Inventory Manual.* New York: Learning Research Associates, 1981, pp. 45–53.

Cavanaugh, D. Student learning styles: A diagnostic/prescriptive approach to instruction. *Kappan,* November, 1981, 64(3), 202-3.

Cody, C. Learning styles, including hemispheric dominance: A comparative study of average, gifted, and highly gifted students in grades five through twelve. Unpublished doctoral dissertation, Temple University, 1983.

Dean, W. L. A comparison of the learning

styles of educable, mentally retarded students and learning disabled students. Doctoral dissertation. The University of Mississippi.

Della Valle, J. An experimental investigation of the relationship(s) between preference for mobility and the word recognition scores of seventh grade students to provide supervisory and administrative guidelines for the organization of effective instructional environments. Unpublished doctoral dissertation, St. John's University, 1984.

Dunn, K. Madison prep: Alternative to teenage disaster. *Educational Leadership*, February, 1981, 38(5), 386–7.

Dunn, K. What administrators should know about learning styles. *Catalyst*, Winter, 1982, 5, 2.

Dunn, K. Measuring the productivity styles of adults. *Student Learning Styles and Brain Behavior*. Reston, Virginia: National Association of Secondary School Principals, 136–142, Chapter 4.

Dunn, K. Small-group techniques for the middle school. *Early Years*, 15, 5 (January, 1985), 41–43.

Dunn, R. Looking into education's crystal ball. *Instructor*. Dansville, New York: Instructor Publications, August, 1977, l(LXXXVII), 39.

Dunn, R. Learning: a matter of style. *Educational Leadership*. Washington, D. C.: Association for Supervision and Curriculum Development, March, 1979, 430–432.

Dunn, R. Learning: A matter of style. Alexandria, Virginia: Association for Supervision and Curriculum Development Discussion Guide and Videotape, 1979.

Dunn, R. Teaching in a purple fog: What we don't know about learning styles. *NASSP Bulletin*. Reston, Virginia: National Association of Secondary School Principals, March, 1981, 33–36.

Dunn, R. A learning styles primer. *Principal*. Arlington, Virginia: National Association of Elementary School Principals, May, 1981, 31–34.

Dunn, R. The sum and substance of learning styles. *Early Years*. Darien, Connecticut: Allen Raymond, Inc., January, 1982, 12(5), 30–31, 80–82.

Dunn, R. Would you like to know your learning style—and how you can learn more and remember better than ever? *Early Years*. Darien, Connecticut: Allen Raymond, Inc., October, 1982, 13(2), 27–29, 70.

Dunn, R. Teaching students through their individual learning styles: A research report. *Student Learning Styles and Brain Behavior*. Reston, Virginia: National Association of Secondary School Principals, 1982, Chapter 15.

Dunn, R. Can students identify their own learning styles? *Educational Leadership*. Alexandria, Virginia: Association for Supervision and Curriculum Development, February, 1983, 40(5), 60–62.

Dunn, R. You've got style—now's the time to find out what it is. *Early Years*. Darien, Connecticut: Allen Raymond, Inc., January, 1983, 13(5), 25–31, 58–59.

Dunn, R. Now that you know your learning style—how can you make the most of it? *Early Years*. February, 1983, 13(6), 49–54.

Dunn, R. Now that you understand your learning style, what are you willing to do to teach your students through their individual styles? *Early Years*. Darien, Connecticut: Allen Raymond, Inc., March, 1983, 13(7), 41–43, 62.

Dunn, R. Learning style and its relationship to exceptionality at both ends of the spectrum. *Exceptional Children*. Reston, Virginia: The Council for Exceptional Children, April, 1983, 49 (6), 496–506.

Dunn, R. Learning style: State of the science. *Theory Into Practice*. Columbus, Ohio: The Ohio State University, Winter, 1984, 10–19.

Dunn, R. Teacher-made materials, In *Instructional Leadership Handbook*, Reston, Virginia: National Association of Secondary School Principals, 1984, 28–29.

Dunn, R. How should students do their homework? Research vs. opinion. *Early Years*, 1984, 15, 41, 43–45.

Dunn, R. and Bruno, A. Learning through the tactual/kinesthetic senses. *Momentum*. Washington, D. C.: National Catholic Education Association, December, 1982, XIII(4), 40–42.

Dunn, R., Bruno, A., and Gardiner, B. Put a cap on your gifted program. *Gifted Child Quarterly*. New York: The Association for Gifted Children, Spring, 1984, 28(2), 70–72.

Dunn, R. and Carbo, M. The reading gamble: How to increase the odds for every youngster. *Learning.* Palo Alto, California: Education Today Co., Inc., August/September, 1979, 8(1), 34–43.

Dunn, R. and Carbo, M. Modalities: An open letter to Walter Barbe, Michael Milone, and Raymond Swassing. *Educational Leadership.* Alexandria, Va.: Association for Supervision and Curriculum Development, February 1981, 38 (5), 381–382.

Dunn, R., Carbo, M., and Burton E. Breakthrough: How to improve early reading instruction. *Kappan.* Indiana: Phi Delta Kappa, May, 1981, 675.

Dunn, R., Cavanaugh, D., Eberle, B., and Zenhausern, R. Hemispheric preference: The newest element of learning style. *The American Biology Teacher.* Reston, Virginia: National Association of Biology Teachers, May, 1982, 44(5), 291–294.

Dunn, R., DeBello, T., Brennan, P., and Murrain, P. Learning style researchers define differences differently. *Educational Leadership,* February, 1981, 38(5), 372–5.

Dunn, R., Gregorc, A., Hunt, D., Kolb, D., et al. On mixing and matching of teaching and learning styles. *Practical Applications of the Research.* Bloomington, Indiana: Phi Delta Kappa's Center on Evaluation, Development and Research, December, 1980, 3(2), 1–4.

Dunn, R. and Griggs, S. A. Selected case studies of the learning style preferences of gifted students. *Gifted Child Quarterly,* 1984, 28, 3, 115–119.

Dunn, R. and Dunn, K. Seeing, hearing, moving, touching: Learning packages. *Teacher Magazine.* Greenwich, Connecticut: MacMillan Professional Magazine, Inc., May/June, 1977, 48–51.

Dunn, R. and Dunn, K. Be a better teacher: How to diagnose learning styles. *Instructor.* Dansville, New York: Instructor Publications, September, 1977, 2(LXXXVII), 122–144.

Dunn, R. and Dunn, K. How to redesign your classroom in approximately one hour. *Instructor.* Dansville, New York: Instructor Publications, October, 1977, 3(LXXXVII), 124–130.

Dunn, R. and Dunn, K. Educational accountability in our schools. *Momentum.* Washington, D. C.: National Catholic Educational Association, October, 1977, VIX(3), 10–16.

Dunn, R. and Dunn, K. *Administrator's guide to new programs for faculty management and evaluation.* West Nyack, New York: Parker Publishing Division of Prentice-Hall Publications, 1977.

Dunn, R. and Dunn, K. *Teaching students through their individual learning styles: A practical approach.* Reston, Virginia: Reston Publishing Company, 1978.

Dunn, R. and Dunn, K. How to create hands-on materials. *Instructor.* Dansville, New York: Instructor Publications, March, 1978, 7(LXXXX), 134–141.

Dunn, R. and Dunn, K. How to construct multisensory learning packages. *Instructor.* Dansville, New York: Instructor Publications, April, 1978, 8(LXXXXI), 90–99.

Dunn, R. and Dunn, K. Learning styles/teaching styles: Should they . . . can they . . . be matched? *Educational Leadership.* Washington, D. C.: Association for Supervision and Curriculum Development, January, 1979, 238–244.

Dunn, R. and Dunn, K. Learning styles—practical applications of the research. *Practical Applications of Research.* Bloomington, Indiana: Phi Delta Kappa's Center on Evaluation, Development and Research, March, 1979, 1(3), 2–3.

Dunn, R. and Dunn, K. Using learning style data to develop student prescriptions. *Students Learning Styles: Diagnosing and Prescribing Programs.* Reston, Virginia: National Association of Secondary School Principals, 1979, Chapter 12.

Dunn, R. and Dunn, K. What is your child's learning style. *Parenting.* Columbus, Ohio: The Newsletter of Parenting, January, 1980, 3(1), 4, 5, 8.

Dunn, R. and Dunn, K. Ten ways to make the classroom a better place to learn. *Instructor,* New York, 1984,4, XCIV, 84–88, 139.

Dunn, R., Dunn, K., and Freeley, M. E. Practical applications of the research: Responding to students' learning styles—step one. *Illinois School Research and Development Journal,* Normal: Illinois: Illinois State University: Illinois Association for Supervision and Curriculum Development, 1984, 21, 1, 1–21.

Dunn, R., Dunn, K., and Freeley, M. E. Tips to improve your inservice training: Know your learning style. *Early Years*, 15, 8 (April, 1985), 30–31.

Dunn, R., Dunn, K., and Price, G. E. Diagnosing learning styles: A prescription for avoiding malpractice suits against school systems. *Kappan*. Indiana: Phi Delta Kappa, January, 1977, 418–420.

Dunn, R. and Dunn, K. Identifying individual learning styles. *Student Learning Styles: Diagnosing and Prescribing Programs*. Reston, Virginia: National Association of Secondary School Principals, 1979, Chapter 4.

Dunn, R. and Dunn, K. Learning styles: Research versus opinion. *Kappan*. Indiana: Phi Delta Kappa, May, 1981, 645–646.

Dunn, R., Dunn, K., and Price, G. *Learning style inventory*, 1974, 1979, 1981, 1985). For grades 3–12. Available from Price Systems, Box 3067, Lawrence, KS 66044. Specimen set: $12.

Dunn, R. and Price, G. The learning style characteristics of gifted children. *Gifted Child Quarterly*. Arkansas: The Association for Gifted Children, Winter, 1980, 24(1), 33–36.

Dunn, R., Price, G. E., Bacilious, Z. and Zenhausern, R. Learning style—a predictor of school achievement? *Momentum.* Washington, D. C.: National Catholic Education Association, February, 1982, XIII(1), 47.

Dunn, R., Price, G. E., and Sanders, W. Reading achievement and learning styles. *The Clearing House*. Washington, D.C.: Heldref Publications, January, 1981, 54(5), 223–226.

Dunn, R., Dunn, K., Price, G. E., and Griggs, S. Studies in students' learning styles. *Roeper Review*. Bloomfield Hills, Michigan: Roeper City Country School, November, 1981, 4(2), 38–40.

Fiske, E. Teachers adjust schooling to fit students' individuality. *The New York Times*. December 29, 1981, CXXXI(45), 177, C4–5.

Freeley, M. E. Learning styles and computers: Do they mesh? *Early Years*. Connecticut: Allen Raymond, Inc., April, 1984, 14, *8*, 63, 68.

Freeley, M. E. An experimental investigation of the relationships among teachers' individual time preferences, inservice work-shop schedules, and instructional techniques and the subsequent implementation of learning style strategies in participants' classrooms. Doctoral dissertation, St. John's University, 1984.

Gardiner, B. Stepping into a learning styles program. *Roeper Review*. 1983, 6(2), 90–92.

Gardiner, B. These thinking caps are for real. *Early Years*. January, 1982, 12(5), 39–40.

Griggs, S. A. Counseling the gifted and talented based on learning styles. *Exceptional Children*, 1984, 429–432.

Griggs, S. A. Counseling middle school students for their individual learning styles. *Student Learning Styles and Brain Behavior*. Reston, Virginia: National Association of Secondary School Principals, 1982, 19–24.

Griggs, S. A. and Price, G. E. Learning styles of gifted versus average junior high school students. *Phi Delta Kappan*, 1980, (61), 361.

Griggs, S. A. and Price, G. E. Self-concept relates to learning style in the junior high school. *Phi Delta Kappan*, 1981, (62), 604.

Hart, L. A. *Human brain and human learning*. New York: Longman, 1983.

Hart, L. A. Programs, patterns, and downshifting in learning to read. *The Reading Teacher*, October, 1983, 37(1), 5–11.

Hodges, H. Madison prep: Alternatives through learning styles. *Learning Styles and Brain Behavior*. Reston, Virginia: National Association of Secondary School Principals, 1982, 28–32.

Hodges, H. An analysis of the relationships among preferences for a formal/informal design, one element of learning style, academic achievement, and attitudes of seventh and eighth grade students in remedial mathematics classes in a New York City alternative junior high school. Doctoral dissertation, St. John's University, 1985.

Jenkins, J. Teaching to individual student learning styles. *The Administrator*. Florida, September, 1982 7(1), 10–12.

Johnson, C. D. Identifying potential dropouts. Doctoral dissertation, United States International University, 1984.

Koch, C. A. A comparison of responses of

poor, average and good readers with the reading style inventory. Masters thesis, Emporia State University, 1983.

Krimsky, J. A comparative analysis of the effects of matching and mismatching fourth grade students with their learning style preferences for the environmental element of light and their subsequent reading speed and accuracy scores. Unpublished doctoral dissertation, St. John's University, 1982. Recipient, Association for Supervision and Curriculum Development First Alternate for Best Research Award, 1982.

Kulp, J. J. A description of the processes used in developing and implementing a teacher training program based on the Dunn's concept of learning style. Doctoral dissertation, Temple University, 1982.

LaShell, L. An analysis of the effects of reading methods on reading achievement and locus of control when individual reading style is matched for learning disabled students. Unpublished doctoral dissertation, Fielding University, 1985.

Learning style inventory (LSI) (Dunn, Dunn, & Price, 1974, 1979, 1981, 1985). For students in grades 3–12. Available from Price Systems, Box 3067, Lawrence, KS 66044.

Lee, B. and Rudman, M. K. *Leading to Reading.* New York: Berkley Publishing Company, 1983.

Lemmon, P. Step by step leadership into learning styles. *Early Years*, January, 1982, 12(5), 36, 14.

Lemmon, P. A school where learning styles make a difference. *Principal.* 64, 4 (March, 1985), 26–28.

Levy, Jerre. Children think with whole brains: Myth and reality. *Learning Styles and Brain Behavior.* Reston, Virginia: National Association of Secondary School Principals, 1982, 173–184.

Lynch, P. K. An analysis of the relationships among academic achievement, attendance, and the individual learning style time preferences of eleventh and twelfth grade students identified as initial or chronic truants in a suburban New York school district. Unpublished doctoral dissertation, St. John's University, 1981.

MacMurren, H. A comparative study of the effects of matching and mismatching sixth grade students with their learning style preference for the physical element of intake and their subsequent reading speed and accuracy scores and attitudes. Doctoral dissertation, St. John's University, 1985.

Martin, M. K. Effects of the interaction between students' learning styles and high school instructional environments. Unpublished doctoral dissertation, University of Oregon, 1977.

Murrain, P. G. Administrative determinations concerning facilities utilization and instructional grouping: An analysis of the relationship(s) between selected thermal environments and preferences for temperature, an element of learning style, as they affect word recognition scores of secondary students. Unpublished doctoral dissertation, St. John's University, 1983.

Murray, C. A. The comparison of learning styles between low and high reading achievement subjects in the seventh and eighth grades in a public middle school. Doctoral dissertation, Florida State University, 1982.

Perrin, J. An experimental investigation of the relationships among the learning style sociological preferences of gifted and nongifted primary children, selected instructional strategies, attitudes, and achievement in problem-solving and rote memorization. Doctoral dissertation, St. John's University, 1984.

Perrin, J. The identification of learning styles among young children. *Learning Styles and Brain Behavior.* Reston, Virginia: National Association of Secondary School Principals, 1982, 119–125.

Perrin, J. Who's learning how? *Early Years*, 1982, 12(5), 37–38, 61.

Pizzo, J. An investigation of the relationships between selected acoustic environments and sound, an element of learning style, as they affect sixth grade students' reading achievement and attitudes. Unpublished doctoral dissertation, St. John's University, 1981. Recipient: Association for Supervision and Curriculum Development First Alternate for Research Award, 1981.

Pizzo, J. Quiet versus sound: Under which conditions do your students work best? *Early Years*. Connecticut: Allen Raymond, Inc., 1982, 12(5), 32–33.

Pizzo, J. Small group techniques: Big gains in reading. *Early Years*, 1982, 12(9), 30–31, 72–74.

Price, G. E. Learning style inventory development and continuing research. *Learning Styles and Brain Behavior*, Reston, Virginia: National Association of Secondary School Principals, 1982, Chapter 11.

Raywid, M. A. Bringing alternative schooling to the primary grades. *Early Years*, 1981, 12(3), 17–18.

Ricca, J. Curricular implications of learning style differences between gifted and nongifted students. Doctoral dissertation, State University of New York at Buffalo, 1983, 211 pp.

Shea, T. C. An investigation of the relationship among preferences for the learning style element of design, selected instructional environments, and reading achievement of ninth grade students to improve administrative determinations concerning effective educational facilities. Unpublished doctoral dissertation, St. John's University, 1983.

Sinatra, R. and Stahl-Gemake, J. *Using the right brain in the language arts*. Charles C. Thomas, 1983.

Spiridakis, J. N. Diagnosing the learning styles of bilingual students and prescribing appropriate instruction. *Ethnoperspectives in Bilingual Education Research (III)*, Raymond Padilla (ed.). Ypsilanti, Michigan: Eastern Michigan University, 1981, 307–320.

Spires, R. D. The effect of teacher inservice about learning styles on students' mathematics and reading achievement. Doctoral dissertation, Bowling Green State University, 1983.

Students learn how to study—and like it. *U.S. News & World Report*, December 31, 1979/January 7, 1980, 88(27), 75–6.

Student learning styles and brain behavior. Reston, Virginia: National Association of Secondary School Principals, 1982.

Sudzina, M. An investigation of the relationship between the reading styles of second graders and their achievement in three different basal reader programs. Unpublished doctoral dissertation, Temple University, 1986.

Tappenden, V. J. Analysis of the learning styles of vocational education and nonvocational education students in eleventh and twelfth grades from rural, urban, and suburban locations in Ohio. Unpublished doctoral dissertation, Kent State University, 1983.

Thies, A. A brain-behavior analysis of learning style. *Student Learning Styles: Diagnosing and Prescribing Programs*. National Association of Secondary School Principals, 1979, 55–61.

Trautman, P. An investigation of the relationship between selected instructional techniques and identified cognitive style. Unpublished doctoral dissertation, St. John's University, 1979.

Urbschat, K. A study of preferred learning modes and their relationship to the amount of recall of CVC trigrams. Unpublished doctoral dissertation, Wayne State University, 1977.

Virostko, J. An analysis of the relationships among academic achievement in mathematics and reading, assigned instructional schedules, and the learning style time preferences of third, fourth, fifth, and sixth grade students. Unpublished doctoral dissertation, St. John's University, 1983. Recipient: Kappa Delta Pi National Research Award, 1983.

Wheeler, R. An investigation of the degree of academic achievement evidenced when second grade, learning disabled students' perceptual preferences are matched and mismatched with complementary sensory approaches to beginning reading instruction. Unpublished doctoral dissertation, St. John's University, 1983.

White, R. M. An investigation of the relationship between selected instructional methods and selected elements of emotional learning style upon student achievement in seventh grade social studies. Unpublished doctoral dissertation, St. John's University, 1980. Recipient: Delta Kappa Gamma International Award for best dissertation proposal of 1980.

White, R. M., Dunn, R., and Zenhausern, R. An investigation of responsible students. *Illinois School Research and Development.* Illinois: Illinois Association for Supervision and Curriculum Development, 1982, 19(1), 18–25.

Wingo, L. H. Relationships among locus of motivation, sensory modality and grouping preferences of learning style to basic skills test performance in reading and mathematics. Doctoral dissertation, Memphis State University, 1980.

Wolfe, G. Learning styles and the teaching of reading. Doctoral dissertation, Akron University, 1983.

Zenhausern, R. Education and the left hemisphere. *Student Learning Styles and Brain Behavior.* Reston, Va.: National Association of Secondary School Principals.

Zenhausern, R., Dunn, R., Barretto, R., Ba- cilious, Z., Gemake, J., Griggs S. A., Sanders, W., Schwartz, V., Sinatra, R., Spiridakis, J., and Swanchak, J. *Early Years,* 1984, 15, 1, 46–48.

SELECTED BOOKS FOR USE WITH CHILDREN

Booth, D., Pauli, W., and Phenix, J. *Impressions: Language arts for the '80s.* Toronto, Ontario: Holt, Rinehart, and Winston of Canada, Ltd., 1983. Including: (a) Catch a Rainbow; (b) Fly Away Home; (c) Good Morning Sunshine; (d) How I Wonder; (e) When the Wind Blows; and others.

Fugit, E. D. *He hit me back first. Creative visualization for parenting and teaching.* California: Jalmar Press, 1983.

Vitale, B. *Unicorns are real: A right-brained approach to learning.* California: Jalmar Press, 1982.

Index